Library of
Davidson College

# Loyalists
# &
# Revolutionaries

# Loyalists & Revolutionaries

## POLITICAL LEADERS COMPARED

Mostafa Rejai
Kay Phillips

 PRAEGER

New York
Westport, Connecticut
London

**Library of Congress Cataloging-in-Publication Data**

Rejai, M. (Mostafa)
  Loyalists and revolutionaries : political leaders compared /
Mostafa Rejai, Kay Phillips.
    p.    cm.
  Bibliography: p.
  Includes index.
  ISBN 0-275-92915-9 (alk. paper)
  1. Political leadership.  2. Elite (Social science)
3. Revolutionists.  4. Politicians.  I. Phillips, Kay.  II. Title.
JF1525.L4R45  1988
303.3'4—dc19
                                                    87-27888

Copyright © 1988 by Mostafa Rejai and Kay Phillips

All rights reserved. No portion of this book may
be reproduced, by any process or technique, without
the express written consent of the publisher.

Library of Congress Catalog Card Number: 87-27888
ISBN: 0-275-92915-9

First published in 1988

Praeger Publishers, One Madison Avenue, New York, NY 10010
A division of Greenwood Press, Inc.

Printed in the United States of America

The paper used in this book complies with the
Permanent Paper Standard issued by the National
Information Standards Organization (Z39.48-1984).

10  9  8  7  6  5  4  3  2  1

# Contents

| | |
|---|---|
| List of Tables and Figures | vii |
| Preface and Acknowledgments | ix |
| Introduction | xiii |

**I  THEORY**

| | | |
|---|---|---|
| 1 | Political Leadership: Toward an Interactional Theory | 3 |

**II  FOUNDATIONS**

| | | |
|---|---|---|
| 2 | General Characteristics | 17 |
| 3 | Careers and Crises | 31 |
| 4 | Loyalists and Revolutionaries | 37 |

**III  PROPELLANTS**

| | | |
|---|---|---|
| 5 | Politicization | 45 |
| 6 | Situations | 57 |
| 7 | Psychologies | 71 |
| 8 | Skills | 97 |

**IV  CONCLUSIONS**

| | | |
|---|---|---|
| 9 | Becoming Political Leaders | 107 |
| Appendixes | | 121 |
| Bibliography | | 151 |
| Index | | 185 |
| About the Authors | | 189 |

# List of Tables and Figures

**TABLES**

| | | |
|---|---|---|
| 2.1 | Socioeconomic Status | 19 |
| 2.2 | Father's Primary Occupation | 20 |
| 2.3 | Leader's Primary Occupation | 21 |
| 2.4 | Leader's Age at the Time of Highest Office or Revolution | 23 |
| 2.5 | Membership in Legal Organizations | 24 |
| 2.6 | Membership in Revolutionary Organizations | 24 |
| 2.7 | Arrest/Exile Record: Frequency | 25 |
| 2.8 | Arrest/Exile Record: Duration | 25 |
| 2.9 | Religious Orientation | 26 |
| 2.10 | Ideology | 27 |
| 2.11 | Origin of Ideology | 28 |
| 2.12 | Attitude Toward Human Beings | 29 |
| 2.13 | Attitude Toward Own Country | 29 |
| 3.1 | Q-Factor Analysis by Principal Component Varimax Rotation | 34 |
| 4.1 | Discriminant Patterns | 39 |
| 5.1 | Family as a Source of Politicization | 46 |
| 5.2 | Age Ranking Among Siblings as a Source of Politicization | 50 |
| 5.3 | School as a Source of Politicization | 52 |
| 5.4 | Foreign Travel as a Source of Politicization | 54 |
| 7.1 | Psychological Dynamics of Political Behavior | 76 |

## FIGURES

| 9.1 | Becoming Political Leaders: A Social-Psychological Flowchart of Critical Variables | 116 |
| 9.2 | Becoming Loyalist or Revolutionary Leaders: A Social-Psychological Flowchart of Critical Variables | 117 |

# Preface and Acknowledgments

Some political leaders—the "loyalists"—come to office through peaceful processes, whether appointive or elective. Other individuals—the "revolutionaries"—seize power (or attempt to do so) in violent ways. Who *are* these two groups of individuals? What social backgrounds do they have? What motivates them to seek political office? Are the two groups fundamentally alike or are they radically different?

Conventional wisdom has been founded on the belief that loyalist political elites constitute a distinct type of individual while revolutionary leaders form quite another. Accordingly, received wisdom has projected two sharply contrasting group portraits. With rare exceptions, loyalists are seen as rational, mainstream, upstanding, patriotic citizens out to promote national greatness and public welfare. Revolutionaries, by contrast, are typically viewed as social outcasts, abnormal and fanatical, touched by mysterious afflictions, and out to betray the national will.

Conventional wisdom would seem to have found support, inadvertently perhaps, in social science research. On the one hand, the findings of some scholars have been interpreted to mean that loyalist elites come from normal social backgrounds and are engaged in normal or constructive searches for power, status, achievement, affiliation, recognition, or public service. By contrast, the findings of other scholars have been construed to suggest that revolutionary leaders come from marginal social strata and are driven, simultaneously or alternately, by intense anxiety and insecurity, narcissistic or masochistic behavior, unresolved emotional problems, and generally pathological tendencies.

Whatever the source of received wisdom or popular views concerning loyalists and revolutionary elites, are the two group portraits accurate? Do loyalists and revolutionaries come from fundamentally similar or radically different social backgrounds? Are the two groups moved into action by fundamentally similar or radically different motivations and psychologies? Do loyalists and revolutionaries constitute two separate orders of individuals or the same human beings who experience life in their own ways?

These are some of the intriguing and elusive questions about political leaders and political leadership to which we seek answers throughout this work. We shall go about our task in many ways, employing a variety of data, approaches, and methods. We shall identify similarities between the two groups, and we shall isolate differences. When all is said and done, however, it is the similarities that will command pivotal importance. Our lengthy journey completed, we shall establish, clearly if tentatively, that loyalists and revolutionaries are basically the same individuals, differing most meaningfully in terms of their relative access to positions of power and authority within societies.

A project long in gestation inescapably and rightly incurs a multitude of debts, both individual and institutional. We are happy to have the opportunity to acknowledge them.

Indispensable research assistance was provided by David Arredondo, Pio Celestino, Patrick Costigan, Rosemary Garry, Stuart Gilman, Reuben Johnson, Kitty Kincaid, Beverly Kolb, Jeffrey Kranz, Leslie Kutzleb, Mack Leftwich, Mekki Mtewa, James Muldoon, Brian Murphy, Julius Nyangoro, Otieno Okelo, Tipaporn Phimphisut, Patricia Piperno, Borvorn Praprutidee, Steven Wainscott, and Philip Zampini. Candace Conrad rendered important help with translation of Spanish and Portuguese texts, as did Josette Thévenin with translation of French sources.

Among Miami University librarians particularly resourceful at locating research materials, we note Chris Africa, Sarah Barr, Karen Clift, Martin Miller, Rebecca Morgenson, Richard Quay, Catherine Seitz, and Scott Van Dam.

Shahla Mehdizadeh of Academic Computer Services, Miami University, generously and enthusiastically shared with us her superb data-analytic skills. Very helpful at earlier stages of data analysis were Suzanne Kunkel and Christine Noble.

An exceptionally large number of European and North American colleagues have been generous with a variety of contributions to our work. Impressive indeed were the many scholar-experts who responded to our plea for assistance in connection with the construction of the lists of loyalists and revolutionaries (see Introduction and Appendix A). Richard G. Braungart, Anthony King, J. A. LaPonce, John Meisel, and Jerzy J. Wiatr offered helpful comments on various parts of the study. Our colleague Warren L. Mason and two anonymous reviewers read earlier drafts of the manuscript in entirety and provided comprehensive critiques. Although for various

Preface and Acknowledgments

reasons we have been unable to incorporate all suggestions, we hope we have gone a considerable distance toward meeting our colleagues' criticisms.

Dan Eades of Praeger Publishers was an ideal acquisitions editor, striking a nice balance between resolution and humor. Lisa MacLeman did a very sensitive job of copyediting. Karen O'Brien skillfully steered the manuscript through production.

Some of the research for this work was conducted at the Center for International Affairs, Harvard University, and the Hoover Institution, Stanford University. We are grateful to the officers and staffs of these organizations for superbly productive opportunities.

Miami University has supported our work in every conceivable way throughout the years. Our friend Dorothy S. Pierson "processed" successive drafts of the manuscript with unfailing patience and exemplary good humor.

Throughout the text, we make every effort to explain some very difficult—and, at times, ultimately arbitrary—decisions we were called upon to make. We only hope that future advances in social science research render such decisions easier, if not altogether unnecessary. Meanwhile, we alone remain responsible for any problems or shortcomings associated with this book.

# Introduction

This volume is the culmination of a research project launched in 1970. The results of our earlier endeavors appeared most recently in *World Revolutionary Leaders*.[1] All told, we have reported research findings for 135 leaders from 31 revolutionary movements between the 1640s and the 1970s. The present study focuses on a comparative analysis of revolutionary elites* with their "establishment" or "loyalist" counterparts.

We raise three interrelated sets of questions about political leaders, one dealing with their sociodemographic characteristics and traits, one with their motivation and emergence upon the scene, and one with similarities and differences between loyalists and revolutionaries:

1. Who are men** who assume leadership positions, whether of a loyalist or revolutionary nature? Are they urban dwellers or do they come from rural locations? What level of education do they have? What socioeconomic and occupational backgrounds do they represent? What sorts of family lives do they lead? What ethnic and religious groups do they come from? Where and how do they acquire social awareness and political experience? What ideological postures do they adopt? What attitudes do they hold toward man and society?

---

*Throughout this volume we use "elite" to refer to a single revolutionary group (for example, the French) and "elites" to refer to more than one (for instance, the French and the English). On occasion, as the context makes clear, we use the two words in a generic sense as well.

**We use "men" or "man" generically and for stylistic convenience. Moreover, as we shall see, there is not a single woman in the population of leaders we study.

2. Under what conditions do men seek positions of political leadership, whether of a loyalist or revolutionary nature? What forces or circumstances provide impetus to the emergence of political elites? What socialization patterns do they encounter in childhood and youth? What are the forces or dynamics—social, psychological, situational—that catapult men into political leadership positions? What kinds of skills do political leaders require in order to reach high office or seize power?
3. In what ways are loyalist elites similar to their revolutionary counterparts and in what ways do they differ? Are there leadership traits or qualities that are uniquely loyalist or uniquely revolutionary? Is there a shared constellation of traits that will allow us to focus on leadership in general? Are there varying attributes, politicization patterns, situational considerations, and psychological dynamics that will allow us to project or anticipate which persons are likely to become loyalists and which ones likely to turn to revolution?

The several steps taken in the execution of the study require elaboration.

Defining a "revolutionary" as a person who risks his life by playing a prominent, active, and continuing role throughout the revolutionary process, we relied on judgment of panels of experts at our own institution in order to arrive at our list. Even though we limited ourselves to the more dramatic and the best documented revolutions* and revolutionaries, we encountered a variety of problems in connection with data availability. Not until we had begun data collection for the loyalists, however, did we realize just how much easier, by comparison, our earlier endeavors had been.

We sought to match our list of revolutionaries with one for the loyalists. Defining a "loyalist" as the counterpart of a revolutionary in a key political (elective) or governmental (appointive) position, we went back to the same regions, the same countries, and about the same time periods as the revolutions, in order to identify an equal number of establishment elites. Lacking the necessary expertise to complete the task by ourselves, we turned to our colleagues in and out of academia for assistance.

Between October 1981 and March 1982 we wrote 96 scholars throughout the United States who specialize in various countries or regions, providing them with lists of the appropriate revolutionaries and asking them to identify their loyalist counterparts. We received a total of 52 responses, of which 40 proved usable, enabling us to draw up a matched list, however imperfect, of loyalist leaders. (The list of scholar-experts appears in Appendix A.)

Once we began the process of actual data collection, we realized the near impossibility of the task we had set for ourselves. For one thing, the sheer

---

*We view revolution as the mass violent overthrow of a political regime in the interest of broad societal change. As such, revolution would sharply differ from such related phenomena as rebellion (which is typically reformist) or coup d'etat (which typically seeks political change alone). For elaboration, see M. Rejai, *The Comparative Study of Revolutionary Strategy* (New York: McKay, 1977), chap. 2 and the sources cited therein.

## Introduction

paucity of even plain sociodemographic data was so severe as to discourage even the most enthusiastic researcher. To use the example of the American loyalists, thanks to such scholars as Bernard Bailyn and James K. Hosmer, we know much about Thomas Hutchinson, the last civilian governor of Massachusetts. But what do we know about the other colonial governors? Surprisingly, very little. Even a man like William Tryon, who was governor of North Carolina, 1765-1771, and of New York, 1771-1776, does not rate anything approaching a substantive biography. On the other hand, we do have a book covering architectural history and other details of the period for Governor Tryon's New York mansion.[2] Accordingly, we dropped Tryon from our list.

Similarly, of the five finance ministers who served Louis XVI in the last years of his reign—Louis Charles Breteuil, Etienne Charles de Brienne, Charles-Alexandre Calonne, Jean-Frédéric Maurepas, Jacques Necker, and Anne-Robert-Jacques Turgot—we have significant information only about the last. Curiously, however, what we know about Turgot is not due to his status as Louis XVI's finance minister—even though, given Louis's problems, the post of finance minister was a pivotal one—but rather due to Turgot's status as a philosopher, economist (physiocrat), and literary figure.

Along the same lines, Necker was a Swiss who was brought to Louis's attention because of his financial wizardry, particularly in the field of banking. But, again, we know little about Monsieur Necker. On the other hand, Madame Necker was a social climber who set up her own salon in competition with the other fashionable salons of Paris. Accordingly, we have a work, in two volumes, on Madame Necker's salon.[3]

If sociodemographic information is so difficult to come by, one can only imagine the state of social-psychological data, remembering that social-psychological studies of leaders constitute a relatively recent phenomenon. With rare exceptions, loyalists simply do not possess the dash, luster, or prominence that propel the revolutionaries to the forefront of popular and scholarly attention.

Another reason for the paucity of data on loyalists is that in the cases we studied they are, by and large, the losers. As such, they are dismissed, shunned, and avoided. Thus, for instance, following the American Revolution, writing about the loyalists became proscribed, and few academicians or journalists dared to treat the subject in any detail. As a result, when, nearly a century later, Lorenzo Sabine published a two-volume work on biographical sketches of the American loyalists,[4] he was virtually ostracized.

As our research progressed, we had to resign ourselves to two indisputable facts. One, we could not possibly hope to gather usable data for 135 loyalists for purposes of comparison with the revolutionary leaders.

Two, we could not possibly entertain the luxury of two perfectly matched lists of loyalists and revolutionaries.

Accordingly, we cut our list of revolutionaries to the 50 individuals for whom we had gathered rather comprehensive data in our most recent work, *World Revolutionary Leaders*. And with the help of our scholarly respondents, we identified a group of 50 loyalist leaders. All data for the two groups, we should note, cover the period up to a revolutionary's *power seizure* or a loyalist's *assuming highest office*; what happens to an individual thereafter does not concern us for the purposes of this work.

Organized by region, country, and time, our matched lists of 50 revolutionaries and 50 loyalists are as follows:

| REVOLUTIONARIES* | LOYALISTS* |
|---|---|
| **Africa** | **Africa** |
| ALGERIA | ALGERIA |
|   Ahmad Ben Bella |   Ferhat Abbas |
| ANGOLA | EGYPT |
|   Holden Roberto (José Gilmore) |   Gamal Abdel Nasser |
|  |   Anwar el-Sadat |
| GUINEA-BISSAU | LIBERIA |
|   Amilcar Cabral |   William V.S. Tubman |
| MOZAMBIQUE | SENEGAL |
|   Samora Moises Machel |   Léopold Sédar Senghor |
|   Eduardo Mondlane |  |
| SOUTH AFRICA | SOUTH AFRICA |
|   Stephen Bantu Biko |   Albert John Luthuli |
| ZIMBABWE | TANZANIA |
|   Joshua Nkomo |   Julius Kambarage Nyerere |
|   Ndabaningi Sithole | TUNISIA |
|  |   Habib Ben Ali Bourguiba |
|  | ZAMBIA |
|  |   Kenneth David Kaunda |
| **Asia and the Middle East** | **Asia and the Middle East** |
| CHINA | BURMA |
|   Chou En-lai |   U Nu |
|   Chu Teh |  |
|   Lin Piao | CHINA |
|   Liu Shao-ch'i |   Chiang Kai-shek |
|   Mao Tse-tung |   H. H. (Hsiang-hsi) K'ung |
|  |   T. V. (Tse-ven) Soong |
|  |   Wang Ching-wei |

---

*Designations in parentheses are nicknames, aliases, noms de guerre, or legal names (the last preceded by né).

Introduction

| REVOLUTIONARIES* | LOYALISTS* |
|---|---|
| **Asia and the Middle East (continued)** | **Asia and the Middle East (continued)** |
| LAOS<br>  Souphanouvong | KAMPUCHEA (CAMBODIA)<br>  Norodom Sihanouk Varman |
| "PALESTINE"<br>  Yasir Arafat<br>  George Habash | "PALESTINE"<br>  Musa el-Alami |
|  | PHILIPPINES<br>  Ferdinand Edralin Marcos |
| VIETNAM<br>  Nguyên Sinh Cung (Ho<br>    Chi Minh)<br>  Vo Nguyên Giap | VIETNAM<br>  Ngô Dinh Diêm<br>  Nguyên Van Thieu |
| **Latin America** | **Latin America** |
| BOLIVIA<br>  Víctor Paz Estenssoro | BOLIVIA<br>  Gen. Enrique Peñaranda |
| BRAZIL<br>  Carlos Marighella | BRAZIL<br>  Gen. Eurico Gaspar Dutra |
| COLOMBIA<br>  Camilo Torres Restrepo | CHILE<br>  Eduardo Frei Montalva |
| CUBA<br>  Fidel Castro Ruz<br>  Ernesto (Che) Guevara de la Serna | COLOMBIA<br>  Laureano Eleuterio Gomez |
|  | CUBA<br>  Fulgencio Batista y Zaldívar |
| PERU<br>  Hugo Blanco Gladós<br>  Luis de la Puente Uceda | PERU<br>  Fernando Belaúnde Terry<br>  Gen. Manuel Apolinario Odría |
| URUGUAY<br>  Rául Sendic Antonaccio (Rufo) | URUGUAY<br>  José Batlle y Ordóñez |
| **Europe and North America** | **Europe and North America** |
| AMERICA<br>  John Adams<br>  Samuel Adams<br>  Patrick Henry<br>  Thomas Jefferson<br>  James Otis<br>  George Washington | AMERICA<br>  Cadwallader Colden<br>  Joseph Galloway<br>  Thomas Hutchinson<br>  Frederick North,<br>    Second Earl of Guilford<br>  Jonathan Sewall |
| ENGLAND<br>  Oliver Cromwell<br>  Robert Devereux, Third Earl<br>    of Essex<br>  John Hampden<br>  John Pym | ENGLAND<br>  William Cavendish, Duke<br>    of Newcastle<br>  Edward Hyde, Earl of Clarendon<br>  William Laud, Archbishop of<br>    Canterbury |

| REVOLUTIONARIES* | LOYALISTS* |
|---|---|
| **Europe and North America (continued)** | **Europe and North America (continued)** |
| Henry (Harry) Vane | Prince Rupert of the Rhine |
| | Thomas Wentworth, Earl of Strafford |
| FRANCE | FRANCE |
| Georges Jacques Danton | Jean-Frédéric Maurepas |
| Jean Paul Marat | Comte de |
| Honoré Gabriel Riqueti, Comte de Mirabeau | Jacques Necker |
| | Anne-Robert-Jacques |
| Maximilien François Marie Isidore de Robespierre | Turgot, Baron de l'Aulne |
| MEXICO | MEXICO |
| Doroteo Arango (Francisco Pancho Villa) | José Lázaro Cárdenas del Rió |
| | José de la Cruz Porfirio Díaz |
| Francisco Indelcio Madero | José Vasconcelos |
| Emiliano Zapata | |
| QUEBEC/CANADA | QUEBEC/CANADA |
| François (né Frenec) Schirm | René Lévesque |
| Georges Schoeters | Lester Bowles Pearson |
| Pierre Vallières | Joseph Phillipe Pierre |
| | Yves Elliotte Trudeau |
| RUSSIA | RUSSIA |
| Lev Davidovich Bronstein (Leon Trotsky) | Nikolai Nikolaevich Mladshii, Grand Duke |
| Joseph Vassarionovich Dzhugashvili (Josef Stalin) | Peter Arkadievich Stolypin |
| | Peter Berngardovich Struve |
| Vladimir Ilyich Ulyanov (Nikolai Lenin) | Sergei Iulevich Witte |

The matched lists, to state the obvious, are not perfect. Since perfection is seldom to be had, however, let us offer some comments and clarifications.

As can be seen, from Africa we have eight revolutionaries and nine loyalists, but only two of the countries match: Algeria and South Africa. Asia and the Middle East* yield ten revolutionaries and ten loyalists, but only three countries are identical: China, "Palestine,"** Vietnam. The picture is much brighter for Latin America: eight revolutionaries, eight loyalists, and six out of seven countries. We almost reach perfection in connection with Europe and North America: 24 revolutionaries, 23 loyalists, and all six countries. On the whole,

---

*We dispense with the region conventionally labeled "Middle East and North Africa" because it would incorporate only two of our cases: Algeria and "Palestine."**

**Although as of this writing there is no such country as "Palestine" with recognized international boundaries, we use this designation (with quotation marks) for stylistic convenience.

# Introduction

then, the two matched lists coincide in terms of regions but not always of time periods or countries.[5] It is noteworthy, nonetheless, that the 100 leaders come from 32 countries scattered across five continents and four centuries.

Another notable feature of our two lists is that among the revolutionaries we find former loyalists; and among the loyalists, former revolutionaries. Loyalists-turned-revolutionaries include Ben Bella and Sithole, Nkomo and Souphanouvong, Fidel Castro and Paz Estenssoro, John Adams and George Washington. On the other hand, such loyalists as Abbas, Kaunda, and Nyerere played leading roles in the independence movements of their countries; Chiang Kai-shek and Wang Ching-wei were prominent in the anti-Manchu Chinese Revolution of 1911; Bourguiba and Senghor remained enthusiastic Francophiles for a long time, assimilating wholesale French language and culture.

Loyalists-turned-revolutionaries participate in the legal political processes of their societies, find the system unresponsive, and turn to revolutionary politics. In other words, had it not been for the unresponsiveness of the system, these men might have become members of the establishment elite. To use a single illustration, Castro was an active candidate in the Cuban parliamentary elections of 1952, when Batista's coup suspended the constitution and halted the electoral process, catapulting Castro toward a revolutionary course.

Revolutionaries-turned-loyalists are not uncommon. Many of our scholar/expert respondents noted this fact in various ways. Edmund S. Morgan wrote in connection with the list of American revolutionaries: "The revolutionary leaders you name include several who could also be considered part of the establishment elite." Having provided a list of African leaders, Ronald H. Chilcote observed: "The above persons are both revolutionary and establishment elites. . . . I have no idea how to distinguish between these terms in countries that have recently become independent after revolutionary struggles." And Robert A. Scalapino said of a list of Asian elites: "As you know, many individuals who became part of the establishment began as revolutionary leaders."

Three mechanical aspects of the list are also worth noting. First, we use the Wade-Giles system of romanizing Chinese names in order to maintain consistency with the bibliographical entries, all of which were published before the new system went into effect. Second, since some of the names (for instance, the Palestinians) are spelled in a variety of ways, we have adopted the policy of using the simplest spelling. Third, the Introduction is the only place in the study where all names appear in full; in the balance of the text short or popular names are used.

Before proceeding, it is necessary to consider some potential problems with our lists of loyalists and revolutionaries. Careful as we have been in selecting our two populations, the reader may object that we have allowed, in effect, our choice of revolutions and revolutionaries to predetermine the list of loyalists, and that by fiat (as it were) we have excluded from consideration the millions of loyalists who through the ages have played successful leadership roles in an infinite variety of capacities, as well as the great many revolutionaries who have failed in their attempts to transform the social system.

However, our objective having been the identification of two maximally comparable populations of loyalists and revolutionaries, we are hard put to think of an alternative set of criteria that possibly might have yielded two more comparable groups, from either a logical or an empirical point of view. It goes without saying that *any* population (in contrast to a universe) by definition entails certain limits, since any principle of inclusion functions, at the same time, as a principle of exclusion. Moreover, the two lists include such successful loyalists as Batlle, Belaúnde, Frei, Cárdenas, Lévesque, Pearson, Trudeau, Tubman, and U Nu as well as such failed revolutionaries as Biko, Cabral, de la Puente, Marighella, Schirm, Schoeters, Sendic, Torres, and Vallières. In short, these are the "best" lists we could develop, given the constraints under which we worked.

The reader may further object: How can such leaders as Nasser and Nyerere be considered loyalists, since they played active roles in the antiimperialist movements of their countries, the former having come to power in a coup d'état? Was Washington a loyalist or a revolutionary, since he performed both roles in a stellar fashion? Was Stalin a revolutionary or a loyalist, since he spent more time as the leader of the Soviet state than he did as an antitsarist revolutionary? And in all such instances, who is to decide which is the "real" or the "more important" career, and by what criteria?

We do not pretend to have definitive responses to all possible objections. However, in order to eliminate any residual doubts concerning the integrity of our lists of loyalists and revolutionaries, we examined our data with a view to answering the following questions: (1) Are there meaningful differences between loyalists and revolutionaries-turned-loyalists to advise against their being grouped together? (2) Are there significant differences between revolutionaries and loyalists-turned-revolutionaries to prohibit their being assigned the same classification? (3) Are there meaningful differences between successful and failed loyalists to militate against grouping them together? (4) Are there significant differences between successful and failed revolutionaries to forbid their being placed in each other's company?

Having subjected our data to extensive analysis, we found a series of differences between the aforementioned groupings that had two characteristics. First, they were very few in number. Second, either they carried no theoretical substance or they proved confirmatory of our theoretical posture. Accordingly, we have found empirical justification for grouping

Introduction xxi

the loyalists and revolutionaries as presented in the foregoing pages. A more detailed report on our findings concerning these matters appears in Appendix B.

Four additional clarifications are in order. The first relates to the problem of the functional equivalence of data drawn from such diverse cultures and time periods as represented on our lists. Do things really have the same "meaning" in such radically different contexts? Ever mindful of this pitfall, in all data collection and coding we have sought to err on the side of the most cautious judgments in order to minimize as much as possible the introduction of ethnocentric or otherwise biased materials.

Second, we are acutely aware that both groups of loyalists and revolutionaries are rather small in numbers. Under the circumstances, however, our alternatives are rather limited, if they exist at all.

Third, we know all too well that leadership is a timeless and universal phenomenon, and that all societies at all times have leaders. Accordingly, wherever we use "leaders," "leadership" or "political leadership" we refer only to the two populations of loyalists and revolutionaries we have studied for the purposes of this book.

Fourth, we realize that we do not have a control group of "nonleaders" for purposes of comparative analysis. Even if it were possible to identify such a group, however, the selection would be so arbitrary as to be meaningless. (How, and by what criteria, does one identify *non*leaders? How does one collect data about them?) Accordingly, in the technical language of contemporary social science, ours is a nonrandom purposive sample of political elites with possibilities as well as limitations. To this topic we shall return in Chapter 9.

The gathering of social background data on loyalist and revolutionary elites went hand in hand with the examination of the historical, situational, social, and psychological conditions under which they emerged. These endeavors involved close scrutiny of primary and secondary sources with heavy reliance on autobiographical and biographical materials, to the extent that these were available. Aware of the biases that may be embedded in such literature, both positive and negative, we treated the matter with due caution and referred to as many independent sources as possible.

The questions of validity and reliability of the data collected for this work have been given careful consideration. As for validity, the data items used are adapted from the general literature of elite analysis; in fact, these items are by now part of the conventional wisdom, representing considerable scholarly consensus. Moreover, the variables for which data are collected interrelate to a large extent. Thus, demographic, ideological, attitudinal, psychological, and situational variables not only cohere as distinct groups, they intersect at many points as well.

As far as reliability is concerned, every effort has been made to minimize possible errors. While there is probably no such thing as an error-free study, a series of precautions was taken in data collection and coding. First, as the Bibliography indicates, a wide range of data sources was employed. Second, while the initial data gatherings were in the hands of the research assistants listed in the Acknowledgments, each assistant was provided with a detailed code sheet (see Appendix C) and with detailed instructions. Third, we personally reviewed every data item on every code sheet against the many sources indicated, thus arriving at a final coding determination.

In all instances, problems of conflicting data were resolved by relying on two yardsticks: (1) the frequency with which a datum appeared in independent sources, and (2) the authenticity of the source or person giving the datum. Needless to say, the second yardstick was given preference throughout.

As for the actual coding, most of the socioeconomic variables were relatively straightforward and presented no particular problems. Such matters as age, birthplace, socioeconomic status, ethnicity and religion, number of siblings and age ranking among them, education and occupation, father's education and occupation, travels, publications, and the like, were *relatively* simple to isolate and code. On the other hand, such issues as home and school influences, attitude toward human beings ("nature of man"), attitude toward one's own country, and attitude toward the international community were based on close textual examination of the available source materials, which at times involved judgment calls. As may be expected, coding psychological variables proved the most problematical, a subject to which we return in Chapter 7.

We have made every effort to keep the organization and presentation of our materials as straightforward as possible. Part I sets forth the theoretical foundation of the study. Chapter 1 reviews some prominent theories of leadership and political leadership, arrives at a synthetic, interactional approach in terms of three principal variables—situation, psychology, skill, and states a series of interrelated propositions and hypotheses derived from relevant research findings.

Part II undertakes a quantitative comparative analysis of loyalists and revolutionaries, in the light of the propositions and hypotheses developed in Chapter 1. Chapter 2 identifies a constellation of traits that cuts across the loyalist-revolutionary distinction and applies with equal force to both political elites, and a cluster of differences that helps construct distinctive composite profiles of each group. Using factor analysis in an effort to arrive at a typology of political leaders, Chapter 3 comes across an unanticipated distinction between career and crisis leaders which, on reflection, corresponds to loyalists and revolutionaries. Chapter 4 employs discriminant analysis as a means of identifying those variables and traits that are

Introduction                                                              xxiii

uniquely loyalist or revolutionary. The overall objective of the analysis undertaken in Part II is threefold: (a) identification of sociodemographic characteristics common to all political elites, (b) identification of differences between loyalists and revolutionaries, and (c) identification of social background variables that may be "situational" in nature and hence contribute to our interactional theory of political leadership.

Shifting to a less formal style, Part III presents a qualitative analysis of the social, political, situational, and psychological dynamics underlying the emergence of loyalist and revolutionary leaders. Looking at patterns of politicization, Chapter 5 examines formative years, school socialization, and new experiences and cultures. Analyzing the situational patterns, Chapter 6 focuses on differential access to political power, national crisis or emergency, colonial or neocolonial contexts, "violent countries," and the role of chance. Considering psychological dynamics, Chapter 7 pays particular attention to vanity and egotism, asceticism and puritanism, relative deprivation and status inconsistency, marginality and inferiority complex, oedipal conflict writ large, and estheticism and romanticism. Looking at the range of verbal and organizational skills at the command of loyalist and revolutionary elites, Chapter 8 examines the relative efficacy with which they deploy their talents.

Part IV (Chapter 9) synthesizes the study by reviewing and consolidating the empirical findings, assessing the theoretical import of the work, and offering probabilistic models to account for the emergence of political leaders in general and of loyalist and revolutionary elites in particular.

Although we have endeavored to steer clear of technical jargon throughout our presentations, some use of cant has been unavoidable, particularly in Chapters 3 and 4. The uninterested reader may skip the affected passages.

## NOTES

1. M. Rejai and K. Phillips, *Leaders of Revolution* (Beverly Hills: Sage Publications, 1979); Rejai and Phillips, *World Revolutionary Leaders* (New Brunswick: Rutgers University Press, 1983).

2. Alonzo T. Dill, *Governor Tryon and His Palace* (Chapel Hill: University of North Carolina Press, 1955).

3. Vicomte d'Haussonville, *The Salon of Madame Necker*, 2 vols. (London: Chapman & Hall, Ltd., 1882).

4. Lorenzo Sabine, *Biographical Sketches of Loyalists of the American Revolution*, 2 vols. (Boston: Little, Brown, 1864).

5. We should note that we treat England and "America" prior to 1776 as one country. The Englishmen and women who constituted the great bulk of the population of the 13 colonies considered themselves transplanted Britons—hence, for instance, the relevance of "Taxation without Representation." This situation, to state

the obvious, does not obtain in colonial contexts where the indigenous population is vastly dissimilar in culture, language, and so on, from the imperialist power. Accordingly, for the English and American leaders, whether loyalist or revolutionary, such variables as birthplace, education, and travel have been coded as "domestic."

# I THEORY

# 1 Political Leadership: Toward an Interactional Theory

## THEORIES AND RESEARCH: BACKGROUND

Which components of the many extant theories of leadership are most congenial to the analysis presented in this work? Let us rapidly survey the field in search of an answer.

"Leadership" and "political leadership" have preoccupied philosophers and social thinkers since time immemorial. From Plato's "philosopher king" to Machiavelli's "prince" to Carlyle's "great man" to Nietzsche's "superman" to Freud's "primal father" and Lasswell's "political man," leadership has commanded singular scholarly attention throughout history.

In the postwar period, advances in social and behavioral sciences—and the confluence of such fields as sociology, psychology, management, and political science—subjected leadership to a variety of new approaches and treatments. Ralph M. Stogdill did much to reorient the study of leadership from a preoccupation with trait and great-man schools to one that stressed the salience of situational forces.[1] Cecil A. Gibb developed an interactional theory stressing the interplay of the leader, the followers, the situation, and the goal.[2] Fred E. Fiedler elaborated the interactional perspective into a contingency model arguing, in effect, that all leadership is motivation- and situation-contingent.[3] Edwin P. Hollander developed a transactional theory by combining the situational approach with a social exchange component that focused on reciprocal influence between the leader and the followers.[4]

Among political sociologists, Glenn D. Paige proclaimed leadership "an emerging field" and called for global studies of the subject.[5] An influential constellation of scholars—including Jean Blondel, Mattei Dogan, Lewis J. Edinger, Donald R. Matthews, Robert D. Putnam, William B. Quandt, and

Donald D. Searing—stressed the importance of the comparative approach to leadership studies.[6] Another distinguished group—Alexander L. George, Fred I. Greenstein, Ted Robert Gurr, Margaret G. Hermann, Harold D. Lasswell, James L. Payne and associates, E. Victor Wolfenstein—focused on the psychological dimensions of leadership.[7] Robert C. Tucker equated all politics with leadership, distinguishing between constituted (legal) and nonconstituted (extralegal, reformist, or revolutionary) leaders.[8]

James MacGregor Burns, one of the most influential recent scholars, stressed several aspects of leadership.[9] First, Burns maintained, leadership is dissensual in that it is rooted in conflict and power over the authoritative allocation of values for a society (after David Easton's formulation). Second, leadership is collective in that it involves leader-follower interaction. Third, leadership is causative in that it leads to the creation of ideas, movements, institutions, nations. Fourth, leadership is purposive and goal-oriented. Fifth, and relatedly, leadership takes two forms depending on the goals involved: (1) transactional leadership consists of exchanges between leaders and followers toward meeting mutual needs and wants (for example, exchange of jobs for votes); it aims at such "modal values" as fairness, honesty, and responsibility; (2) transforming leadership, in addition to addressing exchanges of mutual needs, exacts sacrifice from followers; it is morally elevating and it aims at such "end-values" as liberty, equality, and justice.

Recurrent in the literature on leadership is the concept of *situation*, however defined. Recurrent also is the idea of leader traits, personality, or *psychology*. Moreover, some scholars approach traits or personality in such a broad fashion as to incorporate leadership *skills* (as in pursuit of goals and objectives), whereas other writers give the subject of skills independent scrutiny.

Accordingly, in this work we shall integrate the situational and trait approaches to political leadership using situation, psychology, and skills as central analytical categories, and we shall be concerned with the interaction of the three variables. We are fully cognizant of the elemental importance of a fourth variable—followers—in the analysis of political leadership. Indeed, Ronald L. Heifetz has recently spotlighted the role of the followers by reconceptualizing leadership as the mobilization of group resources toward solving group problems and achieving group objectives.[10] While we take for granted the centrality of leader-follower interaction, we have no way of examining or demonstrating this relationship retroactively in the historical contexts with which we deal.

In the pages that follow, we shall define situation, psychology, and skill in explicit terms and we shall apply our interactional perspective to a comparison of a group of loyalist (transactional or constituted) leaders and a group of revolutionary (transforming or nonconstituted) leaders. Throughout, we shall raise such questions as: What kinds of personality traits or psychological forces characterize the loyalists and the revolutionaries? What kinds of skills do loyalists and revolutionaries require in order either to maintain the status quo or to overthrow it? What kinds of situational variables impinge on psychologies and skills? How do the three variables interact and interrelate?

The interactional theory is a revised statement of the "situational" approach, initially designed for application to revolutionary elites in our previous work (see Introduction). We have modified the theory to incorporate loyalist leaders as well, and hence to apply to political elites in general.

Consistent with our theoretical stance, we shall present a series of hypotheses and propositions concerning loyalists and revolutionaries. These statements are drawn from two principal sources: (1) our previous studies of revolutionary elites and the sources cited therein, and (2) studies of characteristics and motivations of loyalist leaders. Before proceeding, it is necessary to highlight the relevant findings.

Studies of characteristics of political leaders (both loyalist and revolutionary) have yielded the following composite results:[11] Consisting almost exclusively of men, loyalist and revolutionary elites are typically in their forties and fifties upon first coming to office or seizing power. Both groups have urban backgrounds or exposures, and become involved in politics quite early in life. Loyalists and revolutionaries belong to mainstream ethnic and religious groups in their societies. Coming from upper, middle, and lower social strata, the two elite groups are highly educated sometimes in exclusive schools. The occupations of loyalists are preponderantly professional: law, teaching, civil service, party politics, journalism, medicine, and the military in the Third World. Radical leaders frequently abandon their conventional careers to become professional revolutionaries.

Among the most notable contributors to the literature of political motivation, Alfred Adler emphasized the will to power.[12] Sigmund Freud highlighted the leader's narcissistic craving for deference.[13] David C. McLelland and David G. Winter focused on the need for achievement, power, and affiliation.[14] Harold D. Lasswell viewed power seeking as a compensatory mechanism for feelings of inadequacy and low self-esteem, a private need that is displaced on public objects and rationalized in terms of the public interest.[15]

In two specific applications of the Lasswellian paradigm, Alexander L. George reaffirmed the compensatory nature of power seeking for political men while E. Victor Wolfenstein argued that the revolutionaries externalize upon the political world their oedipal problem and the conflict with the father.[16] Bruce Mazlish located the genesis of revolutionary behavior in a combination of asceticism and displaced libido, the latter suggesting that the individual has displaced his libidinal ties onto such abstractions as "revolution," "people," "virtue."[17] William H. Blanchard traced the root of the revolutionary vocation to "moral masochism": a sense of moral rectitude one is supposed to experience as a consequence of suffering for the condition of "humanity."[18]

Subjecting some of the foregoing motives or dynamics to systematic empirical investigation, James L. Payne and associates focused on the need for status, achievement, affiliation, approval, deference, and the like.[19] In a recent novel attempt to give Lasswell's political personality a neurochemical foundation, Douglas Madsen argued that what differentiates the power seeker from the nonpower seeker is that the former has an elevated biochemical marker, whole blood serotonin, one of several neuroregulators.[20]

Stimulating though they are, studies of motivations of political leaders have dealt almost exclusively with psychological variables, and they have typically focused on a single motivating factor that is held to be of universal applicability. For one thing, to engage in a discussion of the need for power or achievement or affiliation or deference in connection with political leaders is to engage in the commonsensical or the tautological. Considered individually, such other concepts as oedipal conflict, displaced libido, and moral masochism provide ethereal or at best partial explanations of political motivation. Alternatively, the need for blood samples (to be assayed for serotonin levels) creates a methodological nightmare in the study of political leaders, past and present. It is our position that a mixture of psychological and sociological variables is likely to converge to throw light on the motivations of political elites.

## TOWARD AN INTERACTIONAL THEORY

Support for our interactional theory may be garnered from talmudic times to the present. According to the Talmud, "In every age, there comes a time when leadership suddenly comes forth to meet the needs of the hour. And so there is no man [leader?] who does not find his time, and there is no hour that does not have its leader."[21]

In more recent times, Barbara Tuchman has observed:

The Human Being—you, I, or Napoleon— is unreliable as a scientific factor. In combination of personality, circumstance, and historical moment, each man is a package of variables impossible to duplicate. His birth, his parents, his siblings, his food, his home, his school, his economic and social status, his first job, his first girl, and the variables inherent in all of these, make up that mysterious compendium, personality—which combines with another set of variables: country, climate, time, and historical circumstance.[22]

Dean Keith Simonton concluded his study of *Genius, Creativity, and Leadership* by integrating the great-man and situational theories:

> I have presented ample evidence that both genius and zeitgeist make integral contributions to creativity and leadership. The zeitgeist participates as linear or cyclical trends, as economic or political conditions, and as a backdrop of events that determines the eponymic significance or sociocultural success of a political, military, philosophical, aesthetic, or scientific leader. At the same time, the impact of the situational context is tempered by such individual attributes as intelligence, morality, leadership qualities, productivity, aggressiveness, age, and belief structure, depending on the specific area of endeavor. "Being the right person" is almost as important as "being in the right place at the right time."[23]

An elaborate literature in the field of social psychology has been devoted to similar concerns. A recent contributor organized an entire book, *Toward a Psychology of Situations: An Interactional Perspective*, around three themes: (1) actual or objective environments and situations, (2) perceived or subjective environments and situations, and (3) person/situation interactions.[24] To the person (psychology) and situation we add the important variable of skills in order to arrive at our interactional perspective.

Consistent with our central concerns (see Introduction), and with the literature just reviewed, our theoretical position is stated in terms of two interrelated sets of propositions and hypotheses about political elites: What socioeconomic characteristics and traits do they have? How and why do they arise upon the scene? A third set of concerns relative to similarities and differences between loyalists and revolutionaries is interwoven throughout.

### Characteristics of Political Leaders

As stated in the Introduction, we study the social characteristics of political leaders in order to delineate similarities and differences between loyalists and revolutionaries, and to isolate social background variables that may be "situational" in nature, hence contributing to the interactional theory of political leadership.

Consistent with the findings summarized above, we expect political leadership to be positively correlated with middle age. Leaders of both loyalist and revolutionary persuasions will be in their forties and fifties upon the assumption of highest office or of power seizure. Although both groups may have been exposed to political ideologies—and may have participated in political activities—at much younger ages, the development of the requisite skills and the assumption of leadership positions are likely to require gestation and refinement. There may be instances, however, where crisis or chance play a more compelling role than one might logically suppose.

Political leadership, we anticipate, is positively correlated with the heightened awareness and activism nurtured by urban life. Loyalist and revolutionary leaders either come from the urban centers or, if born and raised in rural environments, they acquire early and sustained exposure to urban cultures. Early involvement in national affairs in urban areas is likely to be pivotal to the development of political elites.

We expect political leadership to correlate positively with the dominant indigenous culture of a society. Political leaders of all persuasions most likely belong to the main ethnic groups in their societies—more so perhaps of loyalists than revolutionaries. The religious backgrounds of the leaders are also of the mainstream variety, though their evolving religious orientations may vary: loyalists remain stable; revolutionaries, unstable.

Being largely self-selected, we project revolutionary leaders to be more representative of their respective social strata than loyalist elites. The former are likely to be predominantly middle class in origin, with significant representation from the upper and lower classes as well. The latter draw heavily upon upper and middle classes, with little or no representation from the lower class.

Should the foregoing propositions be confirmed by the data, it is logical to postulate some differences in the family lives of our two elite groups. Given the high degree of predictability and continuity associated with their circumstances, loyalist leaders are likely to experience more stable and tranquil family lives; revolutionaries are potential candidates for stormy and conflict-riddled childhoods.

Given their urban, social, and cultural backgrounds, we anticipate all political leaders to be highly educated, many having obtained university or other advanced training. Considering the comparative social strata from which they emerge, however, loyalists are likely to be better educated than revolutionaries.

The occupations of loyalists will be consistent with their education: They are likely to be found in law, politics, military, or civil service. Regardless of their formal education—whether teaching, journalism, law, or medicine—many radical elites are likely to become professional revolutionaries, gaining military experience in the course of their revolutions and as a component of their skills. Given their tasks and objectives, revolutionary elites will tend to be more prolific writers, concentrating chiefly (though not exclusively) on matters of revolutionary theory and practice.

Consistent with their social backgrounds, we expect the occupations of fathers of political leaders to vary rather markedly. Loyalists will tend to have higher status fathers in upper and middle class pursuits: landed gentry, government officials, the professions (including the military). Revolutionaries are likely to have lower status fathers in middle and working-class occupations.

Given their objective of undermining the extant political regimes, revolutionary elites tend to have extensive histories of involvement in illegal organizations and activities, and they will compile long records of arrest, imprisonment, and exile. Being regime-supportive, loyalist leaders are likely to participate in legal political activities, and they tend to be free of harassment by the authorities.

Consistent with their social backgrounds, both elite groups are likely to be cosmopolitan in orientation. Considering their differential objectives, however, revolutionary leaders will tend to heighten their cosmopolitanism in greater foreign travel, exposure to various societies and cultures, and maintenance of foreign contacts. Loyalist leaders are more "local" in these respects.

Accordingly, we project the revolutionaries to be more eclectic in their ideologies, combining indigenous and foreign elements; loyalists rely exclusively on indigenous ideologies. Revolutionaries draw on democracy of various forms, nationalism of various types, Marxism of various shades, or some combination of political doctrines. Loyalists internalize the ideologies of their forefathers.

Given their task of transforming political societies, revolutionaries are likely to have a positive and optimistic view of the human beings who constitute those societies; loyalists will tend to have a negative and pessimistic outlook in this regard. Both groups are likely to hold positive attitudes toward their own countries, but their views of the international society will vary: loyalists will incline toward friends; revolutionaries will be on guard against enemies.

Given their higher socioeconomic status, family background and occupation, we expect loyalists to be strategically situated in their societies, commanding ready access to positions of power and authority; revolutionaries will be markedly disadvantaged in this regard. In fact, we expect access to emerge as a major situational variable differentiating the loyalists from the revolutionaries.

### Rise of Political Leaders

The social backgrounds and socialization experiences of political elites imbue them with sets of norms and values and prepare them for the roles they will be called upon to play in the future. By the same token, leaders are in a position to internalize, articulate, and respond to the needs, wishes, desires, and aspirations of their people. Failure to maintain vital ties with the followers will impede or block reaching high office or, having reached it, such failure will spell demise.

Political leadership is in part situational in nature. Situations of crises—whether political, military, social, economic, or psychological—

catapult the leaders into prominence and provide them with ready and willing groups of followers. Political crises may consist of inter-elite rivalries or coups d'état, riots or rebellions, mass violence and civil strife, governmental corruption or ineptitude. Military crises are exemplified by war or army mutiny. Social crises include the disintegration of the prevailing ideology, normative order, and social institutions. Economic crises are represented by severe inflation or depression. Psychological crises may consist of frustration, relative deprivation, or status inconsistency.

A second type of situation may account for the emergence of other political leaders. Specifically, the persistent turbulence and large-scale violence characteristic of the histories of such countries as China, Colombia, Cuba, "Palestine," Peru, and Vietnam facilitate the emergence of political elites.

A third type of situation is to be found in the nationalist movements of the twentieth century, which directly pit the colonizer against the colonized. Coming sooner or later, conflict is inherent in the very nature of a colonial situation and the mere presence of the outsider. This is as true of America of the 1770s as it is of the Algeria of the 1950s, China and Vietnam of the 1930s and beyond, "Palestine" and South Africa of the 1970s and beyond.

A fourth type of situation results from travel—particularly to foreign lands—and exposure to different experiences and cultures. The traveler may observe firsthand some of the problems of everyday life: misery and hunger, cruelty and torture. If he is a colonial, not only will the traveler witness inhumanity, he is likely to experience it personally as well. Moreover, the colonial traveler will witness sharp differences between the conditions of the colony and those of the metropolitan country.

A fifth type of situational dynamic is, simply, the role of chance. Some political leaders are propelled into prominence not as a result of determination and hard work, but of fortuitous circumstances. Being in the right place at the right time has helped determine a variety of political careers.

The foregoing types of situations operate at the societal or historical levels. A final set of situational variables relate to personal traits or characteristics that are "external" to political leaders and over which they have, as individuals, no control. These include: birthplace, exposure to urban culture, socioeconomic status, family life, number of siblings, age ranking among siblings, ethnicity, and religious background.

It is clear that we use the idea of "situation" in three explicit and identifiable senses: (1) a condition of open or latent conflict in which the elements of a contest for power are sufficiently salient to be unavoidable, (2) a condition of luck or chance, and (3) a condition wherein certain personal attributes beyond one's sway set the stage for the assumption of leadership roles.

Though critical, situation alone does not account for the emergence of political elites; it is a necessary but not a sufficient condition. For a political leader to emerge, it is imperative that the situation coincide with the presence of a certain kind of person or personality. This person or personality has two indispensable characteristics: (1) a mental set or psychology that propels him toward political action, and (2) a set of skills—particularly verbal and organizational—that enables him to perform his tasks.

The mental set or psychology to which we refer takes a variety of forms. As may be expected, however, not all psychological dynamics apply with equal force to all loyalists and revolutionaries. The hypotheses and propositions that follow are derived from the literature of political motivation summarized above and from our own previous studies of revolutionary leaders.

All political elites are likely to be motivated by varieties of nationalism and patriotism. Loyalists and revolutionaries seek to maintain the identity and integrity of their nations. They set out to free their lands from the oppression and exploitation of other countries or, having reached this stage, they may seek to expand their national frontiers.

Revolutionaries are driven by visions of justice and corresponding attempts to right the wrongs. Loyalists may institute or participate in programs of social reform and change but primarily in the interest of "national development" or "modernization." Social justice may be a secondary consequence or outcome.

Political elites of all persuasions are likely to be vain, egotistical, and narcissistic—loyalists perhaps more so than revolutionaries. A degree of vanity appears to be an indispensable condition of rising to leadership roles.

Relative deprivation and status inconsistency may serve as motive forces of political action. Where there is a felt discrepancy between aspiration and achievement (relative deprivation), one may set out to address the situation accordingly. Where there is discrepancy between one's socioeconomic status and one's political power (status inconsistency), political action may promise relief.

Some political leaders—whether loyalist or revolutionary—are driven by a compulsion to excel, to prove themselves, to overcompensate. This compulsion is likely due to feelings of inferiority complex or low self-esteem. How this condition comes about requires examination on a case-by-case basis.

The oedipus complex and its attendant consequences may play a role in the emergence of relatively few political leaders, most likely of the revolutionary variety. The displacement of an internal psychological drama onto the political arena may reduce feelings of ambivalence and guilt and make life more manageable. But this too must be examined on an individual basis.

In short, a variety of forces or dynamics play roles in shaping the mental set of political leaders. We hazard the proposition that no single motivation or dynamic is sufficient to explain the formation of all political personalities.

Nor do we anticipate an invariant mix of psychological dynamics universally applicable to all political elites. A mix there shall be, to be sure, but we expect it to vary from leader to leader, from loyalist to revolutionary.

If they are to be successful, political leaders require a set of skills with which to approach their calling. Loyalists must have the ability to perpetuate status quo ideologies and to command the organizational infrastructures of their societies. By contrast, revolutionaries must have the capacity to devise and propagate ideologies of radical change and to create the necessary organizational apparatuses.

Loyalists extol the established order; revolutionaries denounce it, articulating an alternative vision embodying, in their view, a superior (perhaps even utopian) society. The alternative vision, in turn, must find expression in concrete plans and programs promising success in the future.

While loyalists tend to mask popular grievance or discontent, revolutionaries highlight and publicize them. In so doing, the latter undermine regime morale and legitimacy, rally the masses to the cause, and elicit commitment and devotion.

To be most effective, the verbal skills of political leaders must be complemented by an ability to fashion organizations of various kinds—political, military, and paramilitary. Loyalists, needless to say, by definition control the organizations of their societies. Revolutionaries, on the other hand, must build organizations from the ground up.

Organization is critical in that it is the primary medium for translating ideology into action. Ideology helps attract the masses; organization functions to mobilize them, tap their talents and energies, and channel them toward the realization of articulated objectives. Without organization, there can be no leadership, whether of a loyalist or revolutionary nature.

## SUMMARY

Our interactional theory of political leadership is synthetic in that it incorporates the strong points of some extant theories as well as integrating sociological and psychological variables in the analysis of political leaders. The theory focuses on the salience of a series of social-background variables associated with all political leaders and on distinguishing the loyalist elites from their revolutionary counterparts.

The theory also stresses the interplay of situation, psychology, and skill in the rise of political leaders. Taken together, the three variables demonstrate why it is that (1) not all situations give rise to political leaders, and (2) not all persons with the appropriate psychology and skills emerge as political elites.

We now turn to an examination of our theory against both quantitative and qualitative data.

## NOTES

1. Ralph M. Stogdill, *Handbook of Leadership* (New York: Free Press, 1974); Bernard B. Bass, ed., *Stogdill's Handbook of Leadership*, revised and expanded ed. (New York: Free Press, 1981). Both sources contain Stogdill's seminal 1947 survey of leadership traits.

2. Cecil A. Gibb, "An Interactional View of the Emergence of Leadership," *Australian Journal of Psychology*, 10 (1958): 101-10; Gibb, "Leadership," in Gardner Lindzey and Elliot Aronson, eds., *Handbook of Social Psychology*, vol. 4 (Reading, MA: Addison-Wesley, 1969); Gibb, "Leadership: Psychological Aspects," *International Encyclopedia of the Social Sciences*, vol. 9 (New York: Macmillan, 1968).

3. Fred E. Fiedler, *Leadership* (Morristown, NJ: General Learning Press, 1971); Fiedler, "A Contingency Model of Leadership Effectiveness," in Leonard Berkowitz, ed., *Advances in Experimental Social Psychology*, vol. 1 (New York: Academic Press, 1964).

4. Edwin P. Hollander, *Leadership Dynamics* (New York: Free Press, 1978).

5. Glenn D. Paige, ed., *Political Leadership* (New York: Free Press, 1972); Paige, *The Scientific Study of Political Leadership* (New York: Free Press, 1977).

6. Jean Blondel, *Government Ministers in the Contemporary World* (Beverly Hills: Sage Publications, 1985); Blondel, *World Leaders: Heads of Government in the Postwar Period* (Beverly Hills: Sage Publications, 1980); Mattei Dogan, ed., *The Mandarins of Western Europe* (Beverly Hills: Sage Publications, 1975); Lewis J. Edinger, "The Comparative Analysis of Political Leadership," *Comparative Politics* 7 (1975): 253-69; Edinger, ed., *Political Leadership in Industrialized Societies* (New York: Wiley, 1967); Donald R. Matthews, *The Social Background of Political Decision-Makers* (New York: Doubleday, 1954); Robert D. Putnam, *The Comparative Study of Political Elites* (Englewood Cliffs, NJ: Prentice-Hall, 1976); William B. Quandt, *The Comparative Study of Political Elites* (Beverly Hills: Sage Publications, 1970); Donald D. Searing, "Models and Images of Man and Society in Leadership Theory," *Journal of Politics* 31 (1969): 3-31.

7. Alexander L. George, "Power as a Compensatory Value for Political Leaders," *Journal of Social Issues* 3 (1968): 101-10; Fred I. Greenstein, *Personality and Politics: Problems of Evidence, Inference, and Conceptualization* (Chicago: Markham, 1969); Ted Robert Gurr, *Why Men Rebel* (Princeton: Princeton University Press, 1970); Margaret G. Hermann, ed., *A Psychological Examination of Political Leaders* (New York: Free Press, 1977); Harold D. Lasswell, *Power and Personality* [1948] (New York: Viking, 1962); Lasswell, *Psychopathology and Politics* [1930] (New York: Viking, 1960); James L. Payne et al., *The Motivation of Politicians* (Chicago: Nelson-Hall, 1984); E. Victor Wolfenstein, *Revolutionary Personality* (Princeton: Princeton University Press, 1967).

8. Robert C. Tucker, *Politics as Leadership* (Columbia: University of Missouri Press, 1981).

9. James MacGregor Burns, *Leadership* (New York: Harper & Row, 1978).

10. Ronald L. Heifetz and Riley M. Sinder, "Political Leadership: Managing

the Public's Problem Solving," in Robert B. Reich, ed., *The Power of Public Ideas* (New York: Ballinger, 1987).

11. For detailed findings on revolutionaries, see M. Rejai and K. Phillips, *World Revolutionary Leaders* (New Brunswick: Rutgers University Press, 1983) and the sources cited therein. Prominent studies of loyalist leaders include: Joel D. Aberbach, Robert D. Putnam, and Bert A. Rockman, *Bureaucrats and Politicians in Western Democracies* (Cambridge: Harvard University Press, 1981); Blondel, *Government Ministers in the Contemporary World*; Blondel, *World Leaders*; Dogan, ed., *The Madarins of Western Europe*; W. L. Guttsman, *The British Political Elite* (New York: Basic Books, 1964); R. W. Johnson, "The British Political Elite, 1955-1972," *European Journal of Sociology* (Paris) 14 (1973): 35-77; Harold J. Laski, "The Personnel of the British Cabinet, 1801-1924," *American Political Science Review* 22 (1928): 12-31; Donald R. Matthews, *U.S. Senators and Their World* (Chapel Hill: University of North Carolina Press, 1960); Colin Mellors, *The British MP: A Socioeconomic Study of the House of Commons* (Westmead, Farnborough, England: Saxon House, 1978); Herbert Van Thal, ed., *The Prime Ministers*, 2 vols. (London: George Allen & Unwin, 1974, 1975).

12. Alfred Adler, "The Psychology of Power" [1928], *Journal of Individual Psychology* 22 (1966): 166-72.

13. Sigmund Freud, *Group Psychology and the Analysis of the Ego* [1921] (New York: Bantam Books, 1960); Freud, *Moses and Monotheism* (New York: Knopf, 1939).

14. David C. McLelland et al., *The Achievement Motive* (New York: Appleton-Century-Croft, 1953); David G. Winter, *The Power Motive* (New York: Free Press, 1973).

15. Lasswell, *Power and Personality*; Lasswell, *Psychopathology and Politics*.

16. George, "Power as a Compensatory Value for Political Leaders"; Wolfenstein, *Revolutionary Personality*.

17. Bruce Mazlish, *The Revolutionary Ascetic* (New York: Basic Books, 1976).

18. William H. Blanchard, *Revolutionary Morality* (Santa Barbara, CA: ABC-Clio, 1984).

19. Payne et al., *The Motivations of Politicians* (n. 6).

20. Douglas Madsen, "A Biochemical Property Relating to Power Seeking in Humans," *American Political Science Review* 79 (1985): 448-57; Madsen, "Power Seekers Are Different: Further Biochemical Evidence," *American Political Science Review* 80 (March 1986): 261-70.

21. Quoted by Supreme Court Justice Sandra Day O'Connor and reported in the *New York Times*, July 11, 1982.

22. Quoted in Anthony R. DeLuca, *Personality, Power, and Politics* (Cambridge, MA: Schenkman Publishing, 1983), p. xi, capitalization in original.

23. Dean Keith Simonton, *Genius, Creativity, and Leadership* (Cambridge: Harvard University Press, 1984), p. 165.

24. David Magnusson, ed., *Toward a Psychology of Situations: An Interactional Perspective* (Hillsdale, NJ: Lawrence Erlbaum Associates, 1981).

# II FOUNDATIONS

# 2 General Characteristics

In order to test the hypotheses and propositions advanced in Chapter 1 relative to the sociodemographic, experiential, ideological, and attitudinal attributes of loyalist and revolutionary elites, we gathered data from a variety of sources, as discussed in the Introduction and detailed in the Bibliography. In the pages that follow, we report the results of our investigations. We should note that in this chapter and throughout this study, we have come across findings that, although "statistically significant," carry little or no theoretical substance or meaning. In all such instances, we have refrained from reporting our "findings."

One revelation is so evident as to require only a bare mention. Although women have begun to play increasingly more important leadership roles, there is not a single woman among the 100 leaders we studied.

## FINDINGS

A most striking set of findings is the degree of *similarity* that marks the loyalist and revolutionary elites across an unexpectedly large number of sociodemographic dimensions. Specifically, for over two-thirds of the characteristics measured, no significant differences exist between the two types of leaders. For some of these characteristics (for instance, father's birthplace or education), the problem of missing data is so severe as to make inclusion meaningless. Shared characteristics not seriously affected by missing data are (1) native or domestic birth; (2) urban birth, exposure to urban life if rural-born, and age at which so exposed; (3) legitimacy status; (4) number of siblings; (5) age ranking among siblings; (6) character of family life, whether tranquil or stormy; (7) orphanhood—or otherwise separation from one or both parents; (8) age first exposed to political ideology; (9) age first took part in political activity; (10) religious background, status of religious group as majority, parents' religion; (11) ethnicity; (12) military service; (13) education as to type of school (public or private, parochial or secular), domestic or foreign, level attained, and field; (14) foreign travel as to extent, duration, and location; (15) foreign languages spoken; (16) continuing foreign contacts; (17) publication record; and (18) attitude toward the international community. (Further details concerning these variables will be found in Appendix C, General Code Sheet.)

There is an important cluster of traits, then, that cuts across the loyalist-revolutionary distinction and applies to all political leaders. Political elites are typically native born to legal marriages. They are either urban born or, if born and raised in rural areas, they develop early and sustained exposure to urban cultures. Though having a large number of siblings, they tend to be either the firstborn or the lastborn. They tend to have tranquil, peaceful family lives, even though some of them are orphaned or otherwise separated from one or both parents. They are exposed to political ideology, and participate in political activity, early in life, sometimes in their teens. Their ethnic and religious backgrounds are of the mainstream variety. They are highly educated, frequently at exclusive schools. They are cosmopolitan, traveling far and wide, and developing a variety of foreign contacts. They publish on a wide range of subjects. Their attitude toward the international situation is dualistic, distinguishing friends and foes.

In what ways, then, do our loyalist leaders differ from their revolutionary counterparts, and vice versa? Consistent with our theoretical concerns, we group these differences under three headings: (1) situational variables: parental heritage into which a leader is born and over which he has no control; (2) skill variables: political and organizational activity in developing a career and reaching high office; and (3) psychology-skill variables: attitudes and ideologies that affect one's outlook and activity, ideological skills leaders bring to bear in pursuing their objectives.

In the tabular presentations that follow, where data are organized into nominal/nominal or nominal/ordinal categories, Cramer's V is employed. Where data are grouped into ordinal/ordinal categories, gamma is reported. In some of the tables, *totals do not equal 100* because of missing data.

### Situational Variables

Only two interrelated socioeconomic variables emerge as important: socioeconomic (or class) status, father's occupation. Table 2.1 documents the socioeconomic backgrounds of the leaders. While representation from all categories occurs for both loyalist and revolutionary elites, almost half (48 percent) of the loyalists are from upper class backgrounds, and 46 percent come from the middle class, with only one person (Fulgencio Batista) arising from the lower class. Revolution, however, attracts more leaders from the lower class (22 percent), while the largest group is middle class in origin (48 percent), followed by the upper class (28 percent). On the whole, loyalist elites come from upper and middle classes; revolutionary leaders have significant representation from the lower class as well. (The three persons falling into the "Other" category represent tribal royalty: Luthuli of South Africa, Mondlane of Mozambique, Nyerere of Tanzania.)

Associated with the socioeconomic status of a leader is his father's primary occupation, as shown in Table 2.2. Roughly equal proportions of all fathers were either professionals (17 percent for the revolutionaries, 20 percent for the loyalists) or they fell into the politician-businessman-landlord group (30 percent for the revolutionaries, 37 percent for the loyalists). On the other hand, 28 percent of the revolutionaries' fathers had working class or manual occupations, as compared to only 6 percent for the loyalists. Conversely, while almost one-fourth of the loyalists' fathers had careers as civil servants or government officials, not a single revolutionary's father enjoyed such status. In other words, occupations of the fathers afforded many loyalists much readier access to positions of power than revolutionaries.

### Skill Variables

The primary occupations of our leaders prior to power seizure or assuming highest office are rather diverse. Table 2.3 reveals that, their high education notwithstanding, 36 percent of the revolutionary leaders abandoned all endeavors save that of revolution itself: they become professional revolutionaries. By contrast, much like their fathers, 34 percent of the loyalists came up through such established ranks as the civil service or political office. Twice as many loyalists (56 percent to 28 percent) had careers in the

**Table 2.1**
**Socioeconomic Status**

| Leaders | Upper Class N | % | Middle Class N | % | Lower Class N | % | Other N | % | Total N | % |
|---|---|---|---|---|---|---|---|---|---|---|
| Revolutionary | 14 | 28.0 | 24 | 48.0 | 11 | 22.0 | 1 | 2.0 | 50 | 50.0 |
| Loyalist | 24 | 48.0 | 23 | 46.0 | 1 | 2.0 | 2 | 4.0 | 50 | 50.0 |
| Total | 38 | 38.0 | 47 | 47.0 | 12 | 12.0 | 3 | 3.0 | 100 | 100.0 |

Cramer's V = .34    Chi Square = 11.32    $p = 0.01$

**Table 2.2**
**Father's Primary Occupation**

| Leader | Professional | | Politician, Business, Landlord | | Working Class | | Combination | | Tribal Chief | | Civil Servant, Government Official | | Other | | Total | |
|---|---|---|---|---|---|---|---|---|---|---|---|---|---|---|---|---|
| | N | % | N | % | N | % | N | % | N | % | N | % | N | % | N | % |
| Revolutionary | 8 | 17.0 | 14 | 29.8 | 13 | 27.7 | 9 | 19.1 | 1 | 2.1 | 0 | 0.0 | 2 | 4.3 | 47 | 49.0 |
| Loyalist | 10 | 20.4 | 18 | 36.7 | 3 | 6.1 | 2 | 4.1 | 1 | 2.0 | 12 | 24.5 | 3 | 6.1 | 49 | 51.0 |
| Total | 18 | 18.8 | 32 | 33.3 | 16 | 16.7 | 11 | 11.5 | 2 | 2.1 | 12 | 12.5 | 5 | 5.2 | 96 | 100.0 |

Cramer's V = .50      Chi Square = 23.60      p = .0006

**Table 2.3**
**Leader's Primary Occupation**

| Leader | Professional | | Professional Revolutionary | | Politician, Business Landlord | | Working Class | | Combination | | Civil Servant, Government Official | | Other | | Total | |
|---|---|---|---|---|---|---|---|---|---|---|---|---|---|---|---|---|
| | N | % | N | % | N | % | N | % | N | % | N | % | N | % | N | % |
| Revolutionary | 14 | 28.0 | 18 | 36.0 | 5 | 10.0 | 0 | 0.0 | 12 | 24.0 | 0 | 0.0 | 1 | 2.0 | 50 | 50.0 |
| Loyalist | 28 | 56.0 | 0 | 0.0 | 2 | 4.0 | 1 | 2.0 | 1 | 2.0 | 17 | 34.0 | 1 | 2.0 | 50 | 50.0 |
| Total | 42 | 42.0 | 18 | 18.0 | 7 | 7.0 | 1 | 1.0 | 13 | 13.0 | 17 | 17.0 | 2 | 2.0 | 100 | 100.0 |

Cramer's V = .72      Chi Square = 51.26      p = .0000

professions: law, medicine, teaching, the clergy, or the military. Through their occupations, then, many loyalists prepare themselves to protect the status quo; revolutionaries, to overthrow it.

Despite access problems, when it comes to reaching the pinnacle of authority, speed and impatience seem to mark the revolutionaries: nearly two-thirds (64 percent) had seized power *before* age 45 (Table 2.4). Loyalists are significantly older when they step into the highest office: 62 percent *after* age 45. Loyalist leaders, it seems, must observe the protocol of office (for example, seniority) while coming up through the ranks; unhampered by protocol—and enjoying the advantages of youth—revolutionaries appear to take greater risks.

Tables 2.5 and 2.6 give a flavor of membership in legal and revolutionary organizations by the two leadership groups. As may be expected, loyalists overwhelmingly participate in legal organizations (98 percent) and revolutionaries in illegal ones (also 98 percent). However, with rare exceptions, over their entire careers loyalists and revolutionaries participate in both legal and illegal activities. On the other hand, revolutionaries are more likely to cross over to legal organizations (58 percent) than are loyalists to join illegal ones (22 percent).

While some of these findings may appear surprising at first blush, they are quite consistent with our discussion in the Introduction of loyalists-turned-revolutionaries and revolutionaries-turned-loyalists. Moreover, some crossovers may occur as a means of infiltrating and subverting the other side.

Whether legal or illegal, organizations function as reference groups for political leaders. Legal organizations reinforce the prevailing ideologies of the loyalists while illegal ones provide support for the antiregime rationale and behavior of the revolutionaries.

As may be expected, persons involved in illegal activity are likely to develop records of arrest, imprisonment or exile, sometimes extensively. Accordingly, Tables 2.7 and 2.8 demonstrate that a larger number of revolutionaries are arrested with some frequency and they spend from a few months up to 20 years (as in the case of Lenin) in prison or exile.

What may not be immediately expected is the arrest record of the loyalists. While nearly two-thirds have clean records, 35 percent had been arrested at least a few times and were imprisoned for several years. Some of these arrests are related to political activity of the radicals or revolutionaries who subsequently become loyalists. Thus, for instance, Wang of China, Abbas of Algeria, Nasser of Egypt, Bourguiba of Tunisia, and Kaunda of Zambia were detained at one time or another for either anti-imperialist or antiregime agitation. Other arrests were unrelated to political activity, however. Thus, for example, an expert marksman, Marcos of the Philippines was arrested in 1939 on the suspicion of having murdered his father's

**Table. 2.4**
**Leader's Age at the Time of Highest Office or Revolution**

| Leaders | 16 - 19 N | 16 - 19 % | 20 - 24 N | 20 - 24 % | 25 - 34 N | 25 - 34 % | 35 - 44 N | 35 - 44 % | 45 - 64 N | 45 - 64 % | 65+ N | 65+ % | Total N | Total % |
|---|---|---|---|---|---|---|---|---|---|---|---|---|---|---|
| Revolutionary | 1 | 2.0 | 0 | 0.0 | 15 | 30.0 | 16 | 32.0 | 18 | 36.0 | 0 | 0.0 | 50 | 50.0 |
| Loyalist | 1 | 2.0 | 1 | 2.0 | 3 | 6.0 | 14 | 28.0 | 26 | 52.0 | 5 | 10.0 | 50 | 50.0 |
| Total | 2 | 2.0 | 1 | 1.0 | 18 | 18.0 | 30 | 30.0 | 44 | 44.0 | 5 | 5.0 | 100 | 100.0 |

gamma = .49    Chi Square = 15.59    p = .008

**Table 2.5**
**Membership in Legal Organizations**

|  | Membership |  |  |  |  |  |
|---|---|---|---|---|---|---|
|  | No |  | Yes |  | Total |  |
| Leader | N | % | N | % | N | % |
| Revolutionary | 20 | 41.7 | 28 | 58.3 | 48 | 49.0 |
| Loyalist | 1 | 2.0 | 49 | 98.0 | 50 | 51.0 |
| Total | 21 | 21.4 | 77 | 78.6 | 98 | 100.0 |
| gamma = .94 | Chi Square = 20.59 |  |  |  | p = .0000 |  |

political rival; Dîem of Vietnam was taken prisoner by the Vietminh between September 1945 and January 1946; Senghor of Senegal was imprisoned by the Germans during World War II.

On the whole, for loyalists the negative effects of arrest, imprisonment, and exile are likely to be outweighed by the more enduring positive attachments to the political system. For the revolutionaries, these experiences are likely to sharpen and reinforce growing discontent and antiregime activity.

### Psychology-Skill Variables

Before taking up leader ideologies and attitudes, we consider a related matter: religion. While there are no appreciable differences in the religious

**Table 2.6**
**Membership in Revolutionary Organizations**

|  | Membership |  |  |  |  |  |
|---|---|---|---|---|---|---|
|  | No |  | Yes |  | Total |  |
| Leader | N | % | N | % | N | % |
| Revolutionary | 1 | 2.0 | 49 | 98.0 | 50 | 50.0 |
| Loyalist | 39 | 78.0 | 11 | 22.0 | 50 | 50.0 |
| Total | 40 | 40.0 | 60 | 60.0 | 100 | 100.0 |
| gamma = −.98 | Chi Square = 57.04 |  |  |  | p = .0000 |  |

## Table 2.7
### Arrest/Exile Record: Frequency

|  | None | Some (1-3) | Moderate (4-6) | Frequent (7+) | Total |
|---|---|---|---|---|---|
| Leader | N     % | N     % | N     % | N     % | N     % |
| Revolutionary | 17   34.7 | 20   40.8 | 10   20.4 | 2   4.1 | 49   50.0 |
| Loyalist | 32   65.3 | 17   34.7 | 0   0.0 | 0   0.0 | 49   50.0 |
| Total | 49   50.0 | 37   37.8 | 10   10.2 | 2   2.0 | 98   100.0 |

gamma = -.62    Chi Square = 16.84    p = .0008

*backgrounds* into which the two groups of leaders are born, a notable difference occurs in their evolving religious *orientations*. Not unexpectedly, as seen in Table 2.9, almost 38 percent of the revolutionaries turn to atheism while not a single loyalist publicly deviates from traditional religious beliefs.

Table 2.10 elucidates the primary reason for the shift in religious beliefs: 48 percent of revolutionary elites adhere to political doctrines that are antithetical to religion. These ideologies include varieties or combinations of nationalism, socialism, Marxism, communism, and other leftist doctrines. By contrast, only two loyalists—Lévesque of Canada and Struve of Russia—subscribed to leftist (social democratic) ideologies but they remained steadfast in religious beliefs: Lévesque, Catholic; Struve, Russian Orthodox.

## Table 2.8
### Arrest/Exile Record: Duration

|  | None | One Year or Less | Two to Nine Years | Ten or More Years | Total |
|---|---|---|---|---|---|
| Leader | N     % | N     % | N     % | N     % | N     % |
| Revolutionary | 17   34.7 | 10   20.4 | 16   32.7 | 6   12.2 | 49   50.0 |
| Loyalist | 32   65.3 | 12   24.5 | 5   10.2 | 0   0.0 | 49   50.0 |
| Total | 49   50.0 | 22   22.4 | 21   21.4 | 6   6.1 | 98   100.0 |

gamma = -.59    Chi Square = 16.54    p = .0009

**Table 2.9**
**Religious Orientation**

| Leader | Atheist | | Protestant | | Catholic | | Christian, Other | | Muslim | | Buddhist | | Other | | Total | |
|---|---|---|---|---|---|---|---|---|---|---|---|---|---|---|---|---|
| | N | % | N | % | N | % | N | % | N | % | N | % | N | % | N | % |
| Revolutionary | 17 | 37.8 | 14 | 31.1 | 6 | 13.3 | 1 | 2.2 | 2 | 4.4 | 0 | 0.0 | 5 | 11.1 | 45 | 47.0 |
| Loyalist | 0 | 0.0 | 18 | 36.0 | 20 | 40.0 | 4 | 8.0 | 5 | 10.0 | 3 | 6.0 | 0 | 0.0 | 50 | 52.0 |
| Total | 17 | 17.9 | 32 | 33.7 | 26 | 27.4 | 5 | 5.3 | 7 | 7.4 | 3 | 3.2 | 5 | 5.3 | 95 | 100.0 |

Cramer's V = .62  Chi Square = 35.96  p = .0000

**Table 2.10**
**Ideology**

|  | \multicolumn{2}{c}{None} | \multicolumn{2}{c}{Demo-cratic} | \multicolumn{2}{c}{Marxist/Leninist} | \multicolumn{2}{c}{Nationalist/Marxist/Leninist} | \multicolumn{2}{c}{Nationalist/Marxist/Socialist} | \multicolumn{2}{c}{Nationalist/Other} | \multicolumn{2}{c}{Leftist/Other} | \multicolumn{2}{c}{Rightist/Other} | \multicolumn{2}{c}{Other} | \multicolumn{2}{c}{Total} |
|---|---|---|---|---|---|---|---|---|---|---|---|---|---|---|---|---|---|---|---|
| Leader | N | % | N | % | N | % | N | % | N | % | N | % | N | % | N | % | N | % | N | % |
| Revolutionary | 1 | 2.0 | 11 | 22.0 | 2 | 4.0 | 17 | 34.0 | 1 | 2.0 | 10 | 20.0 | 4 | 8.0 | 2 | 4.0 | 2 | 4.0 | 50 | 50.0 |
| Loyalist | 0 | 0.0 | 2 | 4.0 | 0 | 0.0 | 0 | 0.0 | 0 | 0.0 | 22 | 44.0 | 2 | 4.0 | 24 | 48.0 | 0 | 0.0 | 50 | 50.0 |
| Total | 1 | 1.0 | 13 | 13.0 | 2 | 2.0 | 17 | 17.0 | 1 | 1.0 | 32 | 32.0 | 6 | 6.0 | 26 | 26.0 | 2 | 2.0 | 100 | 100.0 |

Cramer's V = .73    Chi Square = 53.01    p = .0000

(Rationale for the particular classification of ideologies in Table 2.10 will be found in our earlier work.)

Alternatively, it may be argued, revolutionaries embrace certain ideologies *because* they are antireligious and, therefore, antiestablishment. Insofar as religion is an integral part of the social order, an antireligious posture may become part and parcel of a revolutionary vocation. On the other hand, it must be remembered that in the English (Puritan) Revolution of the 1640s, the Iranian Revolution of 1979, the spread of "Islamic fundamentalism" in Arab countries, and the continuing sectarian strife in Northern Ireland and elsewhere, religion has played a revolutionary role. In other words, religion appears to function as a two-edged sword, depending on times and contexts.

The origins of ideologies to which the leaders subscribe are depicted in Table 2.11. Nearly two thirds (63 percent) of revolutionary elites borrow a foreign ideology and adapt it to local conditions, while 86 percent of the loyalists accept the prevailing indigenous ideology. Almost 37 percent of the revolutionaries work with indigenous ideologies but, by definition, these doctrines are at variance with the ones adopted and propagated by the establishment regimes they fight.

Tables 2.12 and 2.13 document some significant attitudinal differences between the two groups of elites. Nearly 82 percent of the revolutionaries hold a positive view of human nature, with only 8 percent showing a negative view. The loyalists, on the other hand, are evenly divided (48 percent) between the positive and the negative.

Almost 96 percent of the loyalists and 74 percent of the revolutionaries maintain a positive attitude toward their own countries. However, 22 percent of the revolutionaries vacillate between the positive and the negative, depending on the regime in power.

**Table 2.11**
**Origin of Ideology**

| Leader | Indigenous N | Indigenous % | Foreign N | Foreign % | Foreign/Indigenous N | Foreign/Indigenous % | Total N | Total % |
|---|---|---|---|---|---|---|---|---|
| Revolutionary | 18 | 36.7 | 0 | 0.0 | 31 | 63.3 | 49 | 49.5 |
| Loyalist | 43 | 86.0 | 2 | 4.0 | 5 | 10.0 | 50 | 50.5 |
| Total | 61 | 61.6 | 2 | 2.0 | 36 | 36.4 | 99 | 100.0 |

Cramer's V = .56   Chi Square = 31.02   p = .0000

**Table 2.12**
**Attitude Toward Human Beings**

|  | Attitude | | | | | | | |
|---|---|---|---|---|---|---|---|---|
|  | Negative | | Fluctuating | | Positive | | Total | |
| Leader | N | % | N | % | N | % | N | % |
| Revolutionary | 3 | 7.9 | 4 | 10.5 | 31 | 81.6 | 38 | 45.2 |
| Loyalist | 22 | 47.8 | 2 | 4.3 | 22 | 47.8 | 46 | 54.8 |
| Total | 25 | 29.8 | 6 | 7.1 | 53 | 63.1 | 84 | 100.0 |

gamma = −.68        Chi Square = 16.02        p = .0003

**Table 2.13**
**Attitude Toward Own Country**

|  | Attitude | | | | | | | | | |
|---|---|---|---|---|---|---|---|---|---|---|
|  | Negative | | Fluctuating | | Positive | | Other | | Total | |
| Leader | N | % | N | % | N | % | N | % | N | % |
| Revolutionary | 2 | 4.3 | 10 | 21.7 | 34 | 73.9 | 0 | 0.0 | 46 | 48.9 |
| Loyalist | 0 | 0.0 | 1 | 2.1 | 46 | 95.8 | 1 | 2.1 | 48 | 51.1 |
| Total | 2 | 2.1 | 11 | 11.7 | 80 | 85.1 | 1 | 1.1 | 94 | 100.0 |

Cramer's V = .36        Chi Square = 12.13        p = .007

## SUMMARY

Several of the hypotheses and propositions concerning loyalist and revolutionary elites advanced in Chapter 1 are disconfirmed by the data. We had expected the revolutionaries to have more stormy family lives, to be more prolific writers as well as more cosmopolitan. We had expected the loyalists to be better educated, to participate only in legal organization and activity, and to have a uniformly positive view of international society. We had expected both groups to be about the same ages at the time of power seizure or assuming highest office. None of these holds.

Instead, we find, on the one hand, a large constellation of sociodemographic traits that cuts across the loyalist-revolutionary distinction and applies with equal force to both political elites. In the pages that follow, these similarities enable us to focus on leadership characteristics in general.

On the other hand, we find a series of attributes that sharply separates the two groups. In the pages that follow, these differences enable us to project which men are likely to become loyalists and which ones revolutionaries.

# 3 Careers and Crises

**METHODOLOGICAL NOTE**

As indicated in Chapter 2, a series of variables related to situation, skill, and psychology brings forth significant differences between loyalist and revolutionary elites. In order to highlight further heterogeneity between the two groups, we controlled our data for three independent variables we had found important in our previous work: (1) the time period in which the leaders seized power or assumed highest office: before or after World War II, (2) the region of the world in which the leaders appeared, and (3) the ideologies the leaders held.

Not surprisingly, perhaps, controlling for independent variables did not yield meaningful results in this study. To begin with, whereas World War II provided dramatic impetus to the emergence of new revolutions and revolutionaries, it did not have a similar impact on loyalist elites as well. As for region, a few differences did emerge between the two groups, but they are so inconsequential (for example, probably due to ideological eclecticism, Africa is the only region to have produced no atheists) that we forgo reporting them. Similarly, differences between the ideological stances of the two groups are manifest and self-explanatory (*within* the revolutionaries, however, divergences are considerable, as mentioned in Chapter 2). Finally, we should note, although our (unrepresentative) sample size is rather small, it does not appear that even a much larger one would have changed the picture as far as the foregoing variables are concerned.

Having suspended effort to identify further heterogeneity between the two elite groups, we turned to factor analysis as a method of classifying the 100 leaders into meaningful categories or types, both in terms of attributes and personalities.

A factor, it will be recalled, is an artifically constructed composite variable to which several individual variables are correlated. R-factor analysis was performed in an effort to produce constellations of attributes the leaders may share; Q-factor analysis was intended to produce groupings of the leaders themselves.

In executing the factor analyses, we included the variables listed below because they show variations involving our *entire* set of 100 political leaders and because of relatively low incidence of missing data. Where missing data still remained a problem, we substituted modal values for nominal variables and mean values for ordinal or interval variables. The factor-analytic variables are: (1) age at time of highest office or revolution; (2) age first exposed to political ideology; (3) age first politically active; (4) birthplace: urban or rural; (5) type of country in which the leader is found, whether developed, semideveloped, or undeveloped (using the standard criterion of percent of labor force in agriculture); (6) number of siblings; (7) age ranking among siblings; (8) family status: stable or broken home; (9) character of family life: tranquil or stormy; (10) religious orientation; (11) ethnicity; (12) socioeconomic status; (13) military service; (14) education: type, place, highest level attained, field; (15) father's education; (16) primary occupation: professions, government service, business and industry, military; (17) father's primary occupation; (18) cosmopolitanism: foreign travel (duration, extent, location), foreign languages, continuing foreign contacts; (19) legal and illegal organizational memberships and activities; (20) writings and publications; (21) source of ideology: foreign or domestic; (22) attitudes toward human beings, own country, and international community. (For more details on these variables, see Appendix D, Code Sheet for Factor and Discriminant Analyses.)

Using SPSS[x1] we performed R-factor analysis by principal component varimax rotation. The operation unraveled 17 factors explaining 76.8 percent of the variance in the data set. However, the first and most important factor explained only 10.2 percent of the variance, with the other 16 factors ranging between 9.0 percent and 2.1 percent. None of the 17 factors exhibited appreciable theoretical meaning or implication. Consequently, we have chosen not to report the results of the R-factor analysis at all (copies of the findings are available upon request). We take note, however, of an important negative finding: the attributes of political elites (loyalists and revolutionaries combined) are so similar that no small number of readily identifiable factors emerge.

Using SAS,[2] we executed Q-factor analysis, again, by principal component varimax rotation. Two significant factors developed, the first explaining 46.5 percent of the variance in the data set, the second, 43.4 percent. (A third factor, which explained only 8.9 percent of the variance, is not reported because the highest loading of any leader was an unacceptably low .56.)

## FINDINGS

The results of the Q-factor analysis are displayed in Table 3.1. We list each leader only once, on the factor he loads the higher. This practice determined our cutoff point of .66 for Factor 1 and of .64 for Factor 2 (the actual loadings going all the way down to .31).

Bewilderment is the immediate reaction as one sets out to interpret the data. Most important—and most obvious—is the absence of a direct and simple distinction between loyalists and their revolutionary counterparts. Members of both groups of leaders, it appears, load relatively high on both factors. Accordingly, we are led to conclude not only that most characteristics of the 100 leaders are quite similar but that similarities are distributed across each of the two groups as well. In turn, trait similarities suggest that, as far as our two groups of loyalists and revolutionaries are concerned, leadership must be largely situational in nature.

Although the clear-cut separation we had expected did not materialize, however, the results of the Q-factor analysis are not entirely devoid of pattern. The observed similarities between the two groups must be balanced against the differences in the number and kinds of leaders who load on each factor.

To begin with, of the 51 leaders who load on Factor 1, nearly two-thirds (32) are loyalists and about one-third (19) revolutionaries. Similarly, of the 49 leaders who load on Factor 2, about one-third (17) are loyalists and nearly two-thirds (32) revolutionaries.

Factor 1's tilt toward the loyalists and Factor 2's tilt toward the revolutionaries are further reinforced if we focus on the kinds of leaders that identify most strongly with the two factors. Of the five leaders who load highest on Factor 1, four are loyalists (Maurepas, Laud, Wentworth, Nikolaevich) and one revolutionary (Arafat). Conversely, as chance would have it, of the five leaders who load highest on Factor 2, four are revolutionaries (Adams, Pym, Devereux, Cromwell) and one loyalist (Necker).

How, then, do the two sets of men differ? Principally on two interrelated—and decisive—dimensions: the men of Factor 1 become exposed to political ideology and participate in political activity at *much* earlier ages than the men of Factor 2. Specifically, Maurepas, Laud, Wentworth, and Nikolaevich all developed ideological orientations before age 15; Adams, Pym, Devereux, and Cromwell acquired ideological orientations in their forties and fifties. Similarly, the first group of men became involved in actual political activity, again, in their teens; the second group found themselves active, again, in their forties and fifties.

In short, we have, on the one hand, a group of men that begins very early to set the stage, prepare the way, and construct the building blocks of the political roles they come to play in later life: they are loyalist leaders who are, by and large, *career* oriented. On the other hand, we have a group that bursts

## Table 3.1
## Q-Factor Analysis by Principal Component Varimax Rotation

| Factor | Loading | Percentage variance |
|---|---|---|
| (1) CAREER LEADERS | | 46.5 |
| Maurepas | .91 | |
| Arafat | .89 | |
| Laud | .89 | |
| Wentworth | .87 | |
| Nikolaevich | .86 | |
| Stalin | .85 | |
| Batlle | .85 | |
| Ho Chi Minh | .84 | |
| Diem | .84 | |
| Marighella | .84 | |
| K'ung | .83 | |
| U Nu | .83 | |
| Witte | .82 | |
| Cavendish | .82 | |
| Sithole | .82 | |
| Bourguiba | .81 | |
| Gomez | .81 | |
| Sadat | .81 | |
| Lenin | .81 | |
| Dutra | .80 | |
| Pearson | .80 | |
| Struve | .79 | |
| Giap | .78 | |
| Hutchinson | .78 | |
| De la Puente | .77 | |
| Colden | .77 | |
| Wang | .77 | |
| Habash | .77 | |
| Cárdenas | .77 | |
| Ben Bella | .76 | |
| Souphanouvong | .76 | |
| Nasser | .76 | |
| Díaz | .75 | |
| Stolypin | .74 | |
| Frei | .74 | |
| Schirm | .73 | |
| Schoeters | .73 | |
| Trotsky | .73 | |
| North | .73 | |
| Chou | .72 | |
| Trudeau | .71 | |
| Chu | .71 | |
| Abbas | .70 | |
| Turgot | .70 | |
| Lin | .70 | |
| Tubman | .69 | |
| Mao | .69 | |
| Belaúnde | .67 | |
| Levesque | .67 | |
| Marcos | .67 | |
| Senghor | .66 | |

**Table 3.1** (*continued*)

| Factor | Loading | Percentage variance |
|---|---|---|
| (2) CRISIS LEADERS | | 43.4 |
| Necker | .88 | |
| J. Adams | .88 | |
| Pym | .87 | |
| Devereux | .87 | |
| Cromwell | .87 | |
| Vane | .87 | |
| Zapata | .86 | |
| Odría | .84 | |
| Madero | .84 | |
| Galloway | .83 | |
| Hampden | .82 | |
| Soong | .82 | |
| Liu | .81 | |
| Danton | .80 | |
| Luthuli | .80 | |
| Jefferson | .79 | |
| Robespierre | .79 | |
| Sewall | .79 | |
| Paz | .79 | |
| Sendic | .78 | |
| Villa | .76 | |
| Torres | .74 | |
| Kaunda | .74 | |
| Vallières | .74 | |
| Machel | .73 | |
| Mirabeau | .73 | |
| Castro | .73 | |
| Chiang | .72 | |
| Thieu | .72 | |
| Blanco | .72 | |
| Henry | .71 | |
| Cabral | .71 | |
| Rupert | .71 | |
| Marat | .71 | |
| Biko | .70 | |
| Roberto | .70 | |
| Nyerere | .70 | |
| Nkomo | .69 | |
| Ahmed | .69 | |
| Mondlane | .69 | |
| Vasconcelos | .67 | |
| Hyde | .65 | |
| Washington | .65 | |
| Sihanouk | .65 | |
| Peñaranda | .65 | |
| S. Adams | .65 | |
| Otis | .64 | |
| Guevara | .64 | |
| Batista | .64 | |
| Total variance | | 89.9 |

upon the scene to claim political roles for which they have had no particular preparation: they are revolutionary leaders who are propelled, by and large, by *crisis* situations.

Returning to our idea of differential access, loyalist or career leaders grow to adulthood and maturity in close proximity to sources of power and prestige in societies. Lacking such proximity, revolutionary or crisis leaders spend their lives in pursuit of access to influence and authority, seizing upon such opportunities as may come their way.

## SUMMARY

The characteristics of the 100 leaders do not translate into a ready and easy distinction between loyalists and revolutionaries. Rather, our findings highlight two alternative political types we had not anticipated: career and crisis leaders. However, insofar as career leaders are typically loyalists and crisis leaders typically revolutionaries, the distinction returns us to our notion of differential access: loyalists spend their entire lives in close proximity to positions of power and prestige in societies; revolutionaries seize access as the opportunity comes along.

## NOTES

1. Norman H. Nie et al., *SPSS$^x$ User's Guide* (New York: McGraw-Hill, 1983).

2. *SAS User's Guide* (Cary, NC: SAS Institute, 1982).

# 4 Loyalists and Revolutionaries

## METHODOLOGICAL NOTE

The bivariate and multivariate analyses executed in Chapters 2 and 3 have served to highlight similarities and differences between loyalist and revolutionary elites. However, these analyses offer only limited possibilities of predicting membership in either group. For instance, loyalists are more likely to come from the upper and middle social strata and revolutionaries from the middle and lower, but socioeconomic status is not the only variable defining a loyalist or a revolutionary.

Another multivariate analytical technique, discriminant analysis, is designed with the explicit purpose of investigating differences between two or more groups of subjects on several dimensions or variables simultaneously. More specifically, discriminant analysis is useful in two ways: (1) given a series of significant variables, it helps predict to which group a particular case or subject (here, a leader) belongs, and (2) it helps identify the discriminating power of each variable in determining group membership, thereby providing a ranking of the most important variables.[1]

A discriminant analysis was performed on a subset of our entire data base, employing, as in Chapter 3, SPSS$^x$. The variables listed below were extracted from the larger data base because of the observed *cumulative* variations they generated between loyalist and revolutionary leaders: (1) age at the time of highest office or revolution, (2) age first politically active, (3) religious orientation, (4) socioeconomic status, (5) education level attained, (6) extent of foreign travel, (7) duration of foreign travel, (8) foreign languages, (9) occupation as government official, (10) father's occupation as government official, (11) father's occupation as professional, (12) father's occupation as banker or industrialist, (13) father's occupation as military, (14) father's occupation as landed gentry, (15) father's occupation as peasant or farmer, (16) origin of the ideology to which leader subscribes, (17) attitude toward human beings, (18) attitude toward own country. As with the factor analyses, we addressed the problem of missing data by substituting modal values for nominal variables and mean values for ordinal and interval variables.

We did not include in this analysis variables that would have specifically identified an individual as a member of either the loyalist or revolutionary group (for example, arrest record). We focused instead on those characteristics and traits—demographic, economic, social, attitudinal—that potentially might apply to *any* leader, and yet allow us to predict the probability of a person becoming a loyalist or a revolutionary.[2]

## FINDINGS

A stepwise discriminant analysis run with the aforementioned variables produced a discriminant function composed of ten significant variables, each meeting the entry (or acceptance) criterion of an F of 1.0, as displayed in Table 4.1. Some general comments on this table will set the stage for the discussion of specific findings.

A discriminant function, it will be recalled, can be thought of as the axis of a geometric space, defined by the standardized means ($=0$) of the variables included. The relative importance of each variable in determining the classificatory or predictive power of the discriminant function is indicated by a higher or a lower function coefficient.

Canonical correlation summarizes the relationship between the two groups and the discriminant function; the canonical correlation coefficient of .75 suggests the existence of a strong measure of association. This measure squared produces an eta squared of .56, which represents a significant proportion of the variation in the discriminant function explained by the two groups.

Wilk's lambda denotes the discriminating value of the function, the lower the score, the higher the discrimination. (A lambda of zero would mean perfect discrimination.) The significance level of Chi Square indicates the probability (less than one in 10,000) that differences in the two groups are due to chance.

The direction of the relationship of each of the two groups to the variables included in the discriminant function is determined by the positive or negative sign of the group centroid (or mean), which allows us to interpret each variable for each group. The two group centroids, $-1.11$ for the loyalists and 1.11 for the revolutionaries, refer to the location in multidimensional geometric space of each group's averaged standard score on all ten variables in the discriminant function, relative to the mean axis.

### Table 4.1
### Discriminant Patterns

Standardized Canonical Discriminant Function Coefficients

| | |
|---|---|
| Father Government Official | .52 |
| Atheistic Religious Orientation | -.52 |
| Attitude Toward Country | .37 |
| Father Military | .32 |
| Attitude Toward Human Beings | -.29 |
| Leader Government Official | .29 |
| Father Banker or Industrialist | .27 |
| Father Professional | .24 |
| Father Landed Gentry | .21 |
| Age at Time of Highest Office or Revolution | -.20 |

| | |
|---|---|
| Canonical Correlation Coefficient = | .75 |
| Eta Squared = | .56 |
| Wilk's Lambda = | .44 |
| Chi Square = | 77.96 |
| p = | .0000 |

Canonical Discriminant Function Evaluated at Centroid

| | |
|---|---|
| Loyalists | -1.11 |
| Revolutionaries | 1.11 |

Classification Results

| Actual Group | No. of Cases | Predicted Group Membership | |
|---|---|---|---|
| | | Loyalists | Revolutionaries |
| Loyalists | 50 | 42 (84%) | 8 (16%) |
| Revolutionaries | 50 | 3 (6%) | 47 (94%) |

Percent of "Grouped" Cases Correctly Classified: 89%

(The discriminant function precisely defines a line equidistant from each group centroid.)

As for the classification of results, the percentage of cases classified correctly reflects the percentage of leaders allocated to the appropriate group, using each leader's standardized score on the discriminant function. Random assignment of each of the 100 leaders to either group would have resulted in 50 percent being classified correctly.

Turning to our specific findings, five of the variables that constitute the discriminant function are associated with the occupation of the leader's father, two with social characteristics of the leader himself (occupation as government official, age at the time of highest office or revolution), and three with leader beliefs and attitudes (religious orientation, attitude toward own country, attitude toward human beings). Clearly, the two variables that contribute most to the predictive power of the discriminant function are the leader's religious orientation and the father's occupation as government official. Ranking below these variables are father's occupation in the military, banking or industry, the professions, the landed gentry. In other words, one can predict with some confidence that many loyalist elites are likely to be drawn from families whose fathers held the foregoing occupations, whereas many revolutionary leaders come from families whose fathers did not.

Some of the findings from discriminant analysis are particularly reassuring in that they reiterate and confirm those from the bivariate analysis presented in Chapter 2. A significant number of loyalists are likely to have careers in government service while not a single revolutionary had such an occupation as his *primary* line of activity. Loyalists tend to be older when assuming highest office; revolutionaries are younger at the time of power seizure.

As for beliefs and attitudes, revolutionary leaders frequently abandon their religious backgrounds and turn to atheism; all loyalists remain steadfast in religious beliefs. Revolutionaries are more likely to hold positive views of human nature; loyalist elites, negative ones. Revolutionary leaders fluctuate in their attitudes toward their countries, depending on the regime in power; loyalist leaders are uniformly positive.

Overall, as Table 4.1 documents, the results of discriminant analysis yielded an uncommonly high percentage of correct classifications: 94 percent for the revolutionaries, 84 percent for the loyalists. Using information on the ten variables incorporated in the discriminant function, a combined total of 89 percent of all leaders were correctly classified (42 loyalists, 47 revolutionaries), well above the 50 percent mark that would have occurred by chance.

As can be readily seen, 11 leaders were "misclassified." The three revolutionaries incorrectly grouped as loyalists are Oliver Cromwell and John Pym of England and Stephen Biko of South Africa. The eight loyalists incorrectly grouped as revolutionaries are Batista of Cuba, Cárdenas of Mexico, Kaunda of Zambia, Luthuli of South Africa, Nyerere of Tanzania, Odría of Peru, Senghor of Senegal, and Tubman of Liberia. With only four exceptions, however, there seem to be good reasons for these misclassifications.

Of the revolutionaries misclassified as loyalists, Cromwell was born to a comfortable family, studied mathematics, Latin, and law at Cambridge University, was (as his father) a landlord, and served as a member of parliament both before and during the Long Parliament (1640–1653). Similarly, Pym was a member of the upper class, studied law at Oxford University, was, in addition to being a landlord (again, as his father), deeply involved in the colonizing activities of the Providence Company in the Caribbean and the Americas, in addition to being the acknowledged leader of the Long Parliament. In other words, Cromwell and Pym *were* loyalists in good standing, having been catapulted into revolutionary action in response to situations of national crisis and emergency. As such, these misclassifications are not only understandable, they also suggest that the discriminant function has performed effectively. On the other hand, even though he was born to a middle class family by South African standards, his father having been a government clerk, Biko's case is admittedly an anomaly.

Of the loyalists misclassified as revolutionaries, Presidents Kaunda, Nyerere, and Senghor were, as we have noted in another context, revolutionaries-turned-loyalists. Involved in various ways in anti-imperialist activity, they were instrumental in the independence movements of their countries. As such, their histories resemble more those of the revolutionaries than of the loyalists.

Similarly, Luthuli (1896-1967) was a member of an African aristocracy, his father having been a tribal chief. He was president of African National Congress (ANC) in its peaceful days in the 1950s. Luthuli's leadership of the ANC and his passionate belief in nonviolent resistance and democratic politics won him a Nobel Peace Prize in 1960.

As for Cárdenas (1895-1970), he was an authentic child of the Mexican Revolution of 1910. Lacking a formal education, he joined the revolutionary forces in 1913, becoming a captain in 1914, a colonel in 1915, and a general (under Alvaro Obregón) in 1920. On the political side, he was appointed provincial governor in 1920, minister of interior in 1931, minister of war in 1933; he served as president of Mexico from 1934 to 1940.

Born to a poor family of farm laborers, Batista (1901-1973) attended a Quaker missionary school in Cuba in his early years, coming into contact with pacifist Christian ideas. Having been orphaned and penniless at age 13, he worked at a series of odd jobs, observed first-hand the ruthless and tyrannical rule of president Gerardo Machado (1925-1933), came to identify with the poor and the oppressed, and developed liberal-leftist tendencies. He enlisted in the army in 1924, worked tirelessly to organize the noncommissioned officers, and finally engineered the 1933 coup that brought him to power. Once in office, as it sometimes happens, the liberal reformer turned into a self-centered and self-aggrandizing dictator.

Of the two remaining loyalists misclassified as revolutionaries, Odría (1897-1956) was an obscure colonel who came to power through a coup in 1948 and remained president of Peru until 1956. Having become a high level politician, Tubman (1885-1971) maneuvered a series of "elections" that kept him in power in Liberia from 1943 until his death. These two cases are clear anomalies.

## SUMMARY

Discriminant analysis provided a cutting edge of a cluster of ten traits and characteristics that effectively separated the loyalists from the revolutionaries, with the leader's religious orientation and the father's occupation as government official contributing most to the predictive power of the discriminant function. Using information on all the ten variables constituting the discriminant function, we were able to correctly predict and classify an uncommonly high proportion of loyalist and revolutionary elites.

The differential occupations of the fathers of the 100 leaders—and the differential family prestige and influence that accompany the occupations—constitute situational variables that once again spotlight access as the cutting edge of the distinctions between loyalists and revolutionaries.

**NOTES**

1. See William R. Klecka, *Discriminant Analysis* (Beverly Hills: Sage Publications, 1980).

2. We should note for the record that discriminant analysis assumes interval or ratio levels of measurement as well as a multivariate normal distribution of the population being studied. However, according to the standard reference on discriminant analysis (Klecka, ibid.), even though we have used some nominal and ordinal levels of measurement and even though our population does not have a multivariate normal distribution, these violations are not harmful if the percentage of cases correctly classified is high.

# III PROPELLANTS

# 5 Politicization

In the foregoing chapters we have undertaken quantitative analyses of a relatively large volume of data concerning loyalist and revolutionary elites: their general characteristics, their similarities and differences, the discriminating power of the variables that differentiate the two groups. In this and the following three chapters we present qualitative analyses of changes, forces, or dynamics underlying the emergence of political elites. Our concern is conditions and motivations that propel men toward political leadership.

Specifically, in these chapters we address four interrelated topics: the politicization patterns associated with political leaders for whom we have data, the situational patterns that impel them to leadership positions, the psychological dynamics that may motivate them, and the skill patterns they possess and exhibit. Adopting a less formal presentation style, in each chapter we draw upon leader experiences that most vividly illustrate the topic at hand. Since extensive references for each leader appear in the bibliography, only direct quotations, obscure points or controversial matters are documented.

We treat the patterns of politicization of the leaders under three headings: family politicization, school politicization, and politicization resulting from travel and exposure to new experiences and cultures. (Although we use "politicization" and "socialization" interchangeably, we prefer the former as a means of stressing the learning of explicitly political norms and values.) Throughout, we look for situational variables that may have a bearing on our theoretical concerns.

## FAMILY POLITICIZATION

Family as a source of politicization is a far more powerful attribute of loyalists than revolutionaries. As shown in Table 5.1, fully 80 percent of loyalist leaders are politicized at home, as compared to 50 percent of revolutionary elites.

Loyalists are politicized in two principal ways, both depending, not surprisingly, on the status or occupation of their fathers. Some loyalists come from prominent, illustrious families whose tradition it is to socialize their sons in ways proper to their projected stations in life. Thus, Rupert and Sihanouk were both princes, the former's father having been the king of Bohemia and the latter's, of Cambodia. (Moreover, Rupert's father was married to the sister of Charles I.) Similarly, Nikolaevich was a member of

**Table 5.1**
**Family as a Source of Politicization**

| LOYALISTS | | REVOLUTIONARIES | |
|---|---|---|---|
| Yes (N = 40) | No (N = 10) | Yes (N = 25) | No (N = 25) |
| Abbas | Batista | S. Adams | J. Adams |
| Alami | Cárdenas | Arafat | Ben Bella |
| Batlle | Chiang | Blanco | Biko |
| Belaúnde | Díaz | Castro | Cabral |
| Bourguiba | Dutra | Chou | Cromwell |
| Cavendish | Laud | Chu | Habash |
| Colden | Luthuli | Danton | Hampden |
| Dîem | Nyerere | Devereux | Jefferson |
| Frei | Odría | Giap | Liu |
| Galloway | Senghor | Guevara | Machel |
| Gomez | | Henry | Madero |
| Hutchinson | | Ho | Marighella |
| Hyde | | Lenin | Mondlane |
| Kaunda | | Lin | Nkomo |
| K'ung | | Mao | Paz |
| Lévesque | | Marat | Pym |
| Marcos | | Mirabeau | Roberto |
| Maurepas | | Otis | Sendic |
| Nasser | | De la Puente | Schirm |
| Necker | | Robespierre | Schoeters |
| Nikolaevich | | Souphanouvong | Sithole |
| North | | Trotsky | Stalin |
| Pearson | | Vallières | Torres |
| Peñaranda | | Vane | Villa |
| Rupert | | Washington | Zapata |
| Sadat | | | |
| Sewall | | | |
| Sihanouk | | | |
| Soong | | | |
| Stolypin | | | |
| Struve | | | |
| Thieu | | | |
| Trudeau | | | |
| Tubman | | | |
| Turgot | | | |
| U Nu | | | |
| Vasconcelos | | | |
| Wang | | | |
| Wentworth | | | |
| Witte | | | |

the Russian imperial family, having been the grandson of Nicholas I and the cousin of Nicholas II. Lord North, the British prime minister from 1770 to 1782, was also the second Earl of Guilford. Other English loyalists had noble titles as well: Cavendish was the Duke of Newcastle; Hyde, the Earl of Clarendon; Wentworth, the Earl of Strafford. Maurepas and Turgot came from long lines of aristocrats.

A second way in which loyalists are politicized is that they are born to fathers or families deeply involved in the professions. Among eminent *political* families were those of Batlle, Bourguiba, Dîem, Hutchinson, K'ung, Marcos, Pearson, Sewall, Soong, Stolypin, Tubman, and U Nu. Among families in the *civil service* were those of Abbas, Alami, Belaúnde, Frei, Wang, and Witte. *Military* families include those of Peñaranda, Stolypin, and Thieu. The fathers of Lésveque, Necker, and Trudeau were in the *legal* profession; those of Colden and Kaunda, in the *clergy*.

As for revolutionary elites, although fewer are politicized at home, politicization comes in a somewhat greater variety. Revolutionaries too have their share of illustrious families though to a lesser extent than the loyalists. Souphanouvong was a Laotian prince; Devereux was the third Earl of Essex whose father, the second Earl, was a close advisor to (and by some accounts a lover of) Queen Elizabeth; Comte de Mirabeau was a member of the nobility; Blanco and Washington belonged to the landed gentry.

Other revolutionaries were born to professional families. Among the notable political families were those of the Adamses, Arafat, Giap, Guevara, Henry, Otis, and Vane. Blanco's and Danton's fathers were lawyers; Marat's, a clergyman; Lenin's a tsarist civil servant.

A third way in which revolutionary leaders were politicized is that they found themselves in broken homes (due to parental death or separation) and in custody of a variety of family members. These experiences resulted in a great deal of moving about and the acquisition of political ideas from many sources. Chu, Ho, Lin, and Robespierre fell in this category.

Finally, a few revolutionaries began life in stormy family contexts, typically involving conflict with the father resulting in rebelliousness and politicization. Castro, Mao, Trotsky, and Vallières were in this group.

Whether loyalist or revolutionary, two other aspects of a leader's family life that appear to have a bearing on his future politicization are the number of siblings and his age ranking among the siblings. It is widely believed that both these factors decisively influence the evolution of personality. (Gender position is also considered important, but the requisite data are impossible to locate.)

As noted in Chapter 2, the overall distribution of sibling data between loyalists and revolutionaries is quite similar, there being no significant differences between the two groups. Nonetheless, an analysis of these data will prove consequential for the general phenomenon of political leadership.

As Table 5.2 demonstrates, the 42 loyalists and 43 revolutionaries for whom we have the relevant information came from large families, with an average of seven children in each household. Of the loyalist group, 31 percent (13) were middle children; 49 percent (19), oldest children or oldest sons; 21 percent (9), youngest children; and 2 percent (1), an only son. As for the revolutionaries, 28 percent (12) were middle children; 37 percent (16), oldest children or sons; 19 percent (8), youngest children; and 16 percent (7), only sons. Overall, 31 percent of the loyalists are middle children while 69 percent are oldest, youngest, or only children, the corresponding figures for the revolutionaries being 28 percent and 72 percent. In other words, among political elites middle children are underrepresented; oldest and youngest children, overrepresented. This finding is somewhat startling and the figures are well beyond the realm of chance.

What accounts for this preponderance of oldest, youngest, and only children among political leaders? Generalizing and extrapolating from recent findings in the field of child development throw light on our data.[1] A degree of speculation is unavoidable, however, as these studies do not focus on political elites as such. Moreover, most are culturally biased, dealing, as they do, with child development in the contemporary United States.

Oldest children or sons are typically held to strict and rigorous standards of performance and achievement. Inordinately high parental expectations generate acute anxiety, which requires assurances that are (usually) freely given, which in turn set the stage for success. The firstborns' achievement orientation, in other words, is likely to lead to eminence in their chosen endeavors, politics included.

Typically viewed and treated as "princes," oldest or only sons gradually respond to parental and social expectations by developing auras of command and authority. Moreover, given the fact that parents are likely to be more attentive and patient toward the firstborn, oldest children are likely to experience an orderly and coherent world in their early years. Accordingly, once they are adults and on their own, politics may become a way of introducing order in a chaotic universe.

Oldest children are also likely to experience intense feelings of anxiety over the loss of exclusive parental affection and attention once siblings begin to arrive. Coupled with this anxiety are feelings of guilt over the hostilities the firstborn exhibit toward their siblings. Externalizing and politicizing these feelings of guilt and hostility may be a way of managing one's psychic balance.

The early experiences of *only* children are closer to those of the firstborn than to any other sibling rank. They differ from the oldest children, however, in that they occupy the center stage from beginning to end while at the same time being free from the anxiety and insecurity that the presence of siblings generates. Spending inordinate amounts of time with their parents, only children mature faster and are generally well informed and intelligent. Moreover, they are found to be independent personalities and to make strong leaders who can have difficulty following orders.

Youngest children are more striving and more defiant toward their siblings—and probably toward the world in general. They are more competitive and more vigilant in an effort to maintain their status and possessions in the cruel world that a large family can represent. They may resort to devious means in order to achieve their objectives. Bold and aggressive, they are typically seen as "conquerors." Moreover, being group-oriented, youngest children may see politics as a means of maintaining and enhancing their sense of identity and belongingness.

Middle children are underrepresented among political elites because, as a group, they are not subjected to the same strict parental code and norms of behavior that are applied to the firstborn. Middle children are relatively neglected, and parental expectations are not as high. Being in relatively dependent and vulnerable positions, they tend to be pragmatic and conforming. They are likely to be "diplomats"—either as a means of working their way around older siblings or as a means of acting as mediators between older and younger siblings.

## SCHOOL POLITICIZATION

Nearly all political elites of both loyalist and revolutionary persuasion have some formal education, with 84 percent of the former and 86 percent of the latter progressing beyond high school. However, school as a source of politicization is a striking mark of loyalist elites.

Table 5.3 demonstrates that a staggering 92 percent (46) of the loyalists experienced politicization at school. The four who were not so politicized are Galloway, a self-taught lawyer who apprenticed with others; Rupert, who learned military science by practicing it (as well as from tutors) from early teens; Necker, who was a self-trained banker and financier (the son of a lawyer, he left school at age 15 to become a bank clerk); and Cárdenas, who did not progress beyond an elementary education.

On the other hand, 57 percent (27) of the revolutionaries for whom we have this information were politicized in school and 43 percent (20) were not. (Data are missing for Nkomo, Roberto, and Schirm.) Moreover, revolutionary leaders who were politicized in school are predominantly from Asia, Africa, and Latin America, and they subscribe to a variety of nationalist, Marxist or nationalist-Marxist ideologies.

When we compare the findings of Table 5.3 with those of Table 5.1, a notable pattern emerges: all the loyalists who are politicized in school have also experienced politicization at home. The revolutionaries, on the other hand, divide down the middle: of the 27 who are politicized at school, 14 are

## Table 5.2
## Age Ranking Among Siblings as a Source of Politicization

| Leader | Number of Siblings | Ranking |
|---|---|---|
| LOYALISTS | | |
| Abbas | 13 | Middle child |
| Alami | 1 | Oldest child |
| Batista | 3 | Oldest son |
| Batlle | 1 | Oldest child |
| Bourguiba | 7 | Youngest child |
| Cárdenas | 8 | Oldest son |
| Cavendish | 2 | Youngest child |
| Chiang | 5 | Middle child |
| Díaz | 7 | Middle child |
| Diem | 5 | Middle child |
| Frei | 2 | Oldest child |
| Hyde | ? | Middle child |
| Galloway | 1 | Oldest child |
| Hutchinson | 12 | Middle child |
| Kaunda | 8 | Youngest child |
| K'ung | 1 | Oldest child |
| Laud | 10 | Youngest child |
| Lévesque | 3 | Oldest child |
| Luthuli | 2 | Youngest child |
| Marcos | 3 | Oldest child |
| Nasser | 11 | Oldest child |
| North | 5 | Oldest child |
| Nyerere | 25 | Middle child |
| Pearson | 2 | Middle child |
| Rupert | 8 | Middle child |
| Sadat | 13 | Middle child |
| Senghor | 20-24[a] | Middle child |
| Sewall | 6 | Only son |
| Sihanouk | 4 | Oldest child |
| Soong | 5 | Oldest son |
| Stolypin | 3 | Middle child |
| Struve | 5 | Youngest child |
| Thieu | 4 | Oldest child |
| Trudeau | 2 | Oldest son |
| Tubman | 6 | Oldest child |
| Turgot | 3 | Youngest child |
| U Nu | 1 | Oldest child |
| Vasconcelos | 5 | Oldest child |
| Wang | 10 | Youngest child |
| Wentworth | 11 | Oldest child |
| Witte | 3 | Middle child |

**Table 5.2** (*continued*)

| Leader | Number of Siblings | Ranking |
|---|---|---|
| REVOLUTIONARIES | | |
| Arafat | 4 | Middle child |
| J. Adams | 3 | Oldest child |
| S. Adams | 11 | Oldest son |
| Ben Bella | 6 | Middle child |
| Biko | 1 | Youngest child |
| Castro | 6-8[a] | Middle child |
| Chou | 5 | Middle child |
| Chu | 12 | Middle child |
| Cromwell | 10 | Middle child |
| Danton | 3 | Youngest child |
| Devereux | 3 | Oldest child |
| Giap | 0 | Only child |
| Guevara | 4 | Oldest child |
| Henry | 12 | Middle child |
| Ho | 3 | Middle child |
| Jefferson | 10 | Oldest son |
| Lenin | 5 | Middle child |
| Lin | 4-9[a] | Middle child |
| Liu | 9 | Youngest child |
| Madero | 15 | Oldest child |
| Mao | 4 | Oldest child |
| Marat | 5 | Oldest child |
| Marighella | 0 | Only child |
| Mirabeau | 10 | Youngest child |
| Mondlane | 14 | Youngest child |
| Nkomo | 1 | Oldest child |
| Otis | 13 | Oldest child |
| Paz | 0 | Only child |
| Pym | 2 | Youngest child |
| Roberto | 6 | Oldest child |
| Robespierre | 4 | Oldest child |
| Schirm | 0 | Only child |
| Schoeters | 0 | Only child |
| Sithole | 0 | Only child |
| Souphanouvong | 19 | Youngest child |
| Stalin | 0[b] | Only child |
| Torres | 3 | Youngest child |
| Trotsky | 8 | Middle child |
| Vallières | 2 | Oldest child |
| Vane | 8 | Oldest son |
| Villa | 4 | Oldest child |
| Washington | 6 | Oldest child (of 2nd marriage) |
| Zapata | 4 | Middle child |

[a]Sources disagree on the exact number.
[b]Three older siblings had all died by the time Stalin was born.

**Table 5.3**
**School as a Source of Politicization**

| LOYALISTS | | REVOLUTIONARIES | |
|---|---|---|---|
| Yes (N = 46) | No (N = 4) | Yes (N = 27) | No (N = 20) |
| Abbas | Cárdenas | Arafat | J. Adams |
| Alami | Galloway | Ben Bella | S. Adams |
| Batista | Necker | Biko | Chu |
| Batlle | Rupert | Blanco | Cromwell |
| Belaúnde | | Cabral | Danton |
| Bourguiba | | Castro | Devereux |
| Cavendish | | Chou | Hampden |
| Chiang | | Giap | Henry |
| Colden | | Guevara | Jefferson |
| Díaz | | Habash | Madero |
| Diêm | | Ho | Marat |
| Dutra | | Lenin | Mirabeau |
| Frei | | Lin | Otis |
| Gomez | | Liu | Paz |
| Hutchinson | | Machel | Pym |
| Hyde | | Mao | Robespierre |
| Kaunda | | Marighella | Vane |
| K'ung | | Mondlane | Villa |
| Laud | | De la Puente | Washington |
| Lévesque | | Schoeters | Zapata |
| Luthuli | | Sendic | |
| Marcos | | Sithole | |
| Maurepas | | Souphanouvong | |
| Nasser | | Stalin | |
| Nikolaevich | | Torres | |
| North | | Trotsky | |
| Nyerere | | Vallières | |
| Odría | | | |
| Pearson | | | |
| Peñaranda | | | |
| Sadat | | | |
| Senghor | | | |
| Sewall | | | |
| Sihanouk | | | |
| Soong | | | |
| Stolypin | | | |
| Struve | | | |
| Thieu | | | |
| Trudeau | | | |
| Tubman | | | |
| Turgot | | | |
| U Nu | | | |
| Vasconcelos | | | |
| Wang | | | |
| Wentworth | | | |
| Witte | | | |

also politicized at home, 13 are not. The former cluster either comes from families with a history of antiregime activities (for instance, Arafat, Guevara, and Lenin) or they have experienced stormy childhoods (for example, Castro, Mao, and Trotsky).

That school politicization should be a distinctive mark of the loyalist leaders is not surprising. As a continuation of home politicization, loyalist families of upper and middle social strata feel it incumbent upon themselves to send their sons to the proper schools for the proper preparation and finishing that the sons' future careers would require. And school, needless to say, continues to reinforce the value commitments, attitudinal configurations, and behavior patterns established at home.

## TRAVEL AS A SOURCE OF POLITICIZATION

As noted in Chapter 2, both loyalist and revolutionary elites compile extensive records of foreign travel before assuming highest office or seizing power. As Table 5.4 suggests, 76 percent (38) of loyalists traveled abroad whereas 24 percent (12) did not, the corresponding figures being identical for the revolutionaries. Setting aside the cosmopolitanizing effect of travel, exposure to new experiences and cultures performs two dramatically different functions for the two leadership groups.

Some loyalist elites traveled abroad in connection with their education. Batlle, Belaúnde, Senghor, and Vasconcelos were educated in France; Nyerere, Pearson, and Trudeau, in Britain; Chiang and Wang in Japan; K'ung and Soong in the United States.

Other loyalists traveled abroad on specific missions for their nations and usually for short periods of time. Thus Witte traveled to various European countries, Marcos and Dutra visited the United States, and Gomez went to Europe and Latin America.

Still other loyalists undertook foreign sojourns or tours in a strictly ceremonial fashion, typically at the end of their formal education, while they were in their early twenties. Good examples are Cavendish, Dîem, Sihanouk, Stolypin, Trudeau, Turgot, and Wentworth. The most notable case perhaps is Lord North who, between 1751 and 1754 (he was born in 1732), undertook a leisurely tour of Europe, visiting royalty in Austria, France, Germany, Holland, Italy, Switzerland, and elsewhere.

The most notable exception to the foregoing patterns is René Lévesque, whose travels *within* Canada sensitized him to the dilemma of the French Canadians. Viewing the Canadian Confederation as a "yoke around Quebec's neck," he stated:

To be honestly a Canadian, I shouldn't have to feel like a native leaving his reservation every time I leave Quebec. Outside Quebec, I don't find two great cultures. I feel like a foreigner. First and foremost, I am a Québécois, and second—with a rather growing sense of doubt—a Canadian.[2]

However, Lévesque did not advocate violence as a means of changing the status quo. On the contrary, viewing the Canadian Confederation as a "bad bargain" out of tune with the times, he insisted that one can "get out of it . . . democratically."[3]

**Table 5.4**
**Foreign Travel as a Source of Politicization**

| LOYALISTS | | REVOLUTIONARIES | |
|---|---|---|---|
| Yes (N = 38) | No (N = 12)[a] | Yes (N = 38) | No (N = 12)[a] |
| Abbas | Batista | Arafat | J. Adams |
| Alami | Cárdenas | Ben Bella | S. Adams |
| Batlle | Colden | Biko | Cromwell |
| Belaúnde | Díaz | Blanco | Hampden |
| Bourguiba | Galloway | Cabral | Henry |
| Cavendish | Hutchinson | Castro | Jefferson |
| Chiang | Hyde | Chou | Mao |
| Diêm | Laud | Chu | Otis |
| Dutra | Nasser | Danton | Pym |
| Frei | Sadat | Devereux | Robespierre |
| Gomez | Sewall | Giap | Villa |
| Kaunda | U Nu | Guevara | Zapata |
| K'ung | | Habash | |
| Lévesque | | Ho | |
| Luthuli | | Lenin | |
| Marcos | | Lin | |
| Maurepas | | Liu | |
| Necker | | Machel | |
| Nikolaevich | | Madero | |
| North | | Marat | |
| Nyerere | | Marighella | |
| Odría | | Mirabeau | |
| Pearson | | Mondlane | |
| Peñaranda | | Nkomo | |
| Rupert | | Paz | |
| Senghor | | De la Puente | |
| Sihanouk | | Roberto | |
| Soong | | Schirm | |
| Stolypin | | Schoeters | |
| Struve | | Sendic | |
| Thieu | | Sithole | |
| Trudeau | | Souphanouvong | |
| Tubman | | Stalin | |
| Turgot | | Torres | |
| Vasconcelos | | Trotsky | |
| Wang | | Vallières | |
| Wentworth | | Vane | |
| Witte | | Washington | |

[a]Some of the individuals in these columns traveled <u>after</u> reaching high office or seizing power but not before.

To be sure, foreign travel and exposure to new experiences and cultures help cosmopolitanize loyalist elites. But they also serve to reinforce politicization patterns begun at home and continued through school. With the revolutionaries, the picture is entirely different: such experiences frequently transform their lives.

For revolutionary leaders, foreign travel has a radicalizing influence in many ways. The traveler (would-be revolutionary) may witness oppression, exploitation, and brutality of disquieting proportions. He may see hunger, disease, and death. He may observe—or even personally experience—cruelty, imprisonment, and exile. If he is a colonial (of whom there are many), not only will the traveler witness discrimination and humiliation—he is likely to experience them personally as well. Moreover, the colonial traveler will see stark differences between (1) the conditions of the colony and those of the metropolitan country, and (2) the way the colonists treat one another (with courtesy and civility) and the way they treat the colonized (with derision and contempt). The conclusion becomes unavoidable: Only revolutionary change can alter the existing state of affairs.

Foreign travel has a cosmopolitanizing effect for revolutionaries as well, above and beyond the experience of loyalists. Those who travel gain exposure to a variety of cultures, values, institutions, practices, and ideologies. Revolutionaries develop a set of standards against which to measure their own societies. They share experiences with other revolutionaries and cultivate potential sources of international support.

## SUMMARY

Although home and school politicization are marked features of loyalist elites, a relatively high proportion of all political leaders are so politicized. While both groups are born to large families, they defy the odds by being the oldest, only, or youngest children. As for travel, fully three-fourths of each group experience politicization: loyalists as an important initiation rite, revolutionaries as a transforming venture.

For loyalists and revolutionaries so politicized, home, school, and travel constitute situational variables. Home, needless to say, provides an environment into which one is born and over which one has no control. Similarly, one's schooling (at least initially) is most likely a family decision not entirely within one's own dominion. In addition to its cosmopolitanizing effect, as we postulated in Chapter 1, travel opens one's eyes to a range of problems and issues not afforded by any other experience. Family, school, and travel most likely reflect the social status of the father, another factor over which one holds no sway.

To return to the issue of differential access, high parental status calls for the sorts of politicization experiences that prepare the male offspring for a loyalist orientation to politics; low parental status has no corresponding perquisite or formality.

## NOTES

1. See, for instance, the following works and the sources cited therein: L. Forer and H. Still, *The Birth Order Factor* (New York: David McKay, 1976); H. L. Stewart, "Birth Order and Political Leadership," in Margaret G. Hermann, ed.,

*A Psychological Examination of Political Leaders* (New York: Free Press, 1977); B. Sutton-Smith and B. G. Rosenberg, *The Sibling* (New York: Holt, Rinehart and Winston, 1970); C. A. Broh, "Adler on the Influence of Siblings in Political Socialization," *Political Behavior* 1 (1979): 175-200; Broh, "Siblings and Political Socialization: A Closer Look at the Direct Transmission Thesis," *Political Psychology* 3 (Spring-Summer 1982): 173-83.

It is an index of the growing recognition of its importance that this subject has begun to appear in "high brow" and popular media as well. See, for instance, Didi Moore, "The Only-Child Phenomenon," *New York Times Magazine*, January 18, 1981, p. 26ff.; "Only but Not Lonely," *Newsweek*, June 16, 1986, pp. 66-67.

2. Quoted in Jean Provencher, *René Lévesque: Portrait of a Québécois* (n.p., Canada: Gage Publishing, 1975), p. 199.

3. Quoted in ibid.

# 6 Situations

Other than home, school, and travel, what kinds of situational variables account for the emergence of political elites? To what additional situational stimuli do they respond? Are there specific and recognizable situational patterns that distinguish the loyalists from the revolutionaries?

## THE LOYALISTS

Loyalist leaders appear upon the scene in response to a series of identifiable changes, forces, or dynamics. Conspicuous among these are incidents of national crisis or emergency. World War I, for example, was responsible for bringing Grand Duke Nikolaevich to his highest post: at the age of 58 he was named commander in chief of all Russian forces. Lacking an "appetite for power," the Grand Duke was quite satisfied to have remained the commander of St. Petersburg Military District. But this was not to be:

On August 2, 1914, the tsar suddenly appointed . . . [him] commander in chief. . . . [One writer states] that the monarch declined the supreme command [which he customarily appropriated], assuming that real power would rest elsewhere, and thus Grand Duke Nikolai was picked to fill the need for an attractive figure head. . . . General Yury Danilov . . . , the Grand Duke's deputy chief of staff, argues more plausibly that the tsar intended to command the armies, but developed cold feet at the last moment. In any case, Nikolai Nikolaevich found himself hoisted to a post he had not anticipated, to carry out war plans with which he was barely familiar.[1]

World War II has been responsible, in one way or another, for the rise of other loyalists. Thus, for instance, in the midst of the chaos and uncertainty that gripped Indochina, the French selected Sihanouk to become the puppet king of Cambodia in 1941. Only 18 at the time and a full-fledged bon vivant, Sihanouk was chosen from among the eligible princes because he was thought to be the most malleable. As it turned out, however, he showed an unflinching determination to gain Cambodia's independence, which finally came in 1953. Similarly, it was the Second World War and its aftermath that marked the rise of national revolutionary movements throughout much of Africa and Asia and the emergence of such revolutionaries-turned-loyalists as Bourguiba, Kaunda, and Nyerere.

Ngo Dinh Dîem came to power following the disastrous battle of Dien Bien Phu, his chief qualification having been that he had managed to maintain a certain distance from the contending parties: the French, the puppet emperor Bao-Dai, and the Communists:

At the time of the Dien Bien Phu calamity, Ngo Dinh Dîem was living quietly in Paris. He was ready and willing when the French and Bao-Dai, and even more particularly the Americans—whose involvement had by this time become almost total—having tried everything and everyone else, at last made the decision of despair and turned unconditionally to him.[2]

On June 25, 1954, Dîem returned to Saigon to become prime minister. Two years later he was "elected" president. Except for Dien Bien Phu, these circumstances echo the conditions under which he was succeeded by other South Vietnamese leaders, including the last president Nguyên Van Thieu.

U Nu became the prime minister of Burma (1947–56, 1957–58, 1960–62) initially in response to a situation of national crisis. In preparation for the independence that was to come in the ensuing year, national elections were held in Burma in April 1947. Led by Aung San, the Anti-Fascist People's Freedom League (AFPFL) scored a decisive victory, capturing 170 out of 180 seats in the parliament, which automatically made the party leader prime minister. As fate would have it, Aung San and other party leaders were assassinated in July 1947. U Nu, who, having previously served as vice president of AFPFL, had retired from politics to devote time to his favorite activity of writing, was called upon to form a government. At first he declined but the British governor, who had found U Nu to be conscientious and dedicated, repeatedly pressed him to accept. U Nu yielded reluctantly. A colleague recalled: "He probably had never thought of the possibility of being 'premier,' and the loss of Aung San and his other beloved friends . . . represented a real shock."[3]

A second set of situational variables setting the stage for the appearance of some loyalists is to be found in colonial contexts. As we have already noted such revolutionaries-turned-loyalists as Bourguiba, Kaunda, and Nyerere were products of national liberation movements, which represented responses to colonialism and imperialism. The pattern holds for others as well.

Abbas was born to a family of moderate politicians very active in the Algeria of the 1930s, 1940s, and 1950s. His father was appointed head of a small village and benefited from French largesse. According to one author:

Ferhat Abbas was . . . the son of an influential pro-French "bachaga" [governor or chief] who held the rank of Commander in the Order of the Legion of Honor. The Abbas family was proud of its close ties with France, and made a fetish of speaking French at home (today [1961] Ferhat Abbas speaks haltingly simple Arabic, reverts to French whenever he can). Ferhat Abbas's father wanted his children . . . to be raised as Europeans.[4]

Accordingly, in his early days Abbas stressed the French doctrine of assimilation to the point of denying the reality of Algeria: "This country does not exist. We are products of a new world born out of the spirit and the efforts of the French." Having served with the French Army in World War II, Abbas proudly declared: "I served with the forces because I am French and for no other reason. We are Moslems and we are French. We are natives and we are French." Only in the mid-1950s, following a long history of personal disillusionment and of intensification of French colonial rule, did Abbas join the National Liberation Front. Even then, he continued to remain "the best known . . . of Liberal politicians."[5]

A victim of English colonialism in nearby Egypt was Sadat, who vividly recalled the bedtime stories his mother and grandmother related to him as a child in the early 1920s: "I knew only, at that tender age, that there were forces, called 'the British,' who were alien to us, and that they were evil because [among other things] they poisoned people." He also recalled stories of heroic fighters against the British, particularly one Zahran:

I listened to that ballad night after night, half-awake, half-asleep, which perhaps made the story sink into my subconscious. My imagination roamed free. I often saw Zahran and lived his heroism in dream and reverie—I wished *I* were Zahran.

Lying on the top of the rustic oven in our home in the village, I realized then that something was wrong with our life. Even before I saw the British, I had learned to hate the aggressors who whipped and killed our people.[6]

More than a continent away in more recent times, another victim of British influence was Lévesque, whose feelings of alienation from Quebec society we have noted in another context. Lévesque's first love was writing but the conditions of the French Canadians continued to haunt him from school days:

The division along ethnic lines within the educational system was also evident outside the classroom. It was not just a case of French-speaking kids and English-speaking kids engaging in friendly competition. On the contrary, their games turned into racial struggles, French against English. Naturally there was a lot of scuffling, and a general brawl had usually broken out before the game was even off the ground. It was out-and-out warfare, with neither side ever able to claim lasting victory.[7]

In 1960, at the age of 38, Lévesque joined Quebec's Liberal party above all because he admired the "sense of justice" of its leader Georges-Emile Lapalme. Believing that "the objective of every civilized society . . . [is] the enhancement of human dignity," he gradually became disillusioned with the Liberal party as its leadership changed. In 1966 he declared: "The brute fact we must accept is that economically we are a colony. And only by taking control of our economic life . . . can we guarantee the survival and development of our language and French culture."[8] A year later he founded the Sovereignty-Association Movement (MSA), which was weakened in May 1968 as a result of Trudeau's sweeping victory throughout Canada. Later that year the MSA and *Ralliement National*, another independent political force, came together to form the *Parti Québécois*, which propelled Lévesque to the premiership of Quebec in 1976, a position he was to hold until 1985.

A third constellation of situational considerations setting the stage for the rise of some loyalist leaders is the violent histories of certain countries or the violent circumstances in which the leaders find themselves. The cases of Díaz and Rupert are instructive.

Díaz was born in 1830 in Oaxaca City in southern Mexico, a region known for its violent tradition. While going through the motions of attending a seminary from 1845 to 1849, he was already envisioning himself as a mighty warrior. He carried "a machete under his cape," engaged in an endless series of battles with fellow students, "organized his band in military formation," and "found expansion in fighting."[9] And the environment was not only hospitable, it was strongly encouraging:

Of course, troops were continually passing through Oaxaca, and the young student used to slip off in the evening to join them round the camp fires, where he would follow open-mouthed the tales of valour and strife that made the blood tingle in his veins, and first inspired him with a desire to follow a military career. . . .

His heart beat the faster as he heard yarns of plunder and pillage, of murders and strife, and the flickering flames from the little camp fires . . . played on his features, which were illumined by the enthusiasm of youth as much as, or more than, by the tiny blaze.[10]

As he listened to these tales of horror in that "blood-drenched land," he increasingly saw himself as a military hero. Having obtained a law degree from the Institute of Arts and Sciences in Oaxaca in 1853, he joined the armed forces and distinguished himself as a soldier, rapidly rising in the ranks to become a brigadier general in 1861.

In 1872 Díaz ran for Mexico's highest office against President Benito Juárez. Having lost, he refused to accept defeat, resorted to violence by means of an unsuccessful revolt, and was forced into hiding. He returned to Mexico City later that year when President Juárez died, Vice President Lerdo de Tejada assumed office and declared a general amnesty. Díaz engineered a successful coup against the new president, created a provisional government, and arranged a series of "elections" that kept him in office until 1911.

Prince Rupert was born in Prague, the capital of Bohemia, in 1619, to a family of royalty on both sides: His father was the king of Bohemia; his mother, the sister of Charles I. His absorption in violence and military action was almost instantaneous, as his father lost Bohemia early in the Thirty Years War, in 1621. A biographer comments:

As regards his absorption in things military, Rupert's upbringing played a greater part than heredity. He had been born in time of war; before he was a year old he had been caught up in retreat from battle. Since that day he had grown up in an atmosphere of potential strife, for always the goal before his exiled family was the restoration by force of arms of their hereditary domains if not the kingdom of Bohemia. Rupert with his bellicose temperament looked forward to playing his part in the coming struggle; from his earliest years he was determined to be a soldier.[11]

So single-minded and determined was Rupert in this objective that "at eight years of age he handled his arms with the readiness and address of an experienced soldier."[12] At age 14 (1633) he served with the Prince of Orange at the seige of Rheinberg, and he continued to fight all over the Continent until 1642, when he joined his uncle, Charles I, first as chief of the cavalry and then as commander in chief. In the former capacity, he generated such deference that the loyalists came to be called "Cavaliers." In the latter, he became the counterpart of Cromwell and the New Model Army.

As we have repeatedly seen, a fourth set of situational variables that is crucial to the rise of many loyalists is that by virtue of family and social status they find themselves in positions of access or proximity to political power. Here we document some of the most notable cases. Cavendish, Hyde, North, and Wentworth were all members of high aristocracy with close ties to the royal family and a long tradition of involvement in palace politics. Cavendish was at "courts since the age of sixteen."[13] North became a member of the House of Commons in 1754 (age 22), was appointed chancellor of the exchequer in 1767 and prime minister in 1770. Similar patterns of rapid advancement hold for Hyde and Wentworth as well as for other loyalists.

Maurepas and Turgot came from long lines of aristocratic families and long traditions of public service. Turgot's father and grandfather had both held high public office. "Maurepas started as a child prodigy, succeeding his father as Secretary of the Navy at age fourteen and a half."[14] Born in 1701, he remained an advisor to Louis XV until 1750, when he was dismissed for offending Madame Pompadour. He was recalled by Louis XVI in 1774 and immediately became "The Mentor."

Also born to families with traditions of government service are Witte and Stolypin. Witte began in an unconventional manner: He abandoned the tradition of civil service and joined a large private railroad company in 1868, at the age of 20, compiling 20 years of expertise in that area. The move was fortuitous, for in his capacity as director of the South-West Railways, he frequently accompanied Emperor Alexander III in his travels. A contemporary has recorded:

[T]hanks to his thorough knowledge of railroad operations and management, when [in 1888] he was summoned to St. Petersburg by Emperor Alexander III, as an expert on the railway question that was then so important in Russia, he easily dominated the routine bureaucracy of the capital by his practical experience and good sense.

At St. Petersburg his untiring activity overstepped the bounds of his specialty, and he became an authority, not only on railway matters, but on the whole economic life of the country; his rise in the official hierarchy was marvellously rapid.[15]

Following extensive negotiations over his high salary (half of which eventually came from the government and the other half from the tsar's "own pocket"), Witte was appointed to the newly created post of director of the Department of Railroad Affairs in 1888, to become minister of finance in 1892, president of the Committee of Ministers in 1903, and prime minister in 1905-1906. The last appointment astonished him: "I found myself at the helm, essentially against my own will."[16]

Stolypin's career began earlier and was equally meteoric. Consistent with a family tradition going back to the sixteenth century, he experienced a succession of appointments beginning at age 24: district marshall of Kovno, 1886; provincial marshall, 1889; governor of Grodnov, 1902; governor of Sarat, 1903; minister of interior, 1906; prime minister, 1906-1911. Reflecting on Stolypin's career, a contemporary observed:

His high position, and the unlimited power conferred upon him by the force of circumstances more than by anything else, had imbued him with the conviction that he was indispensable, and that everything would be allowed to him because there was no one to take his place.[17]

Turning to the North American loyalists, Hutchinson entered politics in Boston in 1737. His career developed under the patronage and tutelage of four successive Massachusetts governors: Jonathan Belcher (1737-1740), William Shirley (1740-1756), Thomas Pownall (1756-1760), Francis Bernard (1760-1769). Pownall appointed Hutchinson lieutenant governor in

1758 and, when Bernard departed in 1769, Hutchinson became acting governor until 1771 when he was appointed governor, a post he kept until 1774. Sewall's career followed a similar, but less spectacular, pattern.

Pearson's rise to the prime ministership of Canada was entirely fortuitous. In the summer of 1926 (at age 29), he went to Ottawa to do research on a dissertation on Canadian history for Oxford University. The experience was not only transforming, it also provided him with pivotal contact points:

I spent some evenings that June in the gallery of the House of Commons during the highly dramatic parliamentary discussions that led to the election of 1926. For the first time I sensed the excitement of political and parliamentary life and the privilege of being close to stirring events by living in the capital. That feeling was increased by meeting some men during the summer who were active on the political or official side of our national life.[18]

One of these men was Dr. O. D. Skelton, director of the Department of External Affairs, who encouraged Pearson to accept the post of first secretary in that organization. This appointment, in turn, placed Pearson in a strategic access position to Prime Minister Mackenzie King of the Liberal party. Under the tutelage of King and his successor, Louis St. Laurent, Pearson steadily rose to become ambassador to Washington, secretary of external affairs, and, finally, prime minister (1963-1968). A Methodist minister's son, Pearson "certainly never dreamed of becoming Prime Minister."[19] He himself has acknowledged: "I was clearly not born a politician. . . . I only wish that I had had more talent as a politician and had been able to make more of an event or of a situation that I may in truth have felt about it."[20]

Pearson's successor, Pierre Elliott Trudeau, entered politics quite deliberatively, but his rise to prime ministership was equally circumstantial. Having been elected to the Canadian Parliament in 1965, Trudeau was appointed parliamentary secretary to Prime Minister Pearson, manifestly a vital access point. Upon his retirement in 1968, Pearson selected Trudeau as his successor; Trudeau was elected prime minister in 1968 and remained in office until 1984.

His flamboyant personal style aside, however, in contrast to Pearson, a strong element of opportunism should be noted about Trudeau. For one thing, while studying at the London School of Economics in his late twenties, he became a social democrat under the spell of Ḥarold J. Laski. Accordingly, when he turned to the Liberal party in order to run for office, his socialist friends branded him a "sell out." For another, given the Canadian context, Trudeau made a point of downplaying his paternal French background while accentuating his maternal Anglo-Saxon heritage.[21]

We could continue with this already extended discussion, but enough has been said to establish access as a situational variable in the rise of loyalist elites. The patterns identified in the foregoing pages repeat themselves in the lives of many other leaders. Thus, for example, Charles I appointed Laud Archbishop of Canterbury because of his long service, unflinching loyalty, and increasing influence inside both the royal court and the parliament. (Laud was a highly controversial figure, cherished by some and despised by others.) Batlle came from a most distinguished political family, his father having been the president of Uruguay from 1868 to 1872. President Carlos Ibáñez of Chile catapulted Frei into the national limelight. President Manuel Roxas of the Philippines took Marcos under tutelage.

A major exception to these patterns would appear, at first blush, to be Batista, who came from the lower class and was a mere sergeant when he engineered a successful coup against President Manuel de Céspedes in 1933. It must be recalled, however, for that at least a decade before the coup, Batista deliberately cultivated a series of political and military contacts as a means of setting the stage. In particular, from 1928 until 1933 he was in a relatively lowly—but most sensitive—position in a key military fortress in Havana. This post afforded an additional access point: "Batista's position as a headquarters secretary and his work as court reporter in the [President Gerardo] Machado Councils of War gave him an [insider's] opportunity. . . . The information he was able to pick up became very valuable."[22]

Finally, as we have seen with some frequency, an element of luck or chance coincides with access. Thus, it is not always merely the right man at the right place—the right opportunity counts as well.

## THE REVOLUTIONARIES

With a single and crucial exception, situational variables affecting the emergence of revolutionaries are similar to those accounting for the rise of loyalist elites. Thus, for instance, national crises of various kinds have been responsible for the ascendancy of leaders in the English, American, and French revolutions.

In England of the 1640s, conflicts between the Parliament and the monarch reached a point of no return. A variety of political, economic, and religious issues and interests coalesced around a small group of men who openly challenged the established order. The king's attempt to arrest the leaders only served to unify them, mobilize the masses, and exacerbate the crisis. Thus, as Michael Walzer has persuasively argued, English revolutionary ideology was a response to anarchy and anxiety, and a means of reintroducing order into a chaotic universe.[23] Charles I was executed in 1649, seven years after the beginnings of the upheaval.

The American case is equally instructive. Relying on a set of doctrines based on natural law and natural rights—and formalized in the Declaration of Independence—a group of men succeeded in mounting an effective offensive and gaining independence within a stunningly short period of time. Ironically enough, American revolutionary ideology was borrowed from the enemy, adapted to local needs, and used against the enemy. The movement evolved with a momentum all its own: there were no previous models, no blueprints to draw upon. As with the English case, most of the revolutionaries were members of the establishment in good standing and deeply involved in the legal political processes of their societies.

The French Revolution erupted with equal speed. It was not the result of prior work or planning. Again, a series of conflicts between the king and the parliament catapulted a few men into prominence. Thus, for example, Marat, a physician by profession, had "radicalism thrust upon him."[24] Comte de Mirabeau, a full-fledged member of the nobility, has been characterized as "The Revolutionary Despite Himself."[25]

A major contributing factor to the Russian Revolution was World War I. The war deflected attention from major societal needs and concerns, diverted resources to a massive conflict, highlighted the corruption and ineptitude of the tsarist regime, undermined and demoralized the tsar's supporters, and thoroughly alienated the people. So much so, in fact, that when the Bolsheviks launched their fateful offensive in November 1917, they themselves were surprised at the ease with which the system collapsed. Regime ineptitude had become so pronounced that Lenin claimed to have found power lying in the streets.

In addition to these specific revolutions, it can be argued that all colonial and neocolonial upheavals are, virtually by definition, situational: These movements would likely not have occurred had it not been for the sheer presence of the outsider. The perennial and crushing environment of oppression, exploitation, and discrimination made radicalization virtually unavoidable.

In this context, World War II played a pivotal role in awakening the colonial peoples and accelerating the revolutionary process in their societies. This theme recurs in the thought of many colonial leaders. Reverend Sithole of Zimbabwe, who is most explicit on this point, deserves quotation at length:

World War II . . . had a great deal to do with the awakening of the peoples of Africa. During the war the African came into contact with practically all the peoples of the earth. He met them on a life-and-death struggle basis. He saw the so-called civilized and peaceful and orderly white people mercilessly butchering one another just as his so-called savage ancestors had done in tribal wars. He saw no difference between the so-called primitive and so-called civilized man. . . .

But more than this, World War II taught the African most powerful ideas. During the war, the Allied Powers taught their subject peoples . . . that it was not right for Germany to dominate other nations. They taught the subject peoples to fight and die for freedom. . . .

The big lesson that the African learned during the last war was that he fought and suffered to preserve the freedom he did not have back home. . . .

The hatred against Hitler was transferred to European colonialism. . . . An Asiatic once told me, "We owe our independence to Adolf Hitler!"[26]

A related consideration in this regard is that once a colonial revolutionary movement succeeds—once a colony attains independence—a contagion effect sets in: other countries' expectations heighten, and the process of consciousness accelerates. Thus, for instance, the attainment of independence by Ghana in 1957 and the success of the Algerian Revolution in 1962 served as inspirations to revolutionary or potentially revolutionary leaders throughout much of Africa. Similarly, the success of the Chinese Revolution set an example for Asia; of the Cuban Revolution, for Latin America.

There is another type of situation—much different from the ones mentioned above—that may incline men toward revolution. The turbulent political histories of such countries as China, Colombia, Cuba, Mexico, "Palestine," Peru, and Vietnam, for example, set the stage for the ready emergence of revolutionary elites.

The Palestinian situation is illustrative. Since the formation of Israel in 1947 and the Arab-Israeli War of 1948, the area has been racked by uninterrupted violence, both declared and undeclared. Thus, George Habash readily acknowledged that these events constituted personal as well as national traumas, setting him on a revolutionary course:

I have no personal motive (to participate in the political struggle in the area) except that which every Palestinian citizen has. Before 1948 I was . . . far from politics. . . . [In view of the circumstances, however,] you cannot but become a revolutionary and fight for the cause. Your own cause as well as that of your people.[27]

For Yasir Arafat, these two events were exacerbated by a third: the unilateral diversion by Israel of the upper waters of the Jordan River in 1963. He told his biographer in the mid-1970s:

The timing could not have been more perfect. . . .[I]t was precisely [Israeli] arrogance that blinded them to the true consequences of their action. It would be accurate to say that everything that has happened in the Middle East in the last twelve years stems from the Jordan diversion. The Israeli action gave us in the liberation movement a specific focus around which to build our cause. It put flesh on the skeleton of our ideology. It gave us the power and influence we had been struggling to achieve. It gave us a specific strategy and tactical approach that we could shape to our needs. But most important, it settled the issue once and for all—that is, that there would never be peace in the Middle East until the Palestinian people were given their rights, as individuals and as a nation.[28]

We should also note that in some violent countries there are identifiable locales famous for their revolutionary tradition from which some leaders emerge. Such hotbeds of radicalism include Mao's birthplace of Hunan, Ho's Nghe-An, Giap's Quang Binh, Zapata's Anenecuilco, Castro's Oriente. It has been said of Castro, for example: "Political violence and extremism are as Cuban as the palm trees, and Fidel Castro was a product, rather than a cause, of the profound and unresolved tensions in Cuban society."[29]

There is yet another type of situation that may catapult men toward revolutionary action. Just as the privileged social status of loyalist leaders may provide ready access to high office and channels of power, the relatively low social status of revolutionary elites may lead to painful experiences and profound radicalization. (This pattern has been vividly detailed by Vallières, for instance.)

A child of Montreal slums, tough neighborhoods, and gang fights, Vallières identified the poverty associated with his lower class status as an intrinsic source of radicalization. He wrote:

Money [or lack thereof] had turned all of us into perpetual rebels who rebelled in vain. Protesting victims, how could we seriously believe in our freedom when we knew that freedom was based on money? And how could we not protest, when we knew that money was being stolen from us every day? But our protest changed absolutely nothing. . . . We had to act, not protest. And in order to act effectively, we had to unite, to confront the systematic organization of exploitation with an even stronger organization.[30]

Vallières proceeded to depict the working-class family as the working class writ small:

The terrible thing about the working-class family is the function, imposed on it by the present system, of renewing and perpetuating the supply of slaves, of niggers, of cheap labor to be exploited, alienated, and oppressed. . . . The proletarian child . . . revolts against his parents, but very early his revolt turns against the condition of his class and those who are responsible for that condition. . . .

It is an understatement to say that the working-class family is a double or quadruple monstrosity. This "possessing unit"—as Engels calls it—is a hell, a room with no exit, in which the self-destruction of human beings is accomplished mechanically.[31]

As with the loyalists, a final set of situational dynamics has to do with the role of chance. Thus it happens that at age 12 Georges Schoeters—an illegitimate child who was abandoned by both parents—joined and worked for Belgian partisans in the forests of Ardennes during the German occupation. Examining his condition, a Canadian psychoanalyst wrote:

He observed the Belgians defending themselves against the Nazis with lies, deceit, fraud, civil disobedience, underground bombs, and murder. It is not surprising, therefore, that a young man brought up in these circumstances . . . would have a difficult time after the war in adapting himself to an orderly life in which fraud, sabotage, violence, and insurrection were no longer acceptable.[32]

Similarly, Joshua Nkomo was propelled into the limelight, not as a result of determination and hard work, but of fortuitous circumstances. Having returned to Zimbabwe following training as a social worker in South Africa, Nkomo was appointed as Rhodesia Railways' first African welfare worker.

African employees liked Nkomo well enough to select him in 1951 as the first full-time general secretary of the Rhodesia Railways African Employees' Association, then the best situated, if not the most powerful, of Central Africa's fledgling unions. He was not a particularly energetic or successful union organizer, but very soon Nkomo found himself, unexpectedly, a national political figure.[33]

## SUMMARY

With a single and major exception, there is great overlap between the situational dynamics that catapult loyalists and revolutionary elites into prominence: national crisis or emergency, colonial or neocolonial contexts, "violent countries," and luck or chance. The critical situational variable distinguishing the loyalists from the revolutionaries is that by virtue of their social and family standing, the former frequently find themselves in positions of access or proximity to political power; the latter do not.

## NOTES

1. *Biographical Dictionary of World War I*, edited by Roger H. Hernig and Neil M. Heyman (Westport, CT: Greenwood Press, 1982), p. 264; cf. Richard Pipes, *Struve: Liberal of the Right, 1905-1944* (Cambridge: Harvard University Press, 1980), p. 369.

2. Willard A. Hanna, *Eight Nation Makers* (New York: St. Martin's Press, 1964), p. 163.

3. Quoted in Richard Butwell, *U Nu of Burma* (Stanford: Stanford University Press, 1963), pp. 57-58.

4. Edward Behr, *The Algerian Problem* (New York: W. W. Norton, 1961), p. 45.

5. Quotations and characterizations in this paragraph are from the following sources: Michael K. Clark, *Algeria in Turmoil* (New York: Praeger Publishers, 1959), p. 17; Rolf Italiaander, *The New Leaders of Africa* (Englewood Cliffs: Prentice-Hall, 1961), pp. 20-24; William B. Quandt, *Revolution and Political Leadership: Algeria 1954-1968* (Cambridge: MIT Press, 1969), p. 29; Ronald Segal, *African Profiles* (Baltimore: Penguin Books, 1962), p. 290; Ronald Segal, *Political*

*Africa: A Who's Who of Personalities and Parties* (London: Stevens & Sons, 1961), p. 1.

6. Anwar el-Sadat, *In Search of Identity: An Autobiography* (New York: Harper & Row, 1977), pp. 5-6.

7. Jean Provencher, *René Lévesque* (n.p.: Gage Publishing, 1975), p. 14.

8. All quotations and characterizations are from ibid., pp. 134, 196, 227.

9. Carleton Beals, *Porfirio Díaz* (Philadelphia: J. B. Lippincott, 1932), pp. 60-61.

10. E. Alec-Tweedie, *The Maker of Modern Mexico* (New York: John Lane, 1906), pp. 7-8.

11. Patrick Morrah, *Prince Rupert of the Rhine* (London: Constable & Co., 1976), p. 25.

12. Ibid., p. 24.

13. Mark Bence-Jones, *The Cavaliers* (London: Constable & Co., 1976), p. 25.

14. Vincent Cronin, *Louis and Antoinette* (London: William Collins & Sons, 1974), p. 70.

15. Alexander Iswolsky, *Recollections of a Foreign Minister: Memoirs of Alexander Iswolsky* (New York: Doubleday, Page & Co., 1921), p. 109.

16. Count Sergei Witte, *The Memoirs of Count Witte* (New York: Doubleday, Page & Co., 1921), pp. 31, 317-18.

17. Count Paul Vassili, *Behind the Veil at the Russian Court* (New York: John Lane, 1914), p. 355.

18. Lester B. Pearson, *Mike: The Memoirs of the Right Honorable Lester B. Pearson*, 2 vols. (Toronto: University of Toronto Press, 1972, 1973), I: 56.

19. Peter Stursberg, *Lester Pearson and the Dream of Unity* (Toronto: Doubleday Canada, 1978), p. 18.

20. Pearson, *Mike*, II: 12, 19. Cf. Pearson, *Mike*, I: passim; Bruce Thodarson, *Lester Pearson: Diplomat and Politician* (Toronto: Oxford University Press, 1974), passim.

21. See, for example, John D. Harbron, *This is Trudeau* (Don Mills, Ontario: Longmans Canada, 1968), p. 37; Walter Stewart, *Trudeau in Power* (New York: Outerbridge & Dienstfreng, 1971), p. 9; Martin Sullivan, *Mandate '68* (Toronto: Doubleday Canada, 1968), p. 359.

22. Edmund A. Chester, *A Sergeant Named Batista* (New York: Henry Holt & Co., 1954), p. 27.

23. Walzer, *The Revolution of the Saints* (Cambridge: Harvard University Press, 1965).

24. Louis R. Gottschalk, *Jean Paul Marat: A Study in Radicalism* (New York: Benjamin Blom, 1966), p. 194.

25. Louis Madelin, *Figures of the Revolution* (Freeport, NY: Books for Libraries Press, 1968), Ch. 2.

26. Ndabaningi Sithole, *African Nationalism*, 2nd ed. (New York: Oxford University Press, 1968), pp. 47-49, 53.

27. Quoted in Walid W. Kazziha, *Revolutionary Transformation in the Arab World: Habash and His Comrades from Nationalism to Marxism* (New York: St. Martin's Press, 1975), pp. 17-18.

28. Quoted in Thomas Kiernan, *Arafat: The Man and the Myth* (New York: W. W. Norton, 1976), p. 229.

29. Rolando E. Bonachea and Nelson P. Valdés, eds., "Introduction," *Revolutionary Struggle 1947-1958: The Selected Works of Fidel Castro* (Cambridge: MIT Press, 1972), I: 27.

30. Pierre Vallières, *White Niggers of America* (New York: Monthly Review Press, 1971), p. 122.

31. Ibid., pp. 85-86, 87.

32. Gustav Morf, *Terror in Quebec: Case Studies of the FLQ* (Toronto: Clarke, Irwin, 1970), pp. 20-21.

33. Robert Rotberg, "From Moderate to Militant: The Rise of Joshua Nkomo and Southern Rhodesian Nationalism," *Africa Report*, 7 (March 1962), p. 3.

# 7 Psychologies

**METHODOLOGICAL NOTE**

The personality development of loyalist and revolutionary elites is conditioned not only by their social, economic, political, cultural, and situational experiences discussed in the preceding chapters but also by the interaction of a series of psychological forces or dynamics, some of which the two groups share and some that sharply differentiate them. These forces are: (1) vanity, egotism, narcissism, (2) asceticism, puritanism, virtue, (3) relative deprivation and status inconsistency, (4) marginality, inferiority complex, and compulsion to excel, (5) oedipal conflict writ large, and (6) estheticism and romanticism.

These psychological attributes, far from being new to our work, have been used frequently by a variety of writers and scholars in the analysis of major political, social, and religious figures. Vanity has been emphasized explicitly in the writings of Sigmund Freud and Lucille Iremonger and implicitly in the works of Alfred Adler, Karen Horney, Harold D. Lasswell, Donald R. Matthews, and James L. Payne and associates.[1] Asceticism has been stressed by such scholars as William H. Blanchard, Bruce Mazlish, and Michael Walzer.[2] Relative deprivation has been subjected to thorough analysis by Ted Robert Gurr and Iremonger, among others.[3] Marginality has been highlighted by a number of writers, including Adler, Horney, Erik H. Erikson, Alexander L. George, Iremonger, and Lasswell.[4] Oedipal conflict has been stressed in E. Victor Wolfenstein's treatment of Lenin, Trotsky, and Gandhi.[5] Estheticism, though perhaps not as conspicuous as the other variables, has received attention in Iremonger's study of British prime ministers and our own investigations of revolutionaries.[6]

Coding psychological variables is among the most demanding tasks social scientists are called upon to undertake, full of hazards and pitfalls, and capable of producing misleading results. The standard technique for the kind of psychological investigation at hand is content analysis. Under this method, the social scientist identifies representative passages from a leader's autobiographical writings or other pronouncements bearing on the topic(s) under study and then, under a rigorous set of controls, subjects the writings to coding, quantification, analysis, and interpretation.

Its many problems notwithstanding, the method of content analysis is infeasible for the purposes of this work. The main reason is straightforward: we have no way of locating comparable passages of the kind described on the six sets of relevant psychological variables for the 100 leaders. Moreover, since social and historical conditions under which a statement is made are likely to color or shape the statement itself, we have no way of establishing the comparability of these conditions for the 100 leaders across time and space.

Strictly speaking, then, we are left with nonscientific ways of proceeding with our analyses. Although autobiographies, diaries, and memoirs have been rare to come by, we have been able to locate a large collection of biographical studies supplemented by historical works and journalistic accounts (see Bibliography). We have subjected our source materials to close scrutiny in search of evidence for the six sets of psychological variables we have identified. Following is a listing of the kinds of evidence we sought in connection with each variable.

Vanity: Excessive pride in one's own qualities or accomplishments; self-aggrandizement, ostentatiousness, smugness.

Asceticism: The consistently austere approach to life; self-denial, self-discipline, devotion to hard work.

Relative deprivation: Perception of discrepancy between (economic or political) values sought and values attained.

Marginality: Significant or perceptible deviation from commonly accepted norms, whether physical, social, or psychological.

Oedipal conflict: Rebelliousness or ambivalence toward the father; history of intrafamily contention and discord.

Estheticism: Sensitivity to things of beauty; emotional attachment or receptivity to art, music, poetry, literature.

Contrary to our expectations, some of the psychological variables lent themselves to relatively unambiguous coding. For example, when John Adams repeatedly insists on displaying his vanity (see below), we tended to take that acknowledgment at face value. We accorded similar credibility to such matters as Lenin's legendary and obsessive preoccupation with asceticism and puritanism ("Tartar Marxism," as some have called it); George Washington's deep personal frustration generated by the 1767 royal proclamation that forbade the settlers' further annexation of Indian territory; the pervasive sense of marginality and inferiority experienced by such diverse figures as Cromwell and Lord North, Mao Tse-tung and Chiang Kai-shek, Stalin and Stolypin, Hutchinson and Ho Chi Minh; acknowledgment of early history of rebelliousness and potential oedipal problems by such a figure as Trotsky; the romanticism embedded in Jefferson's infatuation with music, the poetry of such a leader as Mao Tse-tung, and the Don Quixote complex of such a figure as Ernesto Guevara.

At times the psychological variables were difficult to code, requiring exhaustive searches of the available source materials and judgment calls rooted in extensive prior research. Accordingly, in this chapter we give our psychological variables more extended treatment than we have accorded other topics in this book, in order to share with the reader the "flavor" of the source materials with which we worked. We urge the reader to be sensitive to the limitations of our findings and to exercise due caution and skepticism. At the same time, we ask the reader to share with us the possibilities inherent in the presentations that follow.

## FINDINGS

Before examining the six sets of psychological forces, it is instructive to discuss the loyalists and revolutionaries in the light of two important mental attributes: a sense of justice, a commitment to nationalism.

With the possible exception of such loyalists-turned-revolutionaries as the Adamses, Washington, Cromwell, and Devereux, the typical revolutionary is driven by a vision of justice and a corresponding attempt to right the wrongs. This sense of justice may be derived from personal experiences or it may be perceived in societal conditions (oppression and humiliation at home and abroad, for instance). Whatever its source, and whatever form it might take, the sense of justice is ubiquitous among revolutionaries.

Of the loyalist elites only a few exhibit a sense of justice and as such they constitute clear exceptions. In general, only loyalists with humanistic (including democratic socialist) orientations and ideologies express a concern with justice. Thus, for instance, Batlle remained committed to the "love of justice." To Cárdenas, "the thing most precious . . . was the dignity of the common folk." And Frei sought to unite his ideology of social democracy with the humanism of Jacques Maritain.[7] (Lévesque's concern with this subject has been noted in Chapter 6.)

While an abiding belief in justice is virtually a defining feature of revolutionaries, an unalterable commitment to nationalism and patriotism describes almost all political elites, loyalist and revolutionary. Political leaders uniformly seek to maintain the independence and integrity of their countries. They set out to free their nations from the oppression and exploitation of other nations. They act to improve the status, power, and prestige of their homelands.

As might be expected, however, even here there are exceptions. Of the loyalists, two cannot be labeled nationalist: Necker and Rupert. Necker, it will be recalled, was a Swiss financial wizard with the sole charge of helping Louis XVI with his financial problems; he had no particular identification with French society or culture. Similarly, Rupert was a warrior prince, without an identifiable nationalist ideology.

As chance would have it, two of the revolutionaries are not nationalists either: Guevara and Schoeters. Guevara was an internationalist soldier of fortune, a Don Quixote, as we shall see, out to tilt at windmills wherever he found them. Schoeters was a Belgian and a radical Marxist-humanist who, having emigrated to Canada and having joined the Quebec National Liberation Front, found himself scornful of Quebec nationalism.

We are now in a position to turn to the more specifically psychological factors that appear to motivate political leaders. In order to keep the discussion manageable, and to avoid repetition, we limit the treatment of each of these psychological variables to a relatively few—but we hope representative and instructive—instances of their manifestations among loyalist and revolutionary elites. The entire picture is summarized in Table 7.1, wherein "x" denotes the psychological attribute(s) a leader shares. (Since extensive references for each leader appear in the Bibliography, only direct quotations, obscure points, or controversial matters are documented.)

### Vanity, Egotism, Narcissism

Vanity and egotism of various forms are found with much greater frequency among loyalists than revolutionaries: 74 percent (37) and 54 percent (27), respectively.

Such diverse loyalists as Bourguiba, Chiang, Diem, Hutchinson, Hyde, Laud, Marcos, Nasser, Necker, North, Peñaranda, Sadat, Stolypin, Struve, Trudeau, Turgot, Vasconcelos, Wentworth, and Witte are variously described as egomaniacal, vain, dogmatic, aloof, cold, insensitive, arrogant, haughty, conceited, and the like. Laud was a "firm believer" in his own "destiny." Necker "was never averse to being hero-worshipped." Convinced of his own indispensability, Stolypin reminded a contemporary of a famous "Persian grand vizier."[8]

Chiang's vanity traced its origins to his childhood. His mother used to tell him that

> the Chiangs were descended from no less a person than Tan, Duke of Chou, the great innovator, the man who founded the fortunes of the Chou dynasty in the

twelfth century B.C. . . . To claim descent from Tan, Duke of Chou, was to claim connection with one of the greatest characters in Chinese history. He was a sage, a statesman, a warrior, a scholar . . . [and] the reputed author of . . . the oldest surviving document on Chinese statecraft.[9]

Chiang behaved accordingly. Even as a child, "his manner [was] haughty, his gait lordly."[10] Later, he would consider himself a most exceptional man and would insist on being addressed as the Generalissimo.

Bourguiba claimed to be "the creator of Tunisia. . . . The system? I am the system." He believed that "If my life were taken, the people would suffer an irreparable loss in losing not so much their leader and moral counselor as the fruit of all their past sacrifices."[11] In a similar vein, Sadat began his autobiography in a grandiose fashion:

I, Anwar el-Sadat, . . . present this book to readers everywhere.
This is the story of my life, which is at the same time the story of Egypt since 1918—for so destiny has decreed. . . . I therefore tell my story in full . . . as an Egyptian whose life has been intimately bound up with that of Egypt.[12]

Sadat's predecessor, Nasser, went one step further by seeing himself as the "God-summoned liberator of all Arab people."[13]

Turning to the revolutionaries, it is said of Cromwell, for example, "that in the day-time, lying melancholy in his bed, he believed that a spirit appeared to him and told him that he should be the greatest man (not mentioning the word king) in his kingdom."[14]

John Adams was surprisingly candid—and quite repetitious—about his vanity. Thus: "Reputation ought to be the perpetual subject of my Thoughts, and Aim of my Behaviour. How shall I gain a Reputation! How shall I Spread an Opinion of myself as a Lawyer of distinguished Genius, Learning, and Virtue." And again: "Vanity, I am sensible, is my cardinal Vice and cardinal Folly, and I am in continual Danger, when in Company, of being led an ignis fatuus Chase by it, without the strictest Caution and watchfulness over my self."[15]

Similarly, "Marat . . . was especially susceptible to love of glory. 'From my infancy,' he said, 'I have been devoured by the love of glory, a passion which has changed its object during the various periods of my life but which has not left me for an instant.'"[16] Danton speculated that, "The people will revere my head even when the guillotine has severed it from my shoulders!"[17]

Leon Trotsky was given to monumental self-aggrandizement, particularly in the intellectual field. He persistently sought recognition of his personal superiority. Stalin's vanity was legendary as well as pathological. Morbid and vindictive, he was sensitive to the minutest slight to his position, status, authority.

Pierre Vallières's narcissism repeatedly surfaces in his autobiographical work, *White Niggers of America*. Instructive in this regard is his recounting of his feelings as a budding writer in his late teens:

## Table 7.1
## Psychological Dynamics of Political Behavior

| Leaders | Vanity | Asceticism | Relative Depr. | Marginality | Oedipal Conf. | Estheticism |
|---|---|---|---|---|---|---|
| **LOYALISTS** | | | | | | |
| Abbas | | | x | x | | x |
| Alami | | | x | x | | x |
| Batista | x | | x | x | | x |
| Batlle | | | | x | | x |
| Belaúnde | | | | | | |
| Bourguiba | x | | x | x | | x |
| Cárdenas | | x | x | x | | x |
| Cavendish | x | | | | | x |
| Chiang | x | | x | x | | x |
| Colden | x | | | x | | |
| Díaz | x | | x | x | | x |
| Dîem | x | | | x | | x |
| Dutra | x | | | | | |
| Frei | | | x | x | | |
| Galloway | x | | | / | | |
| Gomez | x | | | | | |
| Hutchinson | x | | | x | | |
| Hyde | x | | | x | | x |
| Kaunda | | | x | x | | x |
| K'ung | x | | | x | | x |
| Laud | x | | x | x | | x |
| Lévesque | | | x | x | | x |
| Luthuli | | x | x | x | | x |
| Marcos | x | | | | | |
| Maurepas | x | | | | | x |
| Nasser | x | x | x | | | x |
| Necker | x | | x | x | | |
| Nikolaevich | x | | | | | x |
| North | x | | | x | | x |
| Nyerere | | | x | x | | x |
| Odria | x | | x | x | | |
| Pearson | x | | | | | x |
| Peñaranda | x | | | x | | |
| Rupert | x | | x | x | | x |
| Hadnt | x | | x | x | | |
| Senghor | | | x | x | | x |
| Sewall | x | | x | | | |
| Sihanouk | | | | x | | x |
| Soong | x | | | x | | x |
| Stolypin | x | | | x | | x |
| Struve | x | | | x | | x |
| Thieu | x | | | x | | |
| Trudeau | x | | | x | | x |
| Tubman | x | | | | | |
| Turgot | x | | | x | | x |
| U Nu | | | x | x | | x |
| Vasconcelos | x | | x | x | | x |
| Wang | x | x | | | | x |
| Wentworth | x | | | x | | |
| Witte | x | | x | x | | x |
| TOTAL | 37 | 4 | 23 | 37 | 0 | 34 |

76

**Table 7.1** (*continued*)

| Leaders | Vanity | Asceticism | Relative Depr. | Marginality | Oedipal Conf. | Estheticism |
|---|---|---|---|---|---|---|
| REVOLUTIONARIES | | | | | | |
| J. Adams | x | x | | x | | x |
| S. Adams | x | | x | x | | |
| Arafat | x | x | x | x | | |
| Ben Bella | x | x | x | x | | x |
| Biko | | | | x | | x |
| Blanco | | x | x | x | | x |
| Cabral | | | x | x | | |
| Castro | | x | x | x | | |
| Chou | x | x | | | | x |
| Chu | | | | x | | x |
| Cromwell | x | x | | x | | x |
| Danton | x | | | x | | |
| Devereux | x | x | x | | | |
| Giap | x | x | | | | |
| Guevara | | x | | x | | x |
| Habash | | x | x | | | |
| Hampden | x | x | | | | |
| Henry | x | x | | | | x |
| Ho | x | x | x | x | | x |
| Jefferson | x | x | | | | x |
| Lenin | | x | | x | x | x |
| Lin | x | x | | x | | |
| Liu | | x | | | | x |
| Machel | | x | x | | | x |
| Madero | | | x | x | | |
| Mao | | x | | x | x | x |
| Marat | x | | x | x | | x |
| Marighella | | x | | x | | |
| Mirabeau | | x | | x | | |
| Mondlane | | x | x | x | | |
| Nkomo | x | | x | | | |
| Otis | x | | x | | | |
| Paz | x | x | x | | | |
| De la Puente | | x | | | | x |
| Pym | x | x | | | | |
| Roberto | | x | x | | | |
| Robespierre | x | x | | x | | |
| Schirm | | x | x | x | | x |
| Schoeters | | | x | x | | |
| Sendic | | x | | x | | |
| Sithole | | x | x | x | | x |
| Souphanouvong | x | x | x | x | | |
| Stalin | x | x | | x | | |
| Torres | | x | | | | x |
| Trotsky | x | x | | x | x | x |
| Vallières | x | x | x | x | | x |
| Vane | x | x | | | | x |
| Villa | x | | x | | | |
| Washington | x | | x | | | |
| Zapata | | | x | x | | |
| TOTAL | 27 | 37 | 25 | 31 | 3 | 23 |

Every evening, every night, I spent long hours writing—or rather, describing myself. During these hours of silence and solitude I lived out my narcissism to the full. . . .

*Noces obscures* [*Dark Weddings*, his first novel] was a book filled with my narcissism. [And I learned] to take responsibility for that narcissism without being ashamed of it.[18]

From early in his formative years Yasir Arafat's influential mentor and great-uncle Yusuf el-Akbar sought to convince the child that he possessed divine powers and was entrusted with a supernatural mission. As he grew up, Arafat became increasingly insensitive. A fellow activist and student at the University of Cairo recalled:

In my opinion, winning the presidency of PSF [Palestine Student Federation, in 1952] turned Yasir into a power maniac. . . . [H]e suddenly began to thrive on his position. He learned what it is to be president of something, to be able to issue orders, form committees, handle money, push people around who disagreed with him. He became arrogant. He became pretentious. He used to say that he could no longer have close friends because there might be times when he had to discipline or dismiss or even punish [them].[19]

Though self-confident and single-minded, some political elites of both loyalist and revolutionary orientation are noted for lack of vanity and egotism. Among the loyalists, for instance, even as a king, Sihanouk maintained an unpretentious, egalitarian posture. In 1947, six years after his selection as king by the French, he transformed an absolute monarchy into a constitutional one. Troubled by the pomp, pageantry, and protocol that surrounded his position, isolated from his people while deeply concerned about their welfare, he abdicated the throne in 1955 in order to "devote myself body and soul to the single service of the people and their well-being."[20]

U Nu was a devout Buddhist, committed to the love of peace. It was not insignificant that he dropped from his name the honorary designation "Takin" ("Sire" or "Lord" or "Master"), originally used to address the British. Similarly, Senghor consistently stressed his humility by referring to himself as a "humble Serer," a reference to his ethnic origin. Batlle, Cárdenas, and Frei exhibited similar qualities.

Among the revolutionaries, it is said of Lenin, for example: "Bragging, self-importance, and putting on airs were completely alien to him both as a boy and as a young man; the very scope of his personality excluded such qualities."[21] Reverend Sithole insisted on maintaining his Christian humility. Father Torres wrote: "I chose Christianity because I found in it the best way to serve my neighbor. I was chosen by Christ to be a priest forever, motivated by the desire to devote myself completely to the love of my brothers."[22]

### Asceticism, Puritanism, Virtue

Not unexpectedly, loyalists are virtually untouched by asceticism and puritanism whereas nearly three-fourths of the revolutionaries practice them with regularity.

Some loyalists are labeled pious or austere (for instance, Chiang, Hutchinson, Hyde, Laud, Sadat, Wentworth), but they do not share the emphasis on self-denial, self-discipline, and hard work that are the distinguishing marks of asceticism. On the contrary, loyalists are typically given to luxury and opulence, pomp and circumstance. Some tend to be notable sportsmen as well, be it riding, fencing, marksmanship, hunting, or racing (Cavendish, Dîem, Kaunda, Marcos, Sihanouk, and Trudeau come immediately to mind).

To be specific, only four loyalists appear to meet the criteria of asceticism and puritanism. Luthuli was a strict self-disciplinarian, living the life of self-denial and hard work. Cárdenas developed a lasting ascetic streak in reaction to the atmosphere of the billiard halls (gambling, liquor, profanity) to which his father took him as a young boy. At age 19, Wang's "puritanical streak" led him to organize the Six No Society (no smoking, no gambling, no drinking, no promiscuity, no corruption, no officialdom); ten years later he helped found the Society for the Promotion of Virtue. Nasser was a devout Muslim who led an unpretentious life under the motto of "discipline, unity, and work."[23]

Turning to the revolutionaries, we find asceticism and puritanism as unmistakable hallmarks. We begin with John Adams, whose asceticism and demand for virtue were just as pronounced as his vanity:

Suppos[e] a nation in some distant Region, should take the Bible for their only law Book, and every member should regulate his conduct by the precepts there exhibited. Every member would be obliged in Conscience to temperance and frugality and industry, to justice and kindness and Charity toward his fellow men, and to Piety and Love, and reverence towards almighty God. In this Commonwealth, no man would impair his health by Gluttony, drunkenness, or Lust—no man would sacrifice his most precious time to cards, or any other trifling and mean amusement—no man would steal or lie or any way defraud his neighbour, but would live in peace and good will with all men—no man would blaspheme his maker or prophane his Worship, but a rational and manly, a sincere and unaffected Piety and devotion, would reign in all hearts. What a Eutopia, what a Paradise would this region be.[24]

A most noteworthy feature of Robespierre's puritanism was that it was directly tied to his notions of virtue and terror. "High priest of a new faith," writes one author, "he believed himself sent on earth by God to establish the reign of virtue."[25] Virtue, in turn, can only materialize through the use of terror. Sinful and evil as men uniformly are, moreover, terror must be societywide in nature.

Puritanical, spartan, and self-disciplined, Lenin epitomized the ascetic revolutionary. He readily accepted the many hardships that revolution brought. There were times when he ate "in almost biblical simplicity." "Revolutions," he declared, "cannot be made with gloves and manicured fingernails."[26]

The simplicity with which Mao ran his life prior to power seizure has been widely noted. Living in the caves of Yenan for years, growing his own tobacco (he was always a chain smoker), demanding no special privileges, he lived a life of utter austerity.

Fidel Castro too led a rugged life in the harsh environment of the Sierra Maestra. After three decades in power, he continues to wear combat boots and battle fatigues as symbols of the continuing struggle. His comrade Che Guevara shared these qualities.

Father Torres, as we have seen, was the very personification of Christian virtue, love, and charity. Even before he formally entered the priesthood, this man of aristocratic background practiced the values he was later to preach. Having become disillusioned with church hierarchy, and having determined to leave the comforts of Bogotá for the life of the guerrilla fighter in October 1965, he announced: "I have to take a long and painful trip. I don't know if I will return to Bogotá. We revolutionaries must be prepared to give all—even our lives."[27] The statement proved prophetic: Torres was killed in combat in February 1966.

Arafat is said to have manifested asceticism from early on. His disdain for luxury and his abstinence from rich food or wine were consistent with religious precepts. Arafat himself summed up the matter succinctly: "But I was a *fedayeen* [literally, those who are prepared to sacrifice themselves for a cause], so sacrifice meant nothing. . . . To die at the hands of the real enemy, that would make me proud."[28]

## Relative Deprivation and Status Inconsistency

Relative deprivation and status inconsistency have been instrumental in shaping the motivation of an almost equal number, as it turns out, of loyalists (23) and revolutionaries (25). Briefly, relative deprivation refers to one's *perception* of discrepancy between one's value expectations (aspiration) and one's value capabilities (achievement). Status inconsistency denotes a perceived discrepancy between one's economic status and one's political power (more generally, social position).

Batista is the only loyalist to have come from the lower class and to have experienced relative deprivation in a direct and immediate manner. He began to work in the sugar cane fields at age eight. His poverty was compounded by the fact that he saw "the well-fed, neatly dressed children of the sugar mill owners, who rode into the settlement now and then on plump little ponies." It did not help matters that one night "he watched his young brother die of tuberculosis, for lack of adequate medical care and hospital facilities."[29]

Díaz was born in 1830 to a middle class family by nineteenth-century Mexican standards, his father having functioned variously as a veterinarian, an innkeeper, a soldier, a farmer, and the like. But the father's death in 1833 changed life rather drastically. The entire family had to sacrifice to send Díaz to the seminary and then to law school. His obsessive drive to become a skilled warrior (to which we have previously referred) had to await fruition until much later.

Some loyalists experience relative deprivation and status inconsistency because they are born to distinguished but impecunious families. Thus, it is said of Sewall: "Wealth, which made a man master of the other advantages, was missing. . . . It was enough, throughout his childhood and youth, that the family name saved him from the poverty and obscurity to which his own lack of inheritance doomed him."[30] Similarly, Rupert lived a life of comparative poverty from age two, when his father was ousted as the king of Bohemia. The troubles and anxieties that marked his childhood and youth were in part responsible for turning him into a warrior prince and a soldier of fortune. Likewise, the early death of Witte's father created considerable financial difficulties for the family, forcing the son to abandon the tradition of public service and join a private railroad company (see Chapter 6).

Relative deprivation and status inconsistency may be said to characterize the revolutionaries-turned-loyalists who initially found themselves in colonial contexts: Abbas, Bourguiba, Kaunda, Luthuli, Nasser, Sadat, U Nu, and possibly others. The mere presence of a foreign power and the attendant oppression and exploitation have proven more than sufficient to generate perceptions of economic, political, and social discontinuity.

In short, loyalist leaders experience relative deprivation and status inconsistency in a variety of ways. What is unique about them is that their sense of grievance, frustration, and discontent is later translated into a concern for the self rather than for society. The most notable exceptions in this regard are Bourguiba, Frei, Kaunda, Lévesque, Nasser, and U Nu, all of whom happen to subscribe to varieties of democratic socialist ideologies.

Turning to the revolutionaries, we find comparable patterns of frustration and discontent. A physician by profession, Marat's ambitions as a man of science had been thwarted—most particularly in having been repeatedly denied admission to the prestigious Academy of Sciences. Accordingly, by his own personal admission: "At the outbreak of the Revolution, wearied by the persecution that I had experienced for so long a time at the hands of the Academy of Sciences, I eagerly embraced the occasion that presented itself of defeating my oppressors and attaining my proper position."[31]

Samuel Adams had been trained for the ministry, but an ecclesiastical career did not hold his interest. Then he began the study of law, which he also found unattractive. Then he turned to business, in which he proved a failure as well. Having entered Boston politics, he served undistinguished terms as assessor and tax collector between 1758 and 1764. Assessing Adams's career to this point, a biographer wrote:

At the age of 42 he was faced with the unpleasant realization that he was a failure both in business and in public office. . . .
An experience like this is practically certain to create an inferiority complex, with the resulting hunger for compensation. . . . Much of Adams's career after 1764 may be accounted for by regarding it as a result of his efforts, largely unconscious, to secure compensation and to bring about a more satisfactory adjustment to his environment. Because of his inferiority complex, which served as a stimulus to extra effort to overcome his disadvantages, his activity was sure to be extraordinary, if not abnormal, the kind not infrequently characterized as inspired.[32]

Washington's case was different. His compulsion to expand his landholdings brought him into conflict with English law: by a 1767 proclamation, the king had forbidden further invasion of Indian territory by settlers. But Washington's thirst for more land remained unsatiated. Similarly, his interest in the Stamp and Navigation Acts was more than that of an interested member of the Virginia House of Burgesses. He was personally affected: he owned nearly 10,000 acres and was a heavy exporter to England.

Having failed, in a series of acts of protest and official correspondence, to reform the system, Washington concluded that more potent action was called for. Having been deprived of his rights, having failed to obtain redress in a peaceful manner, Washington's only alternative was to embrace the radicalism that the situation thrusted upon him.

The case of Washington is illustrative of a whole genre of revolutionaries around the globe who begin as reformers and seek to work within the system. Finding the system unresponsive, running into constant frustration and intimidation, they become disillusioned, reject establishment politics, and turn to revolutionary politics. Cases in point include J. and S. Adams, Castro, Cromwell, Madero, Nkomo, Paz, Sithole, Vane (see Appendix B).

Among lower class revolutionaries, Vallières was acutely and obsessively aware of the continued futility of trying to improve his condition in English-dominated Quebec. Brutally candid, he wrote: "My itinerary from lower-class slums to the FLQ was long and tortuous." His childhood was anything but peaceful, secure, or happy. As for school, "the only thing" he learned "was to be ashamed of my—of our—condition." On the whole, he found, his "entire existence was nothing but a daily obscenity." Yet, he continued to strive: "I wanted to *do* something, to become someone." Failing on all fronts, he ended up seeing himself as a "white nigger."

To be a "nigger" in America is to be not a man but someone's slave. For the rich white man of Yankee America, the nigger is a sub-man. Even the poor whites consider the nigger their inferior. They say: "to work as hard as a nigger," "to smell like a nigger," "as dangerous as a nigger," "as ignorant as a nigger." Very often they do not even suspect that they too are niggers, slaves, "white niggers." White racism hides the reality from them by giving them the opportunity to despise an inferior, to crush him mentally or to pity him.[33]

### Marginality, Inferiority, Compulsion to Excel

It is a recurrent theme in the literature of political leadership that political men tend to be marginal in their societies—that is, they deviate in significant and perceptible ways from accepted norms, whether social, psychological, or physical. Perhaps the most influential scholar to advance this proposition was Harold D. Lasswell, who maintained, as we have seen in Chapter 1, that all forms of power seeking represent compensatory mechanisms growing out of inferiority complex, low self-esteem, and a corresponding compulsion to excel. This private need is then displaced onto public objects and rationalized in terms of the public interest. As indicated in Table 7.1, 74 percent (37) of the loyalists and 62 percent (31) of the revolutionaries exhibit some form of marginality.

As with relative deprivation and status inconsistency, one can argue that all loyalist leaders with colonial backgrounds or experiences can be considered marginal, since such experiences invariably inculcate feelings of subordination and inferiority. Abbas, Bourguiba, Kaunda, Luthuli, Nasser, Nyerere, Sadat, Senghor, and U Nu fall in this category.

As we have seen in Chapter 6, even Lévesque protested against what he considered the colonial status of the French Canadians. As early as age six (1928), while going to primary school in his hometown of New Carlisle, he noticed that the Catholics had a one-room schoolhouse while the Protestants had a complete high school. "That high school" became a point of obsession with Lévesque, as it came to symbolize the oppressed position of the French Canadians. As late as 1972, he told his biographer:

Whenever I go back there, I think everything in its proper perspective—everything except that high school. In fact, it seems to get bigger and bigger as years go by. . . . That fine English high school . . . gave its graduates the opportunity to go on to McGill University. My own school . . . led nowhere. It was that simple.[34]

Vasconcelos's experiences were somewhat different, though the consequences were much the same. For a time the Vasconcelos family left their home in Piedras Negras, Mexico, to live in the border town of Eagle Pass, Texas. Going to school with American children, the young Vasconcelos was ridiculed and taunted:

Anxious fears would come over me; for no good reasons, I became profoundly sad. . . . Darkness, helplessness, terrible fears, self-centeredness, such is the summary of the emotional life of my childhood. . . .

And it made me still more angry if some pupil compared the customs of the Mexicans to those of the Eskimos, and said, "Mexicans are a semi-civilized people." At our house, on the other hand, we believed that Yankees had just recently acquired culture.[35]

Some loyalists develop feelings of inadequacy and inferiority as a consequence of psychological traumas. Thomas Hutchinson, for example, came from a family of mental problems: "Both Hutchinson and his father suffered from 'nervous disorders,' probably brought on by the chronic oversensitivity, introspection, and agonizing common to both men."[36] Hutchinson, it will be remembered, was appointed lieutenant governor of Massachusetts in 1758, acting governor in 1769, and governor in 1771. Psychological debility struck at a critical juncture:

[I]n April 1767, well before the major crisis of his career developed, he suffered what appears to have been a nervous breakdown—he was, as he put it, "paralytic" for six or seven weeks—and only gradually regained his health. He was never thereafter free of worry, about himself as well as about the world. Night after night as governor he lay awake . . . worrying if he had the wisdom and the physical and psychic strength to guide the colony to peace. Repeatedly, in the ordeals of the seventies, his energy ebbed, his spirit flagged, and he hovered at the edge of collapse.[37]

Psychological anxieties beleaguered Chiang Kai-shek (1887–1975) from early childhood. Chiang was the first of four children born to his father's third wife, a fact Chiang considered a "blemish." Chiang was flanked by an older brother, who by tradition and custom held the most elevated sibling position, and by a younger brother who, by Chiang's own reckoning, was "endowed with extremely good looks, which none of the others of us had. . . . [H]e was my mother's favorite." As a result, Chiang found himself in a precarious position, felt increasingly rejected, and became distrustful. Moreover,

Chiang was . . . given to fits of ill temper, and he became an object of ridicule in the village. A fortuneteller remarked that he had an abnormally-shaped head, and was "exceptionally strange." He grew up having bouts of weeping and seizures of uncontrolled rage, interspersed by long periods of withdrawal. A tutor who observed his erratic behavior remarked, "One would think he had two different personalities."[38]

In later life, Chiang's political and military actions were "revelatory of the sense of persecution and alienation he often felt during his early adulthood."[39]

Discrepant social status can also generate feelings of marginality and inferiority. A Swiss Protestant, Necker was named Director General of Finance, rather than being given a ministerial title, because of his foreign birth. Hard as he tried, he was never fully accepted at the court of Louis XVI. Rupert of the Rhine had similar experiences at the court of James I.

Struve's grandfather, a world famous astronomer, immigrated from Germany, "became a Russian citizen, received rank of hereditary noble, and was elected to the Academy of Sciences." But Struve's status remained marginal because, in Russian eyes, Germans "never ceased to be 'foreigners,' even if they knew no country other than Russia."[40] Stolypin witnessed similar discrimination, not because of himself but because his wife was a German and a commoner. As a result, "Stolypin avoided Petersburg and court society . . . [because of] the viciousness of the elite."[41]

Some loyalists are made to feel inferior because of their mannerisms or physical and facial features or ill health. Rupert is said to have been "rough and unpolished" from childhood, never picking up "the customs and manners" of British aristocracy.[42] Lord North's biographer summarized his "physical limitations" in the following fashion:

His figure was already [at age twenty-one] beginning to round, his face had the chubby contours of a well-fed infant, his eyes were protuberant, his speech was thick and his pitch and volume badly controlled, and he stood with his feet apart as if braced against a strong wind. His gestures were awkward, and he was extremely near-sighted.[43]

In the following depiction of Struve, the portion in quotation marks is given by a fellow student from St. Petersburg; the balance is added by a biographer:

"He was a slender, tall youth, with a sunken chest. . . . Despite his rather regular features he seemed unattractive because of his unusually pale face, full of freckles, and his moist mouth and white lips." Later on he grew a thick beard to conceal his unappealing mouth and he let his hair reach to the shoulders to hide his equally unattractive thick and protruding ears. His whole appearance as a young man had something utterly helpless about it, and . . . [he was] . . . dubbed . . . the calf.[44]

Equally harsh judgments concerning physical or facial features exist for Batista, Batlle, Bourguiba, Frei, Gomez, K'ung, Laud, Necker, Sadat, Soong, U Nu, Vasconcelos, Wentworth, and Witte.

One's medical condition also matters. A number of loyalists are reported to have been born pallid, puny, frail, and sickly: Bourguiba, Chiang, Hyde, Kaunda, Laud, Struve, Trudeau, Vasconcelos. While the typical loyalist nurtured his frailty or poor health, Trudeau is an exception in that, with his father's encouragement, he instituted a rigorous program of physical activity in order to overcome his vulnerability.

Turning to the revolutionaries, we find the foregoing patterns repeating themselves with surprising regularity. To begin with, all colonial revolutionaries are by definition marginal, since the colonizers systematically infuse them with a sense of inferiority and consider them as subhuman. Thus, for example, Ho Chi Minh tasted bitter personal humiliation as a result of the treatment he received from the French in Vietnam, his experiences as a mess boy on a French liner traveling throughout much of the world, working as a kitchen helper in London, shoveling snow for the London school system, and generally witnessing acts of brutalization and oppression.

Similarly, Ben Bella was quite conscious of the fact that he was a colonial man. Leaving his hometown of Marnia to attend school in Tlemcen helped crystallize his status for him:

[I]n Tlemcen, relations between the several [different] communities did not have the superficial good-heartedness which was to be found in the villages, and which concealed the true state of affairs. At Tlemcen, the gulf between the French world and the Algerian world was obvious. Discrimination hit you in the face, even at school. At Tlemcen I felt, for the first time, that I belonged to a community which was considered inferior by the Europeans. For the first time I realized that I was a foreigner in my own country. . . . I made up my mind that I myself would never submit to it, and it was from that moment that, deep in my heart, I felt myself becoming a rebel.[45]

The revolutionaries experience psychological crisis as well. Cromwell, for instance, was a neurotic youth who underwent a nervous breakdown and a traumatic religious conversion. As a result of the latter, he became convinced that through arduous prayer he could tap divine powers to enable him to overcome the forces of evil and lead England toward a glorious future.

John Adams—that man of supreme vanity and egotism—regularly suffered from self-doubt and feelings of inferiority. Thus, according to one biographer:

If a modern psychologist could have examined unmarried John Adams, he would have found him full of corrosive anxieties, hostilities, and aggressions, slightly paranoid in his suspicion that the hand of man was turned against him, obsessed by an often agonizing inferiority complex which led him to "overcompensate" by defiant, contentious actions, and almost schizophrenic in his dividedness between, on the one hand, the image of a contented rural lawyer and, on the other, the vision of a renowned if restless and harassed philosopher-author-attorney whose brilliance and eloquence were a byword through the land. There were signs, moreover, of the classic manic-depressive, swinging from the heights to the depths, from exultation to black despair. . . . He carried with him a handful of vigorous complexes, from hypochondria to mild paranoia, and lived balanced among them in delicate equilibrium.[46]

Trotsky, a preeminent intellectual of his day, was riddled with feelings of anxiety and a compulsion to prove himself over and over again. His autobiography is studded with instances of humiliation and failure that plagued him in early life. Unable to match his father's skills on the farm, trying to ride a horse and falling off, being scolded for wetting his pants, being laughed at by servants in the household, being scolded by peasant boys for dressing well—all these produced a determination to devote himself entirely to the one area in which he excelled: intellectual prowess. In excelling in school, for example, he proved his special capabilities to his father, to his brother, to school mates, to himself. Years later, revolutionary circles provided him with a platform from which regularly to exhibit his intellectual superiority.

The revolutionaries experience other forms of social marginality as well. Stalin was a Georgian always intensely sensitive about his accent. Mao and Chu were humiliated in school because they came from peasant backgrounds and were poorly dressed. Castro was an illegitimate child whose parents subsequently married. In addition to being illegitimate, Schoeters never knew his father and was abandoned by his mother.

Whether high or low, social class can also have negative consequences. Prince Souphanouvong was the twentieth and youngest son of the viceroy, a hereditary position of a collateral branch of the Laotian royal family. His mother was a commoner, perhaps even a concubine. His father "apparently paid little attention to him and even was rumored not to be his real father." His inferiority vis-à-vis his three older illustrious brothers continued to plague him. Accordingly, "his remarkable vigor, combative, adventurous, and romantic spirit, his strong desire to excel . . . may not be unrelated to the pressures he felt to make up for [his marginal status] . . . in a royal household."[47]

At the opposite end of the social spectrum stands Vallières, whose inferiority complex was just as real and just as intense. His lower class background haunted him as he failed at everything he touched. At the peak of an identity crisis, he turned to religion and felt content as he began "to dream about God." Finding the church hypocritical, he abandoned religion and traveled to France in search of roots and identity. Disillusioned by his experiences in France, he reached the point of contemplating suicide. He concluded: "There was nothing for me to do here [in France]. I could be of no use to anyone. As in Quebec. . . . No one needed me or my services. . . . I am certainly a man who has been flayed alive."[48]

Physical disfigurement is an apparent source of marginality and inferiority complex for some revolutionaries. Mirabeau "is said to have been born with two teeth, to have beaten his nurse at the age of three, and to have shown in early childhood that excess of vitality which drove most of his family to the extremes either of virtue or vice. It was so to the end." His face disfigured by smallpox at age three led his father to consider him "ugly as Satan." And when he went to school, "The boy was not allowed to bear his family name, but was registered in the institution, at his father's request, as Pierre Buffiere, a slight, an ignominy put upon him, that must have irritated his proud nature."[49]

Lenin is supposed to have had Mongolian features and an Asiatic appearance, including slanted eyes. Stalin was born with two toes grown together on his left foot. His face was scarred by smallpox at age seven. A carriage accident produced a chronic stiffness in the right elbow which left that arm seemingly shorter than the other. As a result, he was the object of ridicule from insensitive peers.

According to an older brother, from early childhood, Arafat "was fat, soft, ungainly, and completely unimpressive. He had a very high voice, and was beginning to suffer from comparison to girls. . . . Even my father . . . blamed my mother for much of what he thought was wrong with Rahman [Arafat's given name], saying that her dreaming of a girl had caused Rahman to be born more like a girl than a boy."[50] In a male-dominated culture, this could be psychologically debilitating, setting in motion any number of compensatory mechanisms aimed at power seeking.

Some revolutionaries suffered from ill health. Madero and Guevara were both born puny and frail. Madero had a small stature, a squeaky voice, and a melancholy disposition. Born a month prematurely, Guevara's father devoted himself to improving the child's health through a program of vigorous exercise: "I spent all my time with the boy. I took him shooting, taught him to swim, and got him to play soccer and rugby. I saw to it that he spent about three hours each day in the pool in the summer, to relax his chest muscles and get him breathing well."[51] The father taught Che to regard his frailty as a challenge to be accepted and overcome, rather than a weakness to stand in the way of action. Accordingly, Che developed a passion for sports in order to demonstrate that he could rise above his physical debilities. He kept an asthma atomizer handy throughout his life, however.

### Oedipal Conflict Writ Large

Building on the work of Harold D. Lasswell mentioned above, E. Victor Wolfenstein has developed a theory of revolutionary personality based on the oedipal conflict.[52] According to this theory, the revolutionary externalizes and projects onto the political arena the private conflict with the father, thus moderating his feelings of ambivalence and guilt.

Having examined their early experiences, we found that most loyalists had "normal" family relationships. Some leaders (for example, Díaz, Hyde, Lévesque, and Trudeau) expressed only praise and admiration for their fathers, others (Bourguiba, Chiang, Nasser, Pearson, and Vasconcelos) maintained warm and affectionate relationships with their mothers, and still others (Rupert and Turgot) resented their domineering mothers. One loyalist (Struve) remembered his mother in a most unflattering way and abandoned her when he was 19. In no instance, however, did we find any evidence of father conflict, rebelliousness, ambivalence, and guilt.

Since Wolfenstein's theory is explicitly designed to account for the behavior of revolutionaries, perhaps it is not surprising that we found no evidence of its presence among loyalist leaders. Turning to the group of fifty revolutionaries, we did not find the situation significantly different. Specifically, we can document parental conflict and potential oedipal problems for only three persons: Lenin, Trotsky, Mao. Another three revolutionaries (Castro, Chou, Chu) are potential candidates for this type of analysis, but our knowledge is so inadequate as to render exploration unfruitful. Lenin and Trotsky presenting the more familiar life histories, here we sample the case of Mao.

Mao's father, as the son described him, was a "rich peasant"[53] who was exceedingly demanding of everyone around him. Mao told Edgar Snow:

My father wanted me to begin keeping the family books as soon as I had learned a few [Chinese] characters.... He was a severe taskmaster. He hated to see me idle, and if there were no books to be kept he put me to work at farm tasks. He was a hot-tempered man and frequently beat both me and my brothers.

He gave us no money whatever, and the most meager food. On the fifteenth of every month he made a concession to his labourers and gave them eggs with their rice, but never meat. To me he gave neither eggs nor meat.

In contrast, "My mother was a kind woman, generous and sympathetic, and ever ready to share what she had. She pitied the poor and often gave them rice when they came to ask for it during famines. But she could not do so when my father was present. He disapproved of charity. We had many quarrels in my home over this question."

As a consequence:

There were two "parties" in the family. One was my father, the Ruling Power. The Opposition was made up of myself, my mother, my brother and sometimes even the labourers. In the "United Front" of the Opposition, however, there was a difference of opinion. My mother advocated a policy of indirect attack. She criticized my overt display of emotion and attempts at open rebellion against the Ruling Power. She said it was not the Chinese way....

My dissatisfaction increased. The dialectical struggle in our family was constantly developing....

Reflecting on this, I think that in the end the strictness of my father defeated him. I learned to hate him, and we created a real United Front against him.

Considering the ancient Chinese tradition of filial piety, these are indeed strong words and deeds. Moreover, Mao made a point of siding with the workers whenever they came into conflict with his father. He further defied the father by leaving for Peking at age 18, where he came under the spell of Marxist intellectuals.

### Estheticism and Romanticism

Throughout the preceding pages we have depicted political leaders variously as vain and egotistical, ascetic and puritanical, driven by a variety of passions, tensions, and insecurities. We should now note that 68 percent (34) of the loyalists and 46 percent (23) of the revolutionaries have a gentler, esthetic, romantic side as well. Although strictly speaking not all expressions of estheticism function as psychological dynamics, they help provide a more balanced picture of political elites.

A surprisingly large number of loyalists were serious students of literature, poetry, philosophy, and the arts: Bourguiba, Cárdenas, Cavendish, Chiang, Díaz, Hyde, Laud, Lévesque, Marcos, Nasser, Pearson, Rupert, Struve, Trudeau, U Nu, Vasconcelos, and Wang. North was an accomplished classical scholar; Nyerere and Senghor were world-class philosophers; Turgot was a leading *philosophe* and a contributor to the *Encyclopedie*; Nyerere, Senghor, and U Nu were poets in their own right.

Music lovers include Bourguiba, Laud, Lévesque, Nasser, Senghor, Trudeau, Vasconcelos, and Witte. In addition, Kaunda played the harp and the guitar and sang folk songs. Pearson played the piano and Sihanouk, the saxophone. Stolypin played the violin and composed music.

Bourguiba was a frequent theatergoer. Cavendish, Stolypin, and U Nu were playwrights. Chiang, Diem, Laud, and Lévesque were nature lovers. Lévesque and U Nu had Don Quixote complexes of an episodic nature. Nyerere translated into Swahili *Julius Caesar* and *The Merchant of Venice*. Sihanouk staged plays at the palace and made motion pictures. Stolypin was a sculptor. Turgot translated from the English, Hebrew, German, Greek, Italian, and Latin; he also wrote on chemistry, geology, geography, astronomy, metaphysics, theology, and politics, not to mention economics. Vasconcelos developed a theory of "esthetic monism," seeking to unite the senses, the intellect, and the emotions.

Turning to the revolutionaries, a virtually identical pattern emerges. Some revolutionaries were well-steeped in literature, poetry, philosophy, and the arts: Castro, Guevara, Jefferson, Lenin, Mao, Robespierre, Torres, Trotsky, and Vallières. Even a highly selective list of their favorites would amount to a who's who of world literature and philosophy: Baudelaire, Camus, Dostoyevsky, Einstein, Hegel, Heidegger, Hugo, Kafka, Kierkegaard, Locke, Malraux, Marx, J. S. Mill, Proust, Rousseau, Sartre, Shakespeare, Adam Smith, Tolstoy, Zola. Moreover such an unlikely figure as Vallières wrote three novels before age 18 and destroyed them because he was not satisfied with any.

Some of the revolutionaries were poets in their own right. The best known and most prolific was Mao, of course. Less well known were Ch'en Yi, Chu Teh, Ho Chi Minh, Liu Shao-ch'i, Torres, and Vallières.

Some revolutionaries were infatuated by music. Jefferson called music "the favorite passion of my soul"[54] and played the violin in a string quartet. Biko and Torres composed and performed their own music. Lenin was once observed actually wiping away tears while attending a tragic opera. Particularly fond of Beethoven, he once remarked: "I can listen to Beethoven's *Sonata Pathetique* twenty or forty times, and every time it holds my attention and delights me more and more."[55]

Some revolutionaries were nature lovers. Mao's poetry, for example, frequently depicts the sky, clouds, storm, snow, rain, wind, mountains, rivers, fish, birds, trees, flowers, blossoms, and the like. Father Torres loved all things Colombian: rivers, mountains, flowers, cornfields. He was particularly struck by Los Llanos—the vast sunburnt plains lying on the other side of the mountains from Bogotá. Visiting the place, in fact, transformed his life:

The immensity of that place, the silence, the tropical explosion of life, of sun, impressed me very much. I began to be disturbed. I wanted to be alone. I realized that life as I understood it, as I was living it, lacked meaning. I thought I could be more useful socially. . . . I analyzed the professions one by one: medicine, law, engineering, chemistry . . . ? None of those. What about the seminary? I told myself that the immensity of [Los Llanos] had helped me find God. It was the solution. It seemed to me a total solution. The most logical.[56]

Torres came to count himself among "a handful of [Don] Quixotes"[57]—a condition that afflicts at least two other revolutionaries as well: Blanco and Guevara. Guevara's version is most explicit. Written in 1965 when he was preparing to depart for the Bolivian adventure that led to his death, his farewell letter to his family read in part:

Dear Folks:
Once again I feel Rocinante's bony ribs beneath my legs. Again I begin my journey, carrying my shield.

Almost ten years ago I wrote you another letter of farewell. As I recall, I regretted not being a better soldier and a better doctor. I no longer care about the latter, but I'm not such a bad soldier, now. . . .

Many will call me an adventurer, and I am, but of a different kind—one who risks his skin in order to prove his convictions.

Perhaps this will be my last letter. It is not my intention, but it is within the realm of logical probability. If so, I send you a last embrace. . . .

Give an occasional thought to this little twentieth century *condottiere*. Kisses for Celia, Roberto, Juan Martín, Pototín, for Beatriz, for everyone.

And for you, an embrace from your recalcitrant prodigal son.

Ernesto[58]

## SUMMARY

Examining the mental attributes and psychological dynamics of political leaders, it turns out that as a whole: (1) nationalism-patriotism defines virtually all political elites, (2) a sense of justice, asceticism-puritanism, and oedipal conflict (insofar as it exists) are attributes of the revolutionaries alone, and (3) vanity-egotism, relative deprivation and status inconsistency, marginality, and estheticism apply to both groups, but with differential force.

As far as individual leaders are concerned, as Table 7.1 shows, the particular mix of psychological forces varies from case to case. We should note, however, that, other than nationalism-patriotism, five leaders—loyalists Dutra, Galloway, Gomez, Marcos, and Tubman—are marked by only one psychological dynamic: vanity. A single loyalist, Belaúnde, appears to have no defining feature other than nationalism.

We conclude that loyalist and revolutionary elites are similar in important ways with respect to psychological dynamics, sharing as they do many of the traits we have examined. In particular, next to nationalism-patriotism, marginality emerges as the most ubiquitous characteristic of political elites, whether of loyalist or revolutionary orientation. To this topic we shall return in Chapter 9.

## NOTES

1. Sigmund Freud, *Group Psychology and the Analysis of the Ego* [1921] (New York: Bantam Books, 1960); Lucille Iremonger, *The Fiery Chariot: A Study of British Prime Ministers and the Search for Love* (London: Secker & Warburg, 1970); Alfred Adler, "The Psychology of Power" [1928], *Journal of Individual Psychology* 22 (1966): 166–72; Karen Horney, *The Neurotic Personality of Our Time* (New York: W. W. Norton, 1937); Harold D. Lasswell, *Psychopathology and Politics* [1930] (New York: Viking, 1960); Donald R. Matthews, *U.S. Senators and Their World* (Chapel Hill: University of North Carolina Press, 1960); James L. Payne et al., *The Motivations of Politicians* (Chicago: Nelson-Hall, 1984).

2. William H. Blanchard, *Revolutionary Morality* (Santa Barbara: ABC-Clio, 1984); Bruce Mazlish, *The Revolutionary Ascetic* (New York: Basic Books, 1976); Michael Walzer, *The Revolution of the Saints* (Cambridge: Harvard University Press, 1965).

3. Ted Robert Gurr, *Why Men Rebel* (Princeton: Princeton University Press, 1970); Iremonger, *The Fiery Chariot*.

4. Adler, "The Psychology of Power"; Horney, *The Neurotic Personality of Our Time*; Eric H. Erikson, *Gandhi's Truth* (New York: W. W. Norton, 1969); Erikson, *Young Man Luther* (New York: W. W. Norton, 1962); Alexander George, "Power as a Compensatory Value for Political Leaders," *Journal of Social Issues* 3 (1968): 29–49; Iremonger, *The Fiery Chariot*; Lasswell, *Psychopathology and Politics*.

5. E. Victor Wolfenstein, *The Revolutionary Personality* (Princeton: Princeton University Press, 1967).
6. Iremonger, *The Fiery Chariot*; M. Rejai and K. Phillips, *World Revolutionary Leaders* (New Brunswick: Rutgers University Press, 1983).
7. On Batlle, see Milton J. Vanger, *The Model Country: José Batlle y Ordóñez of Uruguay 1907-1915* (Hanover, NH: University Press of New England, 1980), p. 288; on Cárdenas, Frank Tannenbaum, *Mexico: The Struggle for Peace and Bread* (New York: Alfred A. Knopf, 1950), p. 71; Eduardo Frei, *Latin America: The Hopeful Option* (Maryknoll, NY: Orbis Books, 1978), p. 195 et passim.
8. The characterizations are in the following sources, respectively: Robert Coffin, *Laud: Storm Center of Stuart England* (New York: Brentano's, 1930), p. 41; Vincent Cronin, *Louis and Antoinette* (London: William Collins & Sons, 1974), p. 142; Andrew D. Kalmykow, *Memoirs of a Russian Diplomat* (New Haven: Yale University Press, 1971), p. 180.
9. Robert Payne, *Chiang Kai-shek* (New York: Weybright & Talley, 1969), p. 47.
10. Pinchon Loh, *The Early Chiang Kai-shek* (New York: Columbia University Press, 1971), p. 8.
11. Quotations are from Jean Lacourture, *The Demigods* (New York: Alfred A. Knopf, 1970), pp. 150, 152, 153. See also Rolf Italiaander, *The New Leaders of Africa* (Englewood Cliffs: Prentice-Hall, 1961), pp. 25-30.
12. Anwar el-Sadat, *In Search of Identity: An Autobiography* (New York: Harper & Row, 1977), "Prologue," unpaged; cf. "Epilogue," pp. 314-15.
13. Quoted in Italiaander, *The New Leaders of Africa*, p. 40.
14. Quoted in Mazlish, *The Revolutionary Ascetic* (n. 2), p. 67.
15. L. H. Butterfield, ed., *The Earliest Diary of John Adams* (Cambridge: Harvard University Press, 1966), p. 77; Butterfield, ed., *The Diary and Autobiography of John Adams*, 3 vols. (Cambridge: Harvard University Press, 1961), I:78. In all Adams quotations, the original spelling, capitalization, and punctuation have been retained.
16. Quoted in Henry Beraud, *Twelve Portraits of the French Revolution* (Boston: Little, Brown, 1928), p. 119.
17. Quoted in Robert Christopher, *Danton: A Biography* (New York: Doubleday & Co., 1967), p. 432.
18. Pierre Vallières, *White Niggers of America* (New York: Monthly Review Press, 1971), pp. 145, 152.
19. Quoted in Thomas Kiernan, *Arafat: The Man and the Myth* (New York: W. W. Norton, 1976), p. 184.
20. John P. Armstrong, ed., *Sihanouk Speaks* (New York: Walker, 1964), p. 46; cf. Willard A. Hanna, *Eight Nation Makers* (New York: St. Martin's Press, 1964), pp. 209, 212.
21. Leon Trotsky, *The Young Lenin* (New York: Doubleday & Co., 1972), p. 96.
22. Quoted in Germán Guzmán, *Camilo Torres* (New York: Sheed & Ward, 1969), p. 12.
23. On Luthuli, see Albert Luthuli, *Let My People Go* (New York: McGraw-Hill, 1962), passim. On Cárdenas, see William C. Townsend, *Lázaro Cárdenas: Mexican Democrat* (Ann Arbor, MI: George Wahr Publishing Co., 1952), p. 11. On Wang, see William Morwood, *Duel for the Middle Kingdom* (New York: Everest

House, 1980), pp. 264-65; Howard Boorman, "Wang Ching-wei: A Political Profile," In Chün-tu Hsüeh, ed., *Revolutionary Leaders of Modern China* (New York: Oxford University Press, 1971), p. 301. On Nasser, see Gamal Abdel Nasser, *The Philosophy of the Revolution* (Cairo: Dar Al-Maaref, n.d. [1954?], p. 21 et passim.

24. Butterfield, *The Diary and Autobiography of John Adams* (n. 15), I:9.

25. Gustave Le Bon, *The Psychology of Revolution* (New York: G. P. Putnam's Sons, 1913), p. 240.

26. Trotsky, *The Young Lenin* (n. 21), p. 137; Mazlish, *The Revolutionary Ascetic* (n. 2), p. 129.

27. Quoted in Guzmán, *Camilo Torres* (n. 22), p. 239.

28. Quoted in Kiernan, *Arafat* (n. 19), pp. 231-32.

29. Edmund A. Chester, *A Sergeant Named Batista* (New York: Henry Holt & Co., 1954), pp. 3, 5, 6.

30. Carol Berkin, *Jonathan Sewall: Odyssey of an American Loyalist* (New York: Columbia University Press, 1974), p. 4.

31. Quoted in Louis R. Gottschalk, *Jean Paul Marat: A Study in Radicalism* (New York: Benjamin Blom, 1966), p. 53.

32. Ralph V. Harlow, *Samuel Adams: Promoter of the American Revolution* (New York: Henry Holt & Co., 1923), p. 87.

33. Vallières, *White Niggers of America* (n. 18), pp. 21, 62, 103, 111, 112.

34. Quoted in Jean Provencher, *René Lévesque* (n.p.: Gage Publishing, 1975), p. 14.

35. José Vasconcelos, *A Mexican Ulysses: An Autobiography* (Bloomington: Indiana University Press, 1963), pp. 24-25.

36. William Pencak, *America's Burke: The Mind of Thomas Hutchinson* (Washington: University Press of America, 1982), p. 7.

37. Bernard Bailyn, *The Ordeal of Thomas Hutchinson* (Cambridge: Harvard University Press, 1974), p. 28; cf. ibid., p. 139.

38. Sterling Seagrave, *The Soong Dynasty* (New York: Harper & Row, 1985), p. 153. Other quotations in this paragraph are from Emily Hahn, *Chiang Kai-shek* (New York: Doubleday & Co., 1955), p. 19; Loh, *The Early Chiang Kai-shek* (n. 10), pp. 8, 12.

39. Loh, *The Early Chiang Kai-shek*, p. 29.

40. Richard Pipes, *Struve: Liberal on the Left 1870-1905* (Cambridge: Harvard University Press, 1970), pp. 4, 6.

41. Mary S. Conroy, *Peter Arkadievich Stolypin* (Boulder, CO: Westview Press, 1976), p. 26.

42. Mark Bence-Jones, *The Cavaliers* (London: Constable & Co., 1976), p. 51.

43. Alan Valentine, *Lord North*, 2 vols. (Norman: University of Oklahoma Press, 1967), I:25.

44. Pipes, *Struve* (n. 40), p. 11.

45. Quoted in Robert Merle, *Ahmed Ben Bella* (New York: Walker & Co., 1967), pp. 42-43.

46. C. Page Smith, *John Adams*, 2 vols. (New York: Doubleday & Co., 1962), I:70-71.

47. Paul F. Langer and Joseph J. Zasloff, *North Vietnam and the Pathet Lao* (Cambridge: Harvard University Press, 1970), pp. 29, 230.

Psychologies

48. Vallières, *White Niggers of America* (n. 12), pp. 164, 169, 194, 196.
49. James M. Thompson, *Leaders of the French Revolution* (New York: Harper Colophon, 1967), p. 19; Louis Madelin, *Figures of the Revolution* (Freeport, NY: Books for Libraries Press, 1968), p. 33; Charles F. Warwick, *Mirabeau and the French Revolution* (Philadelphia: J. B. Lippincott Co., 1905), p. 152.
50. Quoted in Kiernan, *Arafat* (n. 19), p. 56.
51. Quoted in John Gerassi, ed., *Venceremos! The Speeches and Writings of Ernesto Che Guevara* (New York: Macmillan, 1968), p. 3.
52. Wolfenstein, *The Revolutionary Personality* (n. 5).
53. All Mao quotations are from Edgar Snow, *Red Star Over China* [1938] (New York: Grove Press, 1961), pp. 125-26.
54. Quoted in Richard B. Morris, *Seven Who Shaped Our Destiny* (New York: Harper & Row, 1973), p. 119.
55. Quoted in Mazlish, *The Revolutionary Ascetic* (n. 2), p. 139.
56. Quoted in Guzmán, *Camilo Torres* (n. 22), p. 14.
57. See ibid., p. 244.
58. In Gerassi, ed., *Venceremos!* (n. 51), p. 412; for Blanco's version, see Hugo Blanco, *Land or Death: The Peasant Struggle in Peru* (New York: Pathfinder Books, 1972), p. 97.

# 8 Skills

The mere fact of becoming a member of the political elite suggests and requires the possession of a range of skills of which verbal and organizational are the most significant. To be sure, some leaders excel in oratory, others in organization building, and still others in both, but some degree of skill is indispensable to political leadership.

## THE LOYALISTS

Among loyalists particularly noted for verbal skill are Batista, Belaúnde, Bourguiba, Galloway, Gomez, Lévesque, Marcos, Nasser, Nyerere, Pearson, Sadat, Sewall, Sihanouk, Stolypin, Trudeau, Turgot, U Nu, Wang, and Wentworth. Thus, for instance, Galloway is said to have been an "eloquent" speaker, a man of "great erudition," and a "master of persuasion."[1] Turgot was given to speaking "with fire and terror"; he was capable of "brilliant orations."[2] An eyewitness remembers Stolypin holding forth with "natural and direct eloquence, and in a powerful voice. . . . [He] made a commanding appearance."[3] Gomez displayed "oratorical ability"; he was "a polemician of the first rank . . . magnetic and forceful."[4]

Bourguiba's talents are described in the following fashion:

Politics to him is rational calculation, a Cartesian activity tempered by common sense, but the man is a fiery bundle of passions and theatrical gestures. It is not only intelligence but determination and personal magnetism . . . that make him an inspirational leader. Like all great actors, Bourguiba, who seems always to be on stage, is able to calculate his gestures and to release the warm spontaneity which draws audiences to him.[5]

At the same time, as a pragmatist, he "can combine fiery Arab oratory with the bargaining skill of a Mediterranean merchant."[6]

Similarly, it has been said of Nyerere: "A powerful speaker with a taste for burning phrases, he is eloquent in Swahili and English"; he carried the title of Mwalimu, "teacher" in Swahili.[7] As for Nasser, "he could communicate with vast throngs and sway them by his oratory—in fact, elicit their admiration, fear and unqualified support. He could practically hypnotize them."[8]

Nasser was a leader excelling in organizational talents as well, which he began to display in school days. In 1939, at age 21, he was the principal force behind the creation of the Free Officers' Association. And he remained the chief architect and strategist of the coup that toppled the regime of King Farouk in 1952.

Similarly, from early on, Díaz showed "a disposition to command, to which his comrades naturally yielded." He "performed marvels of valor and skill" on the battlefield. "With unflinching purpose and boundless energy, he shaped and reshaped armies, against unbelievable odds, carved victories out of defeat."[9]

Cárdenas and Cavendish were superb military leaders and campaigners. Rupert's military exploits became legendary in his own lifetime. Grand Duke Nicholaevich was a man of true ability, in addition to having a distinguished bearing. In fact:

Of imposing presence, over six feet four inches tall, he became an almost legendary figure, and the common soldiers transferred to him much of that personal allegiance they were not able to give . . . Nicholas II. The Grand Duke had the charisma that the Emperor lacked and enjoyed a popularity admitted to even by Bolshevik commentators.[10]

Among loyalists who effectively formed and led political organizations of various kinds we particularly take note of Abbas, Batlle, Bourguiba, Frei, Kaunda, Lévesque, Nyerere, Senghor, U Nu, and Vasconcelos.

**THE REVOLUTIONARIES**

Revolutionary elites also cultivate verbal and organizational skills, even though, being outside the recognized channels of authority, they are in a distinctly less advantageous position than loyalist leaders. Loyalists move to positions of power and authority with relative ease; their job is to maintain the status quo. By definition, revolutionaries typically seize power in violent ways; their job is to smash the status quo. For this reason, verbal and organizational skills assume far greater importance for revolutionary elites.

Such revolutionaries as Ben Bella, Mao, Marighella, Nkomo, and Paz were talented, eloquent communicators. Such others as Castro, Henry, Ho, Lenin, Robespierre, and Trotsky gave mesmerizing speeches, whipping the crowds to frenzied heights.

The verbal skills of the revolutionaries are directed toward creating and propagating political ideologies appropriate to specific times and conditions. A revolutionary ideology has three important components. First, it is based on a thoroughgoing critique of the existing system as corrupt, immoral, and beyond reform. Every revolutionary ideology denounces the existing system through appeal to transcendent norms and principles. Note, for instance, Jefferson's invocation of "the Law of Nature and of Nature's God" in the Declaration of Independence.

Second, a revolutionary ideology articulates an alternative vision of society embodying a superior order. That is, a revolutionary ideology sets forth positive values of its own: liberty, equality, fraternity, humanity. The alternative order frequently embodies a utopian vision or a grand myth— The Fatherland, The Golden Age, The Classless Society—which becomes a rallying cry for the masses. If its mobilizing function is to be maximized, the grand myth must be simplified for popular consumption. Thus note Lenin's slogan of "Land, Peace, and Bread" or Mao's "Serve the People," both of which have been echoed by other revolutionaries as well.

Third, a revolutionary ideology embodies a statement of plans and programs, strategy and tactics, to realize the alternative order. The goals and values of ideology, in other words, are embodied in concrete designs and actions.

Revolutionary ideology performs a number of important functions. First, it articulates social ills and undermines the confidence and morale of the ruling regime. Second, it rationalizes, legitimizes, and justifies the grievances and demands of the revolutionaries; it lends dignity to revolutionary action. Third, ideology gives the revolutionaries a sense of unity, solidarity, and cohesion; it instills zeal, commitment, devotion, and sacrifice. Fourth, ideology serves as an instrument of mass mobilization. The greater the revolutionaries' skill in politicizing the masses, and the greater their ability to create an atmosphere of popular commitment, the greater their chances of success.

Finally, ideology may serve as a cover for personal motives and ambitions of revolutionary leaders. The elite is always in a position to employ ideology to manipulate and control the masses. To this end, ideology may be diluted or misrepresented.

Organization is a fundamental adjunct to ideology, the link between ideology and action. Ideology helps reach the people; organization functions to tap their energies and skills and channel them toward the realization of revolutionary objectives. When combined, ideology and organization make possible full-scale mobilization.

Virtually all revolutionaries must cultivate organizational skills of a military and political nature if they are to survive at all. Some stand out, however.

The Adamses, Henry, Jefferson, Otis, and Washington were variously involved in the Caucus Clubs, the Virginia House of Burgesses, the Committees of Correspondence, and the Continental Congresses; Washington was named commander in chief of the armed forces because of his successful expeditions in French and Indian wars. Cromwell had no military background but he emerged as an effective leader of the New Model Army, of which Hampden and Vane were named regimental commanders. Like his father, Devereux was a professional military man; in addition, he held membership in the Parliament, the Privy Council, and the Council of War; and he functioned as leader of the Parliamentary Army. As early as 1640, Pym began organizing secret meetings in his home to map out revolutionary strategy; he was also the acknowledged leader of the Long Parliament. Lenin and Trotsky, needless to say, were among the master organizers of the Bolshevik Revolution.

Following the disastrous Autumn Harvest Uprising of August 1928, Mao—soon to be joined by Chou, Chu, Lin, and Liu—transformed a bunch of ragtag peasants into one of history's most skilled fighting forces; he also served as a founding member of the Chinese Communist party in 1921, becoming its supreme leader in 1936. Ben Bella and his associates ("the Nine Brothers") divided Algeria into six political-military districts, assigned to each district the "brother" most familiar with the context, and fought the French to eventual independence in 1962. Cabral, Machel, Mondlane, and Roberto were founders or leaders of the political organizations that eventually brought nationhood to their respective lands. Ho and Giap transformed the face of Vietnam; Castro and Guevara, of Cuba. Examples could be multiplied.

Traditionally, in communist and noncommunist theory and practice alike, the military has been an instrument in the service of the political party and subservient to the same. The German military writer Karl von Clausewitz established the principle that the military is an instrument of political policy. Lenin, Mao, Ho, and others insisted on the complete subordination of the military to political organization and they employed political cadres or commissars to institutionalize this arrangement.

Following the Cuban Revolution, Castro, Guevara, and their French admirer Régis Debray flatly challenged this view and sought to reverse the relationship between the party and the army in the Latin American context.[11] Debray, who is most explicit and detailed on this point, argued forcefully that the Cuban experience demonstrates that revolution in Latin America cannot follow the pattern established by other revolutions. The Cuban Revolution is a "revolution in the revolution," different from all revolutions that preceded it. In particular, he maintained, the foremost task throughout the revolution is not politicization and mobilization of the masses but the consolidation of military strength.

Successful revolutionary activity in Latin America requires, according to Debray, that the political apparatus be controlled by the military. While the success of revolution lies in the realization that guerrilla warfare is essentially political, the party and the guerrilla must become one and the same, with the guerrilla in command. The guerrilla cannot tolerate a duality of functions and powers, but must become the political as well as the military vanguard of the movement. The armed destruction of the enemy—the public demonstration of his fallibility—is the most effective propaganda for the local population. Consequently, in Latin America the chief concern must be the development of guerrilla units (*focos*) and not the strengthening of political parties.

The Debray position found adherents among revolutionaries in such countries as Argentina, Bolivia, Brazil, Colombia, Guatemala, Paraguay, Peru, and Venezuela. Significantly, however, those movements have not succeeded. Indeed, Guevara's own 1967 abortive mission in Bolivia (where he lost his life) demonstrates that a small guerrilla force operating in an unfamiliar and hostile environment, and relentlessly pursued by superior government forces, is doomed to defeat.

Accordingly, as early as 1974, Debray repudiated his own position, admitting that he had mistakenly dissociated the military from the political, and that political mobilization was of paramount importance.[12] Indeed, it would appear, beguiled by prospects of quick victory, Debray and others misinterpreted the Cuban revolutionary experience to assert the supremacy of the military over the political and to advance the argument that the military forces played an exclusive role in creating a revolutionary situation. In truth, such a situation prevailed prior to the emergence of the *focos*.

## SKILLS AND THEIR VISCISSITUDES

Some revolutionary movements succeed, others are defeated by superior forces, and still others experience ebbs and flows or periods of activity-dormancy. On the other hand, with the major exception of the revolutionaries-turned-loyalists (most notably, Bourguiba, Kaunda, Nasser, Nyerere, and Senghor), many of the loyalist leaders we have studied turned out to be losers. Why should this be the case?

Some loyalists were defeated because of their excessively narrow, rigid, and inflexible outlook and behavior. Chiang, Colden, Galloway, Hutchinson, Stolypin, and Turgot remained out of touch with reality and blind to changing times and conditions. Thus, for example, Galloway's chief claim to fame was his 1774 "Plan for Union between Great Britain and the Colonies," which represented, by definition, a total misreading of the times: the revolutionaries were not even faintly fathoming "union" at that late date. Hence, in 1778 Galloway went into exile in Britain an embittered man:

I call this country ungrateful, because I have attempted to save it from the distress it at present feels, and because it has not only rejected my endeavors, but returned me evil for good. I feel for its misery; but I feel it is not finished—its cup is not yet full—still deeper distress will attend it.[13]

Similarly, Hutchinson never understood or appreciated the forces at work all about him:

Never having felt deep personal discontent—never having passionately aspired—never having longed for some ideal and total betterment—never having found in some utopian vision a compelling and transforming cause, he never understood the motivations of the miserable, the visionary, and the committed, and he was unprepared to grapple with the politics they shaped. . . .

[F]or all his intelligence, he did not comprehend the nature of the forces that confronted him. . . . He was never able to understand the moral basis of the protests that arose against the existing order. . . . [H]e could not respond to the aroused moral passion and the optimistic and idealistic impulses that gripped the mind of the Revolutionaries and that led them to condemn as corrupt and oppressive the whole system by which their world was governed.[14]

As a result, to the people of the colonies, Hutchinson "was one of the most hated men on earth—more hated than [the British Prime Minister] Lord North, more hated than George III."[15]

Neither comprehending nor acknowledging popular grievance and discontent, loyalists blame their troubles on the warped motivations of their enemies and turn to despotic rule. Thus, "Hutchinson . . . found the dynamics of the revolutionary movement in the envy and ambition of the revolutionary leaders." Accordingly, he called for "an abridgment of so-called English liberties" and institutionalization of strict discipline.[16] Fitting the Hutchinson mold are such divergent loyalists as Batista, Chiang, Díaz, Dîem, Laud, Marcos, Peñaranda, Stolypin, and Thieu.

Still other loyalists fall due to irresolution and indecision. Having been trained from childhood to defer to the judgments of a strong-willed father, North developed a habit of becoming dependent on the views of those around him. According to a contemporary, Maurepas had a "timid, irresolute mind."[17] This quality was shared by such widely divergent leaders as Hutchinson and Dîem.

In short, a point is reached when some loyalists lose touch with their own peoples and circumstances. When that happens, their skills fall short or utterly fail them. Although written about the American Tories, the following is an astute assessment of the dilemmas of the loyalists:

[T]hey found it difficult to regard the mere threat of revolution seriously. Thus at almost any time between 1765 and 1774 it seemed to most of them that the revolutionary movement had nearly run its course, and that matters would shortly be as they had been before the Stamp Act.

Even when they were sure of their cause and sure that it needed their advocacy, the Tories were comparatively ineffective advocates. They could not compete with the Whigs in organization, and they did not try to compete as propagandists [or ideologists?]. . . . [T]he Tory leaders avoided the basic issues of constitutional reform, and concentrated their attention on minor and peripheral matters. . . . They were afraid [of public opinion], for they felt weak. . . . And the weaker they felt themselves to be, the tighter became their allegiance to Britain. The closer they were bound to Britain, the less able were they to support effectively her cause or theirs. So, as the American quarrel with the British government grew more bitter and more deadly, the Tories began slowly, under the guise of loyalty, to sink into a helpless dependence on Britain, an attachment no longer voluntary but growing desperate, and as it became desperate, ceasing to be quite honorable.[18]

## SUMMARY

Political leadership requires verbal and organizational skills. Loyalists and revolutionaries alike excel in oratory, organization building (whether military or political), or both. Verbal and organizational skills are particularly important to the revolutionaries: being outsiders, they must mobilize the people and usually fight their way to the top by violent means. Mobilization requires the propagation of an appropriate ideology to reach the masses and the creation of effective organizations to channel their energies and talents toward the realization of revolutionary goals.

Whether due to rigidity and inflexibility, unrealistic hopes and expectations, denial of the legitimacy of people's grievance and discontent, inability or refusal to respond to changing times and conditions, miscalculating the tempo of events, some loyalists alienate the people and exacerbate a situation already out of hand. A time comes, in short, when some loyalists' skills fail them.

## NOTES

1. Oliver C. Kuntzelman, *Joseph Galloway: Loyalist* (Philadelphia: Temple University, 1941), p. 17; John E. Ferling, *The Loyalist Mind: Joseph Galloway and the American Revolution* (University Park: Pennsylvania State University Press, 1977), p. 27; Benjamin H. Newcomb, *Franklin and Galloway* (New Haven: Yale University Press, 1972), pp. 11-13 et passim.

2. Douglas Dakin, *Turgot and the Ancient Régime in France* (London: Methuen & Co., 1939), pp. 6, 9-10.

3. Nicholas de Basily, *Memoirs* (Stanford: Hoover Institution Press, 1973), p. 58.

4. Robert H. Dix, *Colombia: The Political Dimension of Change* (New Haven: Yale University Press, 1967), p. 109; Vernon L. Fluharty, *Dance of the Millions: Military Rule and Social Revolution in Colombia 1930-1956* (Pittsburgh: University of Pittsburgh Press, 1957), pp. 49, 50.

5. Clement H. Moore, *Tunisia Since Independence* (Berkeley: University of California Press, 1965), pp. 42-43.

6. Ronald Segal, *African Profiles* (Baltimore, MD: Penguin Books, 1962), p. 307.

7. Donald Robinson, *The 100 Most Important People in the World Today* (New York: G. P. Putnam's Sons, 1970), pp. 89, 92.

8. P. J. Vatikiotis, *Nasser and His Generation* (London: Croom Helm, 1978), p. 314.

9. James Creelman, *Díaz: Master of Mexico* (New York: Appleton & Co., 1911), p. 44; Stewart Watt and Harold F. Peterson, *Builders of Latin America* (New York: Harper & Bros., 1942), p. 205; Carleton Beals, *Porfirio Díaz: Dictator of Mexico* (Philadelphia: J. B. Lippincott, 1932), p. 23.

10. Richard Luckett, *The White Generals* (London: Longman, 1971), p. 15; cf. Richard Pipes, *Struve: Liberal of the Right 1905-1944* (Cambridge: Harvard University Press, 1980), p. 368.

11. Castro's views are summarized in Theodore H. Draper, *Castroism: Theory and Practice* (New York: Frederick A. Praeger, 1965). For Guevara, see his *Guerrilla Warfare* (New York: Vintage, 1961). Debray's main work is *Revolution in the Revolution? Armed Struggle and Political Struggle in Latin America* (New York: Grove Press, 1967).

12. Debray, *La Critique des armes* (Paris, 1974), cited in Walter Laqueur, *Guerrilla: A Historical and Critical Study* (Boston: Little, Brown, 1976), p. 340.

13. Quoted in Lorenzo Sabine, *Biographical Sketches of the Loyalists of the American Revolution*, 2 vols. (Boston: Little, Brown, 1864), I: 454.

14. Bernard Bailyn, *The Ordeal of Thomas Hutchinson* (Cambridge: Harvard University Press, 1974), pp. 34, 378. For parallel comments, see William H. Nelson, *The American Tory* (Oxford: Oxford University Press, 1961), p. 24.

15. Bailyn, *The Ordeal of Thomas Hutchinson*, p. 1.

16. Nelson, *The American Tory*, pp. 25, 29.

17. Quoted in Vincent Cronin, *Louis and Antoinette* (London: William Collins & Sons, 1974), p. 72.

18. Nelson, *The American Tory*, pp. 18-20. Cf. Wallace Brown, *The Good Americans* (New York: William Morrow, 1969), p. 223.

# IV CONCLUSIONS

# 9 Becoming Political Leaders

We have been embarked upon a search for answers to three interrelated sets of questions about political elites: Who are they? Why and how do they rise to leadership positions? In what ways are loyalist and revolutionary elites similar and how do they differ? We have cast this search in the light of an interactional theory of political leadership stressing the interplay of three variables: situation, psychology, skill. Of the situational variables, we have stressed differential access to positions of power and authority as crucial in determining a loyalist or a revolutionary orientation. In order to test our hypotheses, propositions, and arguments, we have drawn on a wide range of data for 100 leaders from 32 countries spread over five continents and four centuries. It is now time to consolidate our empirical findings, assess the theoretical import of our work, and propose some possible models to account for the rise of political leaders in general and of loyalists and revolutionaries in particular.

Before proceeding, it is necessary to reiterate some caveats stressed in the Introduction. All our findings are based on relatively small, nonrandom purposive samples of loyalist and revolutionary elites drawn from specific times, places and contexts. We have been further constrained by the lack of a control group of nonleaders and by the absence of women among the leaders we studied.

## QUANTITATIVE RESULTS

Throughout the study, we have identified similarities and differences between loyalist and revolutionary elites, building toward two complementary sets of results. The delineation of the *similarities* has enabled us to identify a single leadership group that transcends the loyalist-revolutionary distinction and allows us to focus on leadership characteristics in general. The elaboration of the *differences* has highlighted a small set of characteristics that has allowed us to anticipate, given the basic components of leadership—situation, psychology, skill—which leaders are likely to work within extant sociopolitical systems and which ones are likely to seek to transform them.

### General Findings

As Chapters 2-4 make clear, some of the hypotheses and propositions we advanced concerning loyalist and revolutionary elites in Chapter 1 were confirmed by the data while others were disconfirmed. For one thing, we found the number and range of similarities between the two groups to be quite striking. An important cluster of sociodemographic characteristics transcends the loyalist-revolutionary distinction and applies to both groups—and hence to political leaders in general. Thus, political elites are typically native born to legal marriages. They are either urban born or, if born and raised in rural areas, they develop early and sustained exposure to urban cultures. Whether relatively tranquil or relatively stormy, their family lives are, in the aggregate, quite similar. They are exposed to political ideology, and participate in political activity, quite early in life. Their ethnic and religious backgrounds are of the mainstream variety. They are highly educated, frequently in prestigious institutions. They are equally cosmopolitan, traveling far and wide and developing foreign contacts. They publish works on a wide range of subjects.

At the same time, the differences between loyalists and revolutionaries yield composite profiles of two distinct groups. Loyalists are members of a privileged collectivity, high in socioeconomic status, likely to hold positions of prestige and influence in public office or civil service, and operate within the sociocultural traditions and institutions of their societies. Bound by the protocols of political life, they are older upon reaching highest office. They hold a positive view of their sociopolitical systems while maintaining a negative view of the human beings who make up those systems.

By contrast, as a group revolutionary elites attract a large proportion of their membership from underprivileged and lower socioeconomic strata, typically lacking access to positions of power and influence. Rejecting the social roles for which their education had prepared them, they put their skills and talents to working outside the sociocultural frameworks and institutions of their societies, many becoming professional revolutionaries. Risk takers by nature, unencumbered by the protocol of office, they are younger upon seizing power. They hold positive or fluctuating views (depending on the regime) of their sociopolitical systems and an optimistic view of the human beings who constitute those systems.

Given their family background and social status, we expected—and found—the loyalists to be strategically situated, commanding easy access to positions of prestige and authority. This more than any other factor (or group of factors) differentiates the loyalists from the revolutionaries.

## Careers and Crises

We turned to factor analysis as a means of classifying the leaders into meaningful types, in terms of both attributes and personalities. The ready distinction we had anticipated between loyalists and revolutionaries did not materialize. Instead, the existence of a large number of shared traits among the 100 leaders generated two unanticipated political types: career leaders, who devote long years of careful grooming to the political roles they eventually come to assume; crisis leaders, who are swept to the forefront without much preparation and typically in response to situations of national emergency. Insofar as career leaders are typically loyalists and crisis leaders typically revolutionaries, the distinction returned us full circle to our theme of differential access to power and prestige in societies. Loyalists maintain access from childhood until such time as they leave office; revolutionaries seize upon access as opportunities present themselves.

## Loyalists and Revolutionaries

We used discriminant analysis as a means of identifying a discriminant function consisting of ten significant variables. The discriminant function helped us predict the group—whether loyalist or revolutionary—to which each of the 100 leaders belonged; in so doing, it effectively separated the loyalists from the revolutionaries, thus confirming some of our earlier findings.

In terms of specific variables, if a leader remains steadfast in religious beliefs; if his father is a government official or in such other occupations as the military, banking and industry, the professions, or landed gentry; if the leader himself is in government service; if he holds a pessimistic view of human nature but a uniformly optimistic view of his own country—under this set of circumstances, the leader is likely to become a loyalist rather than a revolutionary. By contrast, if a leader abandons his religion to become an atheist, if his father has an occupation not included above, if the leader himself is not in government service, if he has an optimistic view of human nature but a fluctuating attitude toward his own country depending on the regime in power—under this set of circumstances the leader is likely to become a revolutionary rather than a loyalist. (Father's occupation as government official and religious orientation, it will be recalled, have the greatest predictive value.) Once again, in other words, access to political power becomes the cutting edge separating the loyalists from the revolutionaries.

Overall, using information on the ten variables incorporated in the discriminant function, discriminant analysis allowed us correctly to predict and classify 47 of the revolutionaries as revolutionaries and 42 of the loyalists as loyalists, for a commanding total of 89 ( = 89 percent), well beyond the realm of chance.

It may be tempting to attribute some of the variations between loyalists and revolutionaries to built-in generational or cohort differences in the formation of political attitudes and perspectives. Being older, it may be argued, the political experiences and cognitive realities of the loyalists antedate those of the revolutionaries, swaying the former toward system-supporting positions and the latter toward system-challenging behavior.

However, while data for leaders of a few countries (primarily, in fact, England, America, France, Russia, and China) may lend themselves to generational analysis, data for most other leaders transcend time or country or both, thus limiting the utility of the generational perspective for this work. Moreover, studies of generational politics constitute a relatively recent scholarly phenomenon in the context of rapid social change in North American and European countries. Prior to, say, the Second World War, most cultures, societies, and socialization patterns tended to be relatively stable, thus constraining the possibilities of generational analysis in the present context.

## THEORETICAL IMPORT

Our quantitative findings relative to loyalist and revolutionary elites have clear bearings on our theoretical concerns, some more so than others. Such variables as social class, education, urban culture, and cosmopolitanism directly account for expediting political consciousness among leaders and enabling them to refine their verbal and organizational skills. Skills, in turn, constitute one of three sets of variables in our interactional theory of political leadership, the other two being situations and psychologies. These variables are interrelated in that without skills, situations and psychologies would be to no avail; without situations, skills and psychologies would lay dormant; without psychologies, situations and skills would go undeployed.

### Situations

Loyalist and revolutionary elites appear upon the scene in response to a series of identifiable—and to a large extent similar—situational variables.

Circumstances of national crisis or emergency have accounted for the emergence of such loyalists as Nikolaevich and Sihanouk, Nasser and U Nu,

Dîem and Thieu. They have also propelled into prominence such revolutionaries as Cromwell and Devereux, the Adamses and Washington, Danton and Robespierre, Lenin and Trotsky.

Colonial or neocolonial contexts have given rise to such loyalists as Bourguiba, Kaunda, Lévesque, Nyerere, and Sadat. They have also produced such revolutionaries as Ben Bella, Biko, Cabral, Machel, and Nkomo.

"Violent countries" have catapulted Díaz and Rupert upon the scene. They have also accounted for the emergence of Arafat and Habash.

Luck or chance have given rise to such loyalists as Pearson and Witte. They have also generated Nkomo and Schoeters.

Home, school, and travel also provide contextual or situational environments in the politicization of elites, loyalists more so than revolutionaries. Considered in this light, family consists of a social situation into which one is born and over which one has no control (at least not initially), including the number of siblings or one's age ranking among them. Schooling, particularly in the earlier years, is bound to be a family decision and not within one's exclusive purview. Beyond cosmopolitanizing both groups, travel serves to reinforce the system-supporting behavior of the loyalists and the system-challenging activity of the revolutionaries. Family, school, and travel most likely reflect the social status of the father, another factor lying outside one's private dominion.

A series of related personal characteristics and traits identified with political leaders are situational in that one can hold no sway over them. These include socioeconomic status, father's occupation, birth place, ethnicity, religious background, and various forms of marginality. High parental position demands politicization experiences that generate a loyalist orientation to politics; low parental position has no corresponding encumbrance.

The major situational variable separating the loyalists from the revolutionaries is that by virtue of their social or family status, the former find themselves in positions of access or proximity to political power. In fact, fully 27 members of the loyalist group are in this position: Abbas, Alami, Batlle, Belaúnde, Cavendish, Chiang, Frei, Galloway, Gomez, Hutchinson, Hyde, K'ung, Marcos, Maurepas, Nikolaevich, North, Rupert, Sewall, Sihanouk, Stolypin, Struve, Tubman, Trudeau, Turgot, Wang, Wentworth, and Witte. Of the revolutionary group, only 11 members are comparably situated: Chou, Cromwell, Devereux, Hampden, Madero, Mirabeau, Paz, Pym, Souphanouvong, Vane, and Washington. Moreover, such loyalists as Chiang, Frei, Hutchinson, K'ung, Laud, Marcos, Pearson, Soong, Trudeau, and Wang enjoyed the patronage or tutelage of some pivotal political figures of their times.

In short, then, situational variables take five principal forms: (1) conditions of open or latent power contests, whether embedded in national or international politics; (2) environmental conditions associated with family life, school, or travel; (3) personal attributes one acquires as a matter of birth; (4) differential access to channels of power and authority; (5) luck or chance.

## Psychologies

We have examined the loyalist and revolutionary leaders in the light of a series of mental attributes or psychological dynamics that is generally considered to be important in shaping the political personality. We found that a firm commitment to nationalism–patriotism—and a concomitant determination to improve the prestige and status of one's land—defines virtually all political elites, whether loyalist or revolutionary. On the other hand, for the most part only the revolutionaries are driven by undeviating visions of justice and corresponding attempts to right the wrongs.

Among the more explicitly psychological dynamics, we discovered that vanity, egotism, and narcissism define nearly three-fourths (37) of the loyalists and over half (27) of the revolutionaries. Such loyalists as Galloway and Gomez, Hutchinson and Hyde, Necker and Nasser, Turgot and Trudeau, Struve and Sadat, Wentworth and Witte are portrayed as aloof, insensitive, haughty, conceited; and they come to see themselves as indispensable savants, knights, warriors, and liberators. These attributes are shared by such revolutionaries as Adams and Arafat, Cromwell and Washington, Danton and Devereux, Hampden and Ho, Otis and Nkomo, Robespierre and Vallières. That loyalists should be more vain and egotistical than revolutionaries is not surprising if for no other reason than the former's higher social status.

Asceticism and puritanism describe only four of the loyalists, in contrast to a commanding three-quarters of the revolutionary elites. For reasons discussed in Chapter 7, only Cárdenas, Luthuli, Nasser, and Wang were touched by ascetic, puritanical streaks, whereas the other 46 were not. This finding, too is not unexpected: the life-styles of the loyalists are lush and opulent. By contrast, lacking access to levers of status and prestige, the lives of the revolutionaries require shunning luxury and comfort, pursuing a spartan course.

Relative deprivation and status inconsistency affect an almost equal number of loyalists (23) and revolutionaries (25). For both groups, these psychological dynamics may take root in colonial contexts or family circumstances (whether relatively humble or distinguished but impecunious) or other social conditions. What distinguishes the loyalists from the revolutionaries in these respects is that the former appear to translate their frustration and discontent into a concern for the self; the latter, for society as a whole.

Marginality and inferiority complex apply to nearly three-quarters of the loyalist elites and two-thirds of the revolutionary leaders. Again, the sources of marginality or inferiority complex are much similar for the two groups: colonial settings, personal or psychological traumas, social disadvantage (for instance, poor origin, unconventional dialect, immigrant status), physical or facial irregularities, and poor health. In these regards the two groups differ little if at all.

Oedipal conflict writ large has little explanatory value as it appears to apply to only three revolutionaries: Lenin, Mao, Trotsky. Both loyalists and revolutionaries maintain warm and affectionate (or at times strained) relations with their mothers but there is no persuasive evidence of father conflict, rebelliousness, ambivalence, and guilt.

Rather than being driven exclusively by tensions, insecurities, and anxieties, political elites have a gentler side as well: one-third of the loyalists and nearly one-quarter of the revolutionaries manifest varieties of esthetic commitments. Loyalists and revolutionaries are students of literature, philosophy, poetry, and the arts—indeed, some are philosophers and poets in their own rights. Others are music lovers. Still others are theater-goers and playwrights, translators, and nature lovers. There are even Don Quixote complexes on both sides, though it is more pronounced among the revolutionaries.

When we examine mental attributes and psychological dynamics as a whole, it is clear that: (1) nationalism-patriotism defines virtually all political elites, (2) a sense of justice, asceticism-puritanism, and oedipal conflict (to the extent that it may exist) are attributes of the revolutionaries, and (3) vanity-egotism, relative deprivation-status inconsistency, marginality, and estheticism apply to both groups, but with somewhat differential force. (It may appear surprising at first blush that next to nationalism-patriotism, marginality emerges as the most ubiquitous trait of all political elites, loyalist as well as revolutionary. To this topic we shall return presently.)

To conclude, as far as psychological dynamics are concerned, loyalists and revolutionaries are similar in many important respects, sharing as they do five of the eight traits we have considered in this work.

**Skills**

Political leadership requires a range of skills, particularly verbal and organizational. Such loyalists as Bourguiba, Galloway, Gomez, Nasser, Nyerere, Stolypin, and Turgot were spellbinding orators, with an ability to attract and hold followers. Others share this talent but to a lesser extent. Among loyalists excelling in organizational skills of a political or military nature were Abbas, Batlle, Bourguiba, Cárdenas, Cavendish, Díaz, Frei,

Kaunda, Lévesque, Nasser, Nikolaevich, Rupert, Senghor, U Nu, and Vasconcelos.

Verbal and organizational skills are signally important for revolutionaries, since as outsiders they must mobilize the people and usually fight their way to the top. Mobilization requires a revolutionary ideology to denounce the existing society as corrupt and immoral, project an alternative vision of a better (even utopian) society, and elaborate the strategy and tactics of power seizure. Revolutionary ideologies function to undermine the morale and confidence of the regime, legitimize and justify the demands of the rebels, bring unity and cohesion to the revolutionary ranks, generate commitment and devotion to the cause. Particularly skillful at fashioning and propagating revolutionary ideologies were Arafat, S. Adams, Ben Bella, Castro, Henry, Ho, Jefferson, Lenin, Madero, Mao, Pym, Robespierre, Trotsky, and Vallières.

Mass mobilization and power seizure are impossible without political and military organizations of various sorts. Organization is a fundamental adjunct to ideology: it enables the leaders to tap the energies, talents, and skills of the masses and to channel them toward the attainment of revolutionary objectives. Since these objectives are primarily political in nature, political organization traditionally has assumed primacy over its military counterpart. Among our revolutionaries with special organizational skills we note S. Adams, Ben Bella, Chu, Castro, Cromwell, Devereux, Giap, Guevara, Hampden, Ho, Lenin, Mao, Pym, Stalin, Trotsky, Vane, and Washington.

Talents and skills notwithstanding, most loyalists end up as losers. Some are defeated because of their rigidity and inflexibility, refusing to come to terms with changing times and conditions or to meet the needs of the people. Instead, portraying their enemies as deranged and pathological, they turn to despotic rule. Despotism, in turn, further alienates the peoples and exacerbates already unfavorable conditions, both playing into the hands of the revolutionaries. In short, a point is reached when the skills of the loyalists desert them: in the language of cognitive psychology, their conceptual complexity—that is, the ability to process new information in a timely and realistic fashion is replaced by conceptual simplicity—that is, rigid and inflexible thought and behavior.[1]

## BECOMING POLITICAL LEADERS: TOWARD PROBABILISTIC MODELS

Throughout this study we have identified a series of similarities and differences between loyalist and revolutionary elites. Is it possible to employ the similarities to construct a probabilistic, composite profile of individuals who in a given society are likely to become political leaders? Is it possible to utilize the differences to arrive at probabilistic, composite profiles of individuals who turn to loyalist or revolutionary politics?

Before proceeding, we should note a major caveat. Since we have relied on a nonrandom purposive sample of political leaders (a control group of nonleaders not being available to us), we can develop, consistent with canons of contemporary social science, only descriptive-historical statements—or "modal models"—of leader traits and attributes. Accordingly, throughout this discussion we use the word "probabilistic" advisedly and with due caution.

Whether or not a person becomes a political leader depends on the possession or acquisition of certain key attributes and experiences. Distilled from the findings presented throughout this book, these variables are charted in Figure 9.1. (Inspiration for this figure—and for the one that follows—came from Joel D. Aberbach, Robert D. Putnam, and Bert A. Rockman.[2])

The flowchart is self-explanatory: One's chances of becoming a political leader are maximized if one fits all the six variables; they are minimized if one does not. What may not be immediately apparent is that the flowchart echoes our interactional theory of political leadership. Variables 1, 2, 3 and 6 are situational in nature: the last refers to the social-historical context while the first three describe social-background attributes over which one has no control. Variable 4, needless to say, pertains to skills; Variable 5, to psychology.

Its apparent ubiquity notwithstanding, we exclude marginality from this analysis because we find it a most troublesome concept. On reflection, the notion is so broad as to apply to virtually the entire population of any country at a given point in time. Thus, in the foregoing pages we have used marginality in a *historical* sense (for example, colonial context), a *social* sense (immigrant status), a *psychological* sense (nervous disorder), an *economic* sense (poverty), a *physical* sense (facial or bodily disfigurement), and a *medical* sense (poor health). Given this all-encompassing approach, it may be that marginality is a *human* characteristic and not an attribute of loyalists or revolutionaries alone. Should this be the case, needless to say, all "findings" concerning marginality are no findings at all.

Returning to Figure 9.1, not only are the six variables interrelated, they imply temporal and logical priority as well. Being a native-born son of an upper or middle class family presupposes, most likely, an urban background and projects a high level of education. Family, urban, and educational experiences, in turn, are likely to facilitate the acquisition of verbal and organizational skills. The resulting gestalt is bound to enhance one's self-concept, for, as we have seen, it takes something of an ego—or at least a well-developed sense of the self, whether real or imagined—for one to aspire to political leadership.

**Figure 9.1**
**Becoming Political Leaders: A Social-Psychological Flowchart of Critical Variables**

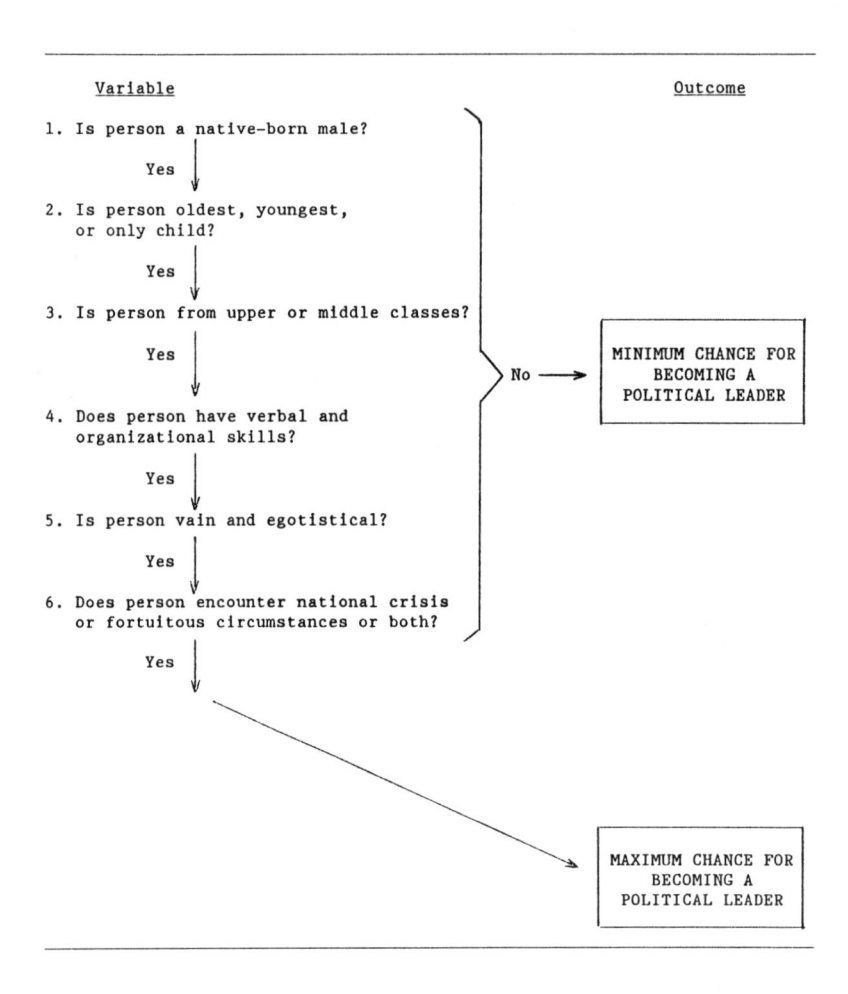

```
       Variable                                              Outcome

1. Is person a native-born male?

      Yes ↓

2. Is person oldest, youngest,
   or only child?

      Yes ↓

3. Is person from upper or middle classes?
                                                    ┌─────────────────────┐
      Yes ↓                                         │ MINIMUM CHANCE FOR  │
                                         No  →      │    BECOMING A       │
4. Does person have verbal and                      │  POLITICAL LEADER   │
   organizational skills?                           └─────────────────────┘

      Yes ↓

5. Is person vain and egotistical?

      Yes ↓

6. Does person encounter national crisis
   or fortuitous circumstances or both?

      Yes ↓

                                                    ┌─────────────────────┐
                                                    │ MAXIMUM CHANCE FOR  │
                                              →     │    BECOMING A       │
                                                    │  POLITICAL LEADER   │
                                                    └─────────────────────┘
```

Whether a person turns to loyalist or revolutionary politics depends on the possession or cultivation of a second set of decisive traits, attitudes, and experiences. These variables are depicted in Figure 9.2.

Again, the flowchart is self-explanatory: One's chances of becoming a loyalist leader are maximized if one conforms to the six variables; one's chances of becoming a revolutionary leader are enhanced to the extent that one departs from them.

And, again, the six variables are interrelated. Home and school politicization encourages the continuity of beliefs, including religious. These

**Figure 9.2**
**Becoming Loyalist or Revolutionary Leaders:**
**A Social-Psychological Flowchart of Critical Variables**

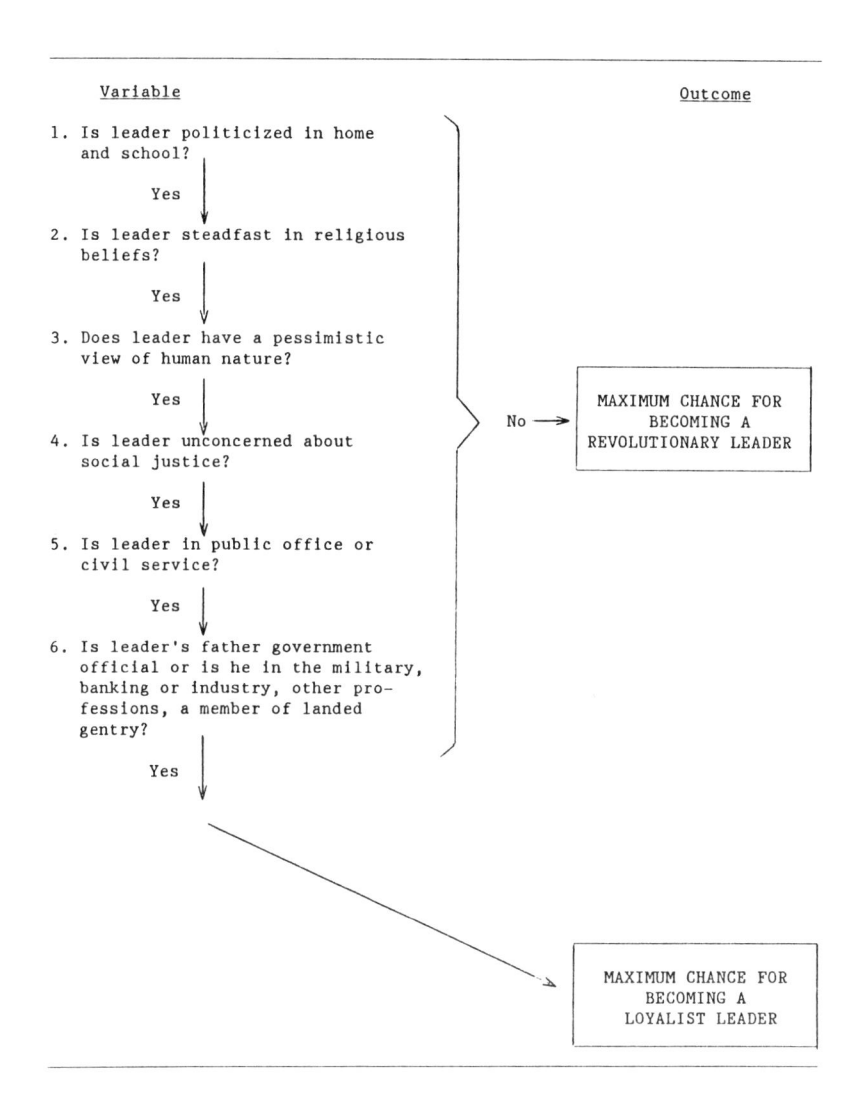

```
        Variable                                          Outcome

1. Is leader politicized in home
   and school?
        Yes ↓

2. Is leader steadfast in religious
   beliefs?
        Yes ↓
                                                    ┌─────────────────────┐
3. Does leader have a pessimistic                   │  MAXIMUM CHANCE FOR │
   view of human nature?                   No →     │     BECOMING A      │
        Yes ↓                                       │ REVOLUTIONARY LEADER│
                                                    └─────────────────────┘
4. Is leader unconcerned about
   social justice?
        Yes ↓

5. Is leader in public office or
   civil service?
        Yes ↓

6. Is leader's father government
   official or is he in the military,
   banking or industry, other pro-
   fessions, a member of landed
   gentry?
        Yes ↓
                                                    ┌─────────────────────┐
                                                    │ MAXIMUM CHANCE FOR  │
                                                    │    BECOMING A       │
                                                    │   LOYALIST LEADER   │
                                                    └─────────────────────┘
```

variables coalesce to reinforce system-supporting behavior on the part of loyalist leaders while their absence would generate system-challenging action on the part of revolutionaries. Similarly, a negative view of human nature and a lack of concern for social justice underscore the loyalists' privileged positions of influence and authority. For the revolutionaries, on the other hand, a positive assessment of human nature and a concern for social justice would combine to highlight distance from the source of power and policy.

While the nature of the variables in Figure 9.2 makes it impossible to address the issue of logical or temporal priority, it helps to spotlight differential access to political influence and authority as a crucial variable in determining a loyalist or a revolutionary political orientation. And access—whether familial, occupational, or both—being the important variable that it turns out to be, it is rather surprising that so little attention has been devoted to the subject.

Some two decades ago, Alexander Groth distinguished between elite-affiliated movements of the right (specifically, the Nazis) and elite-isolated movements of the left (that is, the communists), arguing that the former have an easier time coming to power.[3] In more recent times, in their empirical study of bureaucrats and politicians in Western democracies, Aberbach, Putnam, and Rockman found that "Both sets of elites, particularly in Europe, appear to have inherited a propensity for politics and government, for their relatives were usually involved in political activity or were in government employ."[4] This finding, in turn, echoed Donald R. Matthews' discovery relative to a more sharply defined elite population, the United States senators.[5]

Other than occasional observations, the issue of differential access has gone relatively unrecognized. Our research has laid out, among other things, the path of access to power or lack thereof, documenting the specific differences in opportunities that distinguish those aspirants to political leadership who choose loyalist positions and those who adopt revolutionary stands. As a component of our interactional theory of political leadership, access emerges as a pivotal situational variable differentiating the loyalists from the revolutionaries.

**CLOSING REMARKS**

What, after all is said and done, has been accomplished in this work? This question can be approached at two levels: the broader level of social-science inquiry, the narrower level of specific findings concerning our two elite populations.

Viewed from the broader perspective, we have attempted five things. First, we have endeavored to integrate the trait and the situational approaches in our interactional theory of political leadership. Second, we have sought to reconcile "elite" studies, which tend to be empirical and comparative, with individual leadership studies, which tend to be particularistic and idiosyncratic. Third, we have tried to marshall and blend quantitative (structured) and qualitative (unstructured) data to bear on our empirical and theoretical concerns. Fourth, within an articulated set of constraints, we have offered a comparative analysis of loyalist or "transactional" leaders with their revolutionary or "transforming" counterparts. Finally, we have presented some tentative, probabilistic statements about the emergence of political leaders.

Approached at the narrower level, our specific findings return us full circle to some issues raised in the Preface.

Specifically, what in the light of our findings remains of conventional wisdom or popular understanding concerning loyalist and revolutionary elites? Do the two groups have radically different social backgrounds? Are the two groups catapulted into action by two sharply contrasting psychologies? Do the leaders who maintain the status quo or effect piecemeal political change possess by and large normal personalities whereas those who seek revolutionary transformation are somehow afflicted by mental maladies? Is *e*volutionary change an index of leader health and *re*volutionary change an index of leader pathology?

Given the limited nature of the data available to us, we cannot offer comprehensive or definitive responses to these questions. We are also prepared to acknowledge that the social-psychological mainsprings of political behavior are likely more complex than the findings presented in this book. Nonetheless, we have unraveled enough to demonstrate the untenable nature of received wisdom concerning loyalists and revolutionaries.

Access aside, our multipronged investigations of loyalist and revolutionary leaders have yielded results that highlight the pivotal nature of the similarities between the two groups, relegating the differences to comparatively subordinate positions. Loyalists and revolutionaries, it turns out, are basically the same individuals, separated chiefly along a handful of situational variables.

## NOTES

1. Cf. Margaret G. Hermann, ed., *A Psychological Examination of Political Leaders* (New York: Free Press, 1977), esp. Chapters 8, 12, 13; Peter Suedfeld and A. Dennis Rank, "Revolutionary Leaders: Long-Term Success as a Function of Changes in Conceptual Complexity," *Journal of Personality and Social Psychology* 34 (1976): 169-78.

2. *Bureaucrats and Politicians in Western Democracies* (Cambridge: Harvard University Press, 1981), p. 80.

3. *Revolution and Elite Access: Some Hypotheses on Aspects of Political Change* (University of California, Davis: Institute of Governmental Affairs, 1966).

4. *Bureaucrats and Politicians in Western Democracies*, p. 81.

5. *U.S. Senators and Their World* (Chapel Hill: University of North Carolina Press, 1960), pp. 48-49.

# APPENDIXES

# Appendix A

# List of Scholar-Experts Contacted in Connection with Identification of Loyalist Leaders

Ibrahim Abu-Lughod, Political Science, Northwestern Universtiy
Robert J. Alexander, History, Rutgers University
Walter Arnold, Political Science, Miami University
Bernard Bailyn, History, Harvard University
Paul Bamford, History, University of Minnesota
Frederick Barghoorn, Political Science, Yale University
Samuel Barnes, Political Science, University of Michigan
Gerald J. Bender, International Relations, University of Southern California
Cyril E. Black, History, Princeton University
Newell Booth, Religion, Miami University
Henry L. Bretton, State University of New York, College at Brockport
Bernard Brown, Political Science, CUNY Graduate Center
Bradford Burns, History, University of California, Los Angeles
John F. Cady, History, Ohio University
William Campbell, Political Science, Miami University
Gwendolen Carter, Political Science, Indiana University
Gilbert Chan, History, Miami University
Dewitt Chandler, History, Miami University
Ronald H. Chilcote, Political Science, University of California, Riverside
James B. Christoph, Political Science, Indiana University
James S. Coleman, Political Science, University of California, Los Angeles
Richard Cottam, Political Science, University of Pittsburgh
Philip Curtin, History, Johns Hopkins University
Mattei Dogan, Political Science, University of California, Los Angeles
Martin Dulgarian, Geography, Miami University
Lloyd Eastman, History, University of Illinois
Henry W. Ehrman, Hanover, New Hampshire
Richard Fagen, Political Science, Stanford University

David Fahey, History, Miami University
Steven Feierman, History, University of Wisconsin
Felix V. Gagliano, Ohio University
Joseph R. Goldman, Political Science, Miami University
Jack P. Greene, History, Johns Hopkins University
Kenneth Grundy, Political Science, Case Western Reserve University
Stanley Hoffmann, Government, Harvard University
Irving Louis Horowitz, Sociology, Rutgers University
Ronald Inglehart, Political Science, University of Michigan
Karl D. Jackson, Political Science, University of California, Berkeley
Dan Jacobs, Political Science, Miami University
Norman Jacobson, Political Science, University of California, Berkeley
Richard Jellison, History, Miami University
Chalmers Johnson, Political Science, University of California, Berkeley
Kenneth Jowitt, Political Science, University of California, Berkeley
George McT. Kahin, Government, Cornell University
Michael Kammen, History, Cornell University
F. Kazemzadeh, History, Yale University
Nikki Keddie, History, University of California, Los Angeles
Malcolm Kerr, Political Science, University of California, Los Angeles
Mark Kesselman, Political Science, Columbia University
Paul F. Langer, The RAND Corporation
George Lenczowski, Political Science, University of California, Berkeley
Bernard Lewis, History, Princeton University
John Wilson Lewis, Political Science, Stanford University
Edwin Lieuwin, History, University of New Mexico
Roy Macridis, Politics, Brandeis University
Pauline Maier, History, Massachusetts Institute of Technology
James Malloy, Political Science, University of Pittsburgh
James Kirby Martin, History, University of Houston
Ali Mazrui, Political Science, University of Michigan
John F. McCamant, International Studies, University of Denver
Wilson C. McWilliams, Political Science, Rutgers University
Bruce Menning, History, Miami University
Richard Millett, History, Southern Illinois University
Edward S. Morgan, History, Yale University
Richard B. Morris, History, Columbia University
R. R. Palmer, History, Princeton University
Guy Pauker, The RAND Corporation
Amos Perlmutter, Government and Public Administration, American University
Roy Pierce, Political Science, University of Michigan
Frederick B. Pike, History, University of Notre Dame
Richard Pipes, History, Harvard University
Robert D. Putnam, Government, Harvard University
Lucian Pye, Political Science, Massachusetts Institute of Technology
William B. Quandt, Washington, D.C.
Thomas W. Robinson, McLean, Virginia

# Appendix A

Leo Rose, Political Science, University of California, Berkeley
Robert K. Rotberg, Political Science, Massachusetts Institute of Technology
Robert A Scalapino, Political Science, University of California, Berkeley
Phillipe C. Schmitter, Political Science, University of Chicago
Brenton Smith, History, Miami University
Alfred Stepan, Political Science, Yale University
Maynard Swanson, History, Miami University
Phillip B. Taylor, Jr., Government, University of Houston
Leonard M. Thompson, History, Yale University
Hung-mao Tien, Politicial Science, University of Wisconsin
Robert C. Tucker, Politics, Princeton University
John Turner, Political Science, University of Minnesota
Adam B. Ulam, Government, Harvard University
Herbert Waltzer, Political Science, Miami University
Michael Walzer, Institute for Advanced Study, Princeton
David Werlich, History, Southern Illinois University
James Wilkie, History, University of California, Los Angeles
John Womack, History, Harvard University
William I. Zartman, Political Science, New York University
Joseph Zasloff, Political Science, University of Pittsburgh
Maurice Zeitlin, Sociology, University of California, Los Angeles

## Appendix B
## Empirical Justification for
## The Lists of Loyalist and Revolutionary Leaders

As stated in the Introduction, in order to cast aside any doubt about the discreteness and integrity of our two lists of loyalists and revolutionaries, we subjected our data to a series of additional analyses to produce the following comparisons and results.

### LOYALISTS COMPARED TO REVOLUTIONARIES-TURNED-LOYALISTS

Revolutionaries-turned-loyalists seek to undermine political regimes, typically colonial in nature, by radical means and, then, having succeeded, become members of the established elites. The list includes Abbas, Bourguiba, Chiang, Kaunda, Nasser, Nyerere, Sadat, Senghor, Wang. Are there empirical differences between this small subgroup of nine revolutionaries-turned-loyalists and the larger subgroup of 41 loyalists to prohibit their being assigned the same classification?

Using SPSS$^x$, we analyzed the data to produce standard bivariate distributions, testing for the significance of differences between the two subgroups. We found that revolutionaries-turned-loyalists are: (1) more likely to be Muslims and Buddhists in religious background and orientation whereas the loyalists are more likely to be Christians; (2) more likely to come from larger families than loyalists; (3) more likely to be involved in radical organization and activity than loyalists; (4) more likely to be from Africa, Asia, or the Middle East.

As is readily apparent, these findings, while statistically significant, have little or no theoretical meaning. Moreover, all the findings boil down to the fact that the revolutionaries-turned-loyalists are from developing, formerly colonial lands—hence the variations in religion, family size, illegal activity, and the like. Once the imperialist power withdraws, the resulting system change provides the leaders with enhanced access to positions of authority. Under these circumstances, it is only to be expected that these experienced individuals would fill the loyalist vacuum.

## REVOLUTIONARIES COMPARED TO LOYALISTS-TURNED-REVOLUTIONARIES

Loyalists-turned-revolutionaries participate in the legal political processes of their countries, find the systems unresponsive, and turn to revolutionary politics. The list includes J. Adams, S. Adams, Ben Bella, Castro, Cromwell, Devereux, Hampden, Henry, Jefferson, Madero, Marighella, Nkomo, Otis, Paz, Pym, Sendic, Sithole, Souphanouvong, Vane, Washington, Zapata. Are there significant differences between this smaller subgroup of 21 loyalists-turned-revolutionaries and the larger subgroup of 29 revolutionaries to militate against their being lumped together?

Using SPSS$^x$, we reran the data to produce standard bivariate distributions, testing for the significance of the differences between the two subgroups. We found that loyalists-turned-revolutionaries are: (1) older than their revolutionary counterparts when first exposed to revolutionary ideology and when first engaged in revolutionary activity; (2) more likely to come from stable homes; (3) more likely to belong to mainstream religious groups and less likely to turn to atheism; (4) less likely to become professional revolutionaries; (5) more likely to subscribe to democratic ideologies.

Few in number and largely predictable, these findings serve to confirm our idea of differential access to political power as a major propellant of revolutionary activity. Mainstream in background and moderate in orientation, loyalists-turned-revolutionaries are given to radical action primarily for lack of access to positions of authority. For them, revolutionary activity becomes a means for redressing accumulating grievances against unresponsive political systems they once supported or tried to reform.

## SUCCESSFUL LEADERS (LOYALIST AND REVOLUTIONARY) COMPARED TO FAILED LEADERS

Are there meaningful trait differences between revolutionaries who succeed in their attempts to overthrow the social order and revolutionaries who fail to do so? Are there sociodemographic characteristics that differentiate loyalists who succeed in maintaining the status quo and loyalists who fail to do so? Alternatively, is leadership success (or failure) attributable primarily to situational forces or dynamics?

In an effort to clarify these questions, we separated our lists of both revolutionaries and loyalists into those leaders who had succeeded and those who had failed. We excluded from consideration two revolutionaries (Arafat and Habash) and one loyalist (Sihanouk) because the fate of their movements is yet to be determined.

We used SPSS$^x$ to analyze the data to produce standard bivariate distributions, testing for the significance of the differences between the revolutionaries who had succeeded and those who had failed. We repeated the same operation focusing on the loyalists who had succeeded and those who had failed.

We found no sociodemographic characteristics or traits that differentiated the successful and failed revolutionaries. Rather, the most compelling finding related to the level of development of the country in which the leaders found themselves. Revolutionary leaders in undeveloped countries typically succeeded; those in developed countries uniformly failed.

Appendix B

Not unexpectedly, the level of development of the country turned out to be the single commanding factor that differentiated the successful and the failed loyalists as well. Loyalists in developed countries tended to succeed; those in undeveloped countries tended to fail.

These findings are not surprising. As we found elsewhere, (see M. Rejai, *The Comparative Study of Revolutionary Strategy* [New York: David McKay, 1977] ch. 8) in developing countries revolutions remain possibilities; in developed societies, an impressive array of conditions converge to frustrate political revolution (for example, urbanization and industrialization, efficiency of the ruling regimes, extensiveness of the military and police forces, new technologies of surveillance and control).

Accordingly, revolutionaries are more likely to win in developing countries and to lose in developed ones. Conversely, loyalists are more likely to win in developed societies and lose in developing lands. In any event, leadership success or failure tends to be situationally determined (consistent with our theoretical posture), quite independent of characteristics and attributes leaders themselves may possess.

**CONCLUSION**

We have found empirical justification for grouping together: (1) loyalists with revolutionaries-turned-loyalists, (2) revolutionaries with loyalists-turned-revolutionaries, (3) successful and failed revolutionaries, and (4) successful and failed loyalists. We have established the discreteness and integrity of our two master lists of loyalists and revolutionaries.

## Appendix C
## General Code Sheet

Leader's NAME_____

COUNTRY_____

| Column(s) | Code | Variables and Response Values |
|---|---|---|
| 1 | \_\_\_\_ | (Blank) |
| 2-3-4 | \_\_\_\_ | Leaders (See Introduction) |
| 5 | \_\_\_\_ | Type of Country_____ |

       0    developed
       1    semideveloped    Give % of labor
       2    undeveloped      force in agriculture
       9    unknown

| Column(s) | Code | Variables and Response Values |
|---|---|---|
| 6-7 | \_\_\_\_ | Time of Revolution or of Reaching Highest Office Give actual year _____ |
| 8-9 | \_\_\_\_ | Leader's Age at Time of Revolution or of Reaching Highest Office _____ (exact) |

       93    0-15
       94    16-19
       95    20-24
       96    25-34
       97    35-44
       98    45-64
       99    65 and over

| Column(s) | Code | Variables and Response Values |
|---|---|---|
| 10-11 | \_\_\_\_ | Approximate Age When First Exposed to Political Ideology _____ (exact) |

       93    0-15
       94    16-19
       95    20-24
       96    25-34
       97    35-44
       98    45-64
       99    65 and over
       9     unknown

| Column(s) | Code | Variables and Response Values |
|---|---|---|
| 12-13 | \_\_\_\_ | Approximate Age When First Took Part in Political Activity _____ (exact) |

       93    0-15
       94    16-19
       95    20-24

| Column(s) | Code | Variables and Response Values |
|---|---|---|

|  |  | 96 | 25-34 |
|  |  | 97 | 35-44 |
|  |  | 98 | 45-64 |
|  |  | 99 | 65 and over |
|  |  | 09 | unknown |

14 ____ Sex _____
    0   male
    1   female
    9   unknown

15 ____ Birthplace _____
    0   urban
    1   rural
    9   unknown

16 ____ Exposure to Urban Life (if Born and Raised in Nonurban Areas) _____
    0   none
    1   little (less than one year)
    2   moderate (one to three years)
    3   extensive (four or more years)
    8   other (specify)
    9   unknown/not applicable

17 ____ Age at Which Exposed to Urban Life (if Born and Raised in Nonurban Areas) _____
    0   under 15
    1   15-19
    2   20-24
    3   25-29
    4   30-34
    5   35-39
    6   40-44
    7   45-49
    8   over 50
    9   unknown/not applicable

18 ____ Father's Birthplace _____
    0   same as son
    1   urban, different than son
    2   rural, different than son
    7   foreign
    8   other (specify)
    9   unknown

Appendix C

| Column(s) | Code | Variables and Response Values |
|---|---|---|
| 19 | ____ | Religious Background _____ |
|   |   | 0  atheist |
|   |   | 1  Christian: Protestant |
|   |   | 2  Christian: Catholic |
|   |   | 3  Christian: Other |
|   |   | 4  Jewish |
|   |   | 5  Muslim |
|   |   | 6  Hindu |
|   |   | 7  Buddhist |
|   |   | 8  other (specify) |
|   |   | 9  unknown |
| 20 | ____ | Religious Orientation _____ |
|   |   | 0  atheist |
|   |   | 1  Christian: Protestant |
|   |   | 2  Christian: Catholic |
|   |   | 3  Christian: Other |
|   |   | 4  Jewish |
|   |   | 5  Muslim |
|   |   | 6  Hindu |
|   |   | 7  Buddhist |
|   |   | 8  other (specify) |
|   |   | 9  unknown |
| 21 | ____ | Parent's Religion _____ |
|   |   | 0  same |
|   |   | 3  different |
|   |   | 8  other (specify) |
|   |   | 9  unknown |
| 22 | ____ | Family Life: Number of Siblings _____ |
|   |   | 0  none |
|   |   | 1  one |
|   |   | 2  two |
|   |   | 3  three |
|   |   | 4  four |
|   |   | 5  five |
|   |   | 6  six |
|   |   | 7  seven or more |
|   |   | 8  other (specify) |
|   |   | 9  unknown |
| 23 | ____ | Family Life: Age Ranking Among Siblings _____ |
|   |   | 0  only child |
|   |   | 1  youngest child |
|   |   | 2  middle child (specify) |

| Column(s) | Code | Variables and Response Values |
|---|---|---|
| | | 3    oldest child |
| | | 4    oldest son |
| | | 5    youngest son |
| | | 6    only son |
| | | 8    other (specify) |
| | | 9    unknown |
| 24 | ___ | Family Life: Status of Leader _____ |
| | | 0    legitimate |
| | | 1    illegitimate |
| | | 2    illegitimate, parents subsequently married |
| | | 8    other (specify) |
| | | 9    unknown |
| 25 | ___ | Family Life: Status of Parents _____ |
| | | 0    parents married throughout leader's childhood and beyond |
| | | 1    parents separated before leader left home |
| | | 2    parents separated after leader left home |
| | | 3    parents divorced before leader left home |
| | | 4    parents divorced after leader left home |
| | | 5    parents separated due to a death: before leader left home |
| | | 6    parents separated due to a death: after leader left home |
| | | 7    parents unmarried at time of leader's birth |
| | | 8    other (specify) |
| | | 9    unknown |
| 26 | ___ | Family Life: Character _____ |
| | | 0    broken home |
| | | 1    tranquil |
| | | 2    stormy |
| | | 8    other (specify) |
| | | 9    unknown |
| 27 | ___ | Ethnic Background _____ |
| | | 0    main ethnic group |
| | | 1    ethnic minority: large (specify) |
| | | 2    ethnic minority: small (specify) |

| Column(s) | Code | Variables and Response Values |
|---|---|---|
| | | 8    other (specify) |
| | | 9    unknown |
| 28 | ____ | Socioeconomic Status _____ |
| | | 0    upper class |
| | | 1    middle class |
| | | 2    lower or working class |
| | | 8    other (specify) |
| | | 9    unknown |
| 29 | ____ | Military Service |
| | | 0    none |
| | | 1    some (specify number of years, rank) |
| | | 9    unknown |
| 30 | ____ | Education: Type _____ |
| | | 0    private: secular |
| | | 1    private: church related |
| | | 2    state: secular |
| | | 3    state: church related |
| | | 4    private and state: secular |
| | | 5    private and state: church related |
| | | 6    private and state: secular and church related |
| | | 8    other (specify) |
| | | 9    unknown |
| 31 | ____ | Education: Place _____ |
| | | 0    domestic |
| | | 1    domestic, foreign sponsored or supported institution |
| | | 2    U.S. |
| | | 3    U.S.S.R. |
| | | 4    Europe other than U.S.S.R. (specify) |
| | | 5    Asia (specify) |
| | | 6    Africa (specify) |
| | | 7    Latin America (specify) |
| | | 8    other including combinations (specify) |
| | | 9    unknown |
| 32-33 | ____ | Education: Highest Level Attained _____ |
| | | 15   none, through high school |
| | | 16   some college, to B.A. |
| | | 17   graduate or professional |
| | | 18   military, trade, religious, other |
| | | 19   no formal education |
| | | 09   unknown |

| Column(s) | Code | Variables and Response Values |
|---|---|---|
| 34 | \_\_\_\_ | Education: Highest Level Attained, Characteristics \_ |
| | |   0   private and domestic |
| | |   1   private and foreign (specify) |
| | |   2   state and domestic |
| | |   3   state and foreign (specify) |
| | |   8   other (specify) |
| | |   9   unknown/not applicable |
| 35 | \_\_\_\_ | Education: Field _____ |
| | |   0   professional (specify) |
| | |   4   social sciences, humanities, the arts |
| | |   7   military |
| | |   8   other (specify) |
| | |   9   unknown/not applicable |
| 36-37 | \_\_\_\_ | Father's Education: Highest Level Attained _____ |
| | | 15   none, through high school |
| | | 16   some college, to B.A. |
| | | 17   graduate or professional |
| | | 18   military, trade, religious, other |
| | | 19   no formal education |
| | | 09   unknown/not applicable |
| 38 | \_\_\_\_ | Father's Education: Highest Level Attained: Characteristics _____ |
| | |   0   private and domestic |
| | |   1   private and foreign (specify) |
| | |   2   state and domestic |
| | |   3   state and foreign (specify) |
| | |   8   other (specify) |
| | |   9   unknown/not applicable |
| 39 | \_\_\_\_ | Father's Education: Field |
| | |   0   professional |
| | |   4   social sciences, humanities, the arts |
| | |   7   military |
| | |   8   other (specify) |
| | |   9   unknown/not applicable |
| 40 | \_\_\_\_ | Foreign Languages _____ |
| | |   0   none |
| | |   1   one |
| | |   2   two |
| | |   3   three |
| | |   4   four |
| | |   5   five |

# Appendix C

| Column(s) | Code | Variables and Response Values |
|---|---|---|
| | | 6 six or more |
| | | 8 other, including bilingual (specify) |
| | | 9 unknown |
| 41 | ____ | Foreign Travel Before Revolution or Reaching Highest Office: Extent _____ |
| | | 0 none |
| | | 1 little (one country) |
| | | 2 moderate (two-three countries) |
| | | 3 extensive (four or more countries) |
| | | 8 other (specify) |
| | | 9 unknown |
| 42 | ____ | Foreign Travel Before Revolution or Reaching Highest Office: Duration: _____ |
| | | 0 none |
| | | 1 short (less than one year) |
| | | 2 moderate (one-three years) |
| | | 3 long (four or more years) |
| | | 8 other (specify) |
| | | 9 unknown |
| 43 | ____ | Foreign Travel Before Revolution or Reaching Highest Office: Place _____ |
| | | 0 none |
| | | 1 Europe only |
| | | 2 U.S.A. only |
| | | 4 Asia only |
| | | 5 Africa only |
| | | 6 Latin America only |
| | | 7 combination (specify) |
| | | 8 other (specify) |
| | | 9 unknown |
| 44 | ____ | Continuing Foreign Contacts _____ |
| | | 0 none |
| | | 1 few (one-three) |
| | | 2 some (four-six) |
| | | 3 many (seven or more) |
| | | 8 other (specify) |
| | | 9 unknown |
| 45-46 | ____ | Primary Occupation _____ |
| | | 23 professions (specify) |
| | | 24 professional revolutionary |
| | | 25 politician, business, landlord |
| | | 26 working class |

| Column(s) | Code | Variables and Response Values |
|---|---|---|
| | | 27 combination (specify) |
| | | 28 government official/civil servant |
| | | 19 other (specify) |
| | | 09 unknown |
| 47-48 | ___ | Father's Primary Occupation _____ |
| | | 23 professions (specify) |
| | | 24 professional revolutionary |
| | | 25 politician, business, landlord |
| | | 26 working class |
| | | 27 combination (specify) |
| | | 28 tribal chief |
| | | 29 government official/civil servant |
| | | 19 other (specify) |
| | | 09 unknown |
| 49 | ___ | Membership in Any Organizations: Extent _____ |
| | | 0 none |
| | | 1 few (one-three) |
| | | 2 some (four-six) |
| | | 3 many (seven or more) |
| | | 9 unknown |
| 50 | ___ | Membership in Political Organizations: Traditional or Legal |
| | | 0 no |
| | | 1 yes |
| | | 8 other (specify) |
| | | 9 unknown |
| 51 | ___ | Membership in Political Organizations: Radical or Revolutionary _____ |
| | | 0 no |
| | | 1 yes |
| | | 8 other (specify) |
| | | 9 unknown |
| 52 | ___ | Membership in Trade Union Organizations _____ |
| | | 0 no |
| | | 1 yes |
| | | 8 other (specify) |
| | | 9 unknown |
| 53 | ___ | Membership in Professional Organizations _____ |
| | | 0 no |
| | | 1 yes |

Appendix C

| Column(s) | Code | Variables and Response Values |
|---|---|---|
| | | 8 other (specify) |
| | | 9 unknown |
| 54 | ____ | Membership in Other Organizations (specify) |
| | | 0 no |
| | | 1 yes |
| | | 8 other (specify) |
| | | 9 unknown |
| 55-56 | ____ | Record of Arrests, Imprisonment, Exile, etc. ____ |
| | | 11 none |
| | | 12 some (one-three times) |
| | | 13 moderate (four-six times) |
| | | 14 frequent (seven or more) |
| | | 09 unknown |
| 57-58 | ____ | Duration of Imprisonment or Exile (specify) |
| | | 22 none |
| | | 23 one year or less |
| | | 24 two to nine years |
| | | 25 ten or more years |
| | | 09 unknown |
| 59 | ____ | Publications ____ |
| | | 0 none |
| | | 1 few (one-three) |
| | | 2 some (four-six) |
| | | 3 many (seven or more) |
| | | 9 unknown |
| 60-61 | ____ | Type of Ideology to Which Leader Subscribes ____ |
| | | 24 none |
| | | 30 democratic |
| | | 31 Marxist-Leninist |
| | | 32 nationalist/Marxist-Leninist (Marxist-Leninist-Castroite, nationalist/Marxist-Leninist-Maoist) |
| | | 33 nationalist/Marxist-socialist |
| | | 34 nationalist/other (nationalist, nationalist-socialist, democratic-nationalist) |
| | | 35 leftist/other (utopian socialist, anarchist-socialist, Marxist-socialist, Marxist-anarchist, Trotskyite, Jacobin, Puritan-radical, democratic-socialist) |
| | | 36 rightist/other (Fascist, Nazi, conservative, monarchist, constitutional |

| Column(s) | Code | Variables and Response Values |
|---|---|---|

monarchist)
37 other (specify)
38 vacillating
99 unknown

62 ____ Origin of Ideology _____
0 primarily indigenous
1 primarily foreign
2 primarily foreign but adapted to indigenous conditions
8 other (specify)
9 unknown

63 ____ Personalities the Leader Admires or Identifies with (Excluding Immediate Colleagues) _____
0 none
1 military (specify)
2 scholar/writer/intellectual (specify)
3 revolutionary (specify)
4 philosopher (specify)
5 national hero: own country (specify)
6 national hero: other countries (specify)
7 member of family (specify)
8 other, including combinations (specify)
9 unknown

64 ____ Attitude Toward Human Beings _____
1 negative
2 fluctuating
3 positive
8 other (specify)
9 unknown

65 ____ Attitude Toward Own Country _____
1 negative
2 fluctuating
3 positive
8 other (specify)
9 unknown

66 ____ Attitude Toward International Society _____
1 negative
2 fluctuating
3 positive
5 dualistic
8 other (specify)
9 unknown

# Appendix D

# Code Sheet for Factor and Discriminant Analyses

| Column(s) | Variables and Response Values* |
|---|---|
| 1 | (Blank) |
| 2-3-4 | Leaders (See Introduction) |
| 5 | Type of Country<br>    0    undeveloped<br>    1    semideveloped<br>    2    developed<br>    9    missing data (hereinafter "MD") |
| 6-7 | Time period<br>    01    before 1700<br>    02    1701-1750<br>    03    1751-1800<br>    04    1801-1850<br>    05    1851-1900<br>    06    1901-1950<br>    07    1951-1980<br>    99    MD |
| 8-9 | Leader's age at the time of revolution or highest office<br>    Code exact age<br>    99    MD |
| 10-11 | Approximate age when first exposed to political ideology<br>    Code exact age<br>    99    MD |
| 12-13 | Approximate age when first took part in political activity<br>    Code exact age<br>    99    MD |
| 14 | Birthplace<br>    0    rural<br>    1    urban<br>    9    MD |

---

*In some cases of dummy variables, the loading may have been changed from positive to negative (or vice versa) to facilitate interpretation. In all such cases, the referenced dummy variable has been correspondingly adjusted.

| Column(s) | Variables and Response Values |
|---|---|
| 15 | Exposure to urban life<br>    0    none<br>    1    little (less than 1 year)<br>    2    moderate (1-3 years)<br>    3    extensive (4+ years)<br>    9    MD |
| 16 | Age at which exposed to urban life<br>    0    under 15<br>    1    15-19<br>    2    20-24<br>    3    25-29<br>    4    30-34<br>    5    35-39<br>    6    40-44<br>    7    45-49<br>    8    over 50<br>    9    MD |
| 17 | Father's birthplace<br>    0    rural<br>    1    urban<br>    9    MD |
| 18 | Religious background<br>    0    atheist<br>    1    nonatheist<br>    9    MD |
| 19 | Religious orientation<br>    0    atheist<br>    1    nonatheist<br>    9    MD |
| 20 | Parent's religion<br>    0    same as leader's<br>    1    different than leader's<br>    9    MD |
| 21 | Family life: number of siblings<br>    0    none<br>    1    one<br>    2    two<br>    3    three<br>    4    four<br>    5    five<br>    6    six |

| Column(s) | Variables and Response Values |
|---|---|
|  | 7     seven or more |
|  | 9     MD |
| 22 | Family Life: age ranking among siblings |
|  | 0     youngest child |
|  | 1     middle |
|  | 2     oldest |
|  | 3     only child |
|  | 9     MD |
| 23 | Family life: status of leader |
|  | 0     legitimate child |
|  | 1     illegitimate child |
|  | 9     MD |
| 24 | Family life: status of parents |
|  | 0     married through leader's life |
|  | 1     separated during leader's life |
|  | 2     divorced during leader's life |
|  | 9     MD |
| 25 | Family life: character |
|  | 0     tranquil |
|  | 1     none |
|  | 2     stormy |
|  | 9     MD |
| 26 | Ethnic background |
|  | 0     member of ethnic minority |
|  | 1     member of ethnic majority |
|  | 9     MD |
| 27 | Socioeconomic status |
|  | 0     lower class |
|  | 1     middle class |
|  | 2     upper class |
|  | 9     MD |
| 28 | Military service |
|  | 0     none |
|  | 1     non-officer but service experience |
|  | 2     lower officer |
|  | 3     middle officer |
|  | 4     higher officer |
|  | 8     other |
|  | 9     MD |

| Column(s) | Variables and Response Values |
|---|---|
| 29 | Education: type<br>  0  private institutions<br>  1  combination of private and state institutions<br>  2  state institutions<br>  9  MD |
| 30 | Education: place<br>  0  domestic institutions<br>  1  foreign (any foreign education exposure)<br>  9  MD |
| 31 | Education: religious orientation<br>  0  secular<br>  1  secular and church related<br>  2  church related<br>  9  MD |
| 32 | Education: highest level attained<br>  0  less than high school degree<br>  1  high school degree or equivalent<br>  2  some college<br>  3  BA degree or equivalent<br>  4  BA to MA (inclusive)<br>  5  post MA<br>  9  MD |
| 33 | Education: field 1<br>  0  professional<br>  1  nonprofessional<br>  9  MD |
| 34 | Education: field 2<br>  0  social sciences, humanities, the arts<br>  1  not social sciences, humanities, the arts<br>  9  MD |
| 35 | Father's education: highest level attained<br>  0  less than high school degree<br>  1  high school degree or equivalent<br>  2  some college<br>  3  BA degree or equivalent<br>  4  BA to MA (inclusive)<br>  5  post MA<br>  9  MD |
| 36 | Father's education: place<br>  0  domestic<br>  1  foreign<br>  9  MD |

# Appendix D

| Column(s) | Variables and Response Values |
|---|---|
| 37 | Father's education: field 1<br>    0    professional<br>    1    nonprofessional<br>    9    MD |
| 38 | Father's education: field 2<br>    0    social sciences, humanities, the arts<br>    1    not social sciences, humanities, the arts<br>    9    MD |
| 39 | Foreign languages<br>    0    none<br>    1    one<br>    2    two or more<br>    9    MD |
| 40 | Foreign travel before revolution or reaching highest office: extent<br>    0    none<br>    1    short<br>    2    moderate<br>    3    extensive<br>    9    MD |
| 41 | Foreign travel before revolution or reaching highest office: duration<br>    0    none<br>    1    short<br>    2    moderate<br>    3    extensive<br>    9    MD |
| 42 | Foreign travel before revolution or reaching highest office: place<br>    0    none<br>    1    to undeveloped countries<br>    2    to developed countries<br>    3    to both developed and undeveloped countries<br>    9    MD |
| 43 | Continuing foreign contacts<br>    0    none<br>    1    few<br>    2    some<br>    3    many<br>    9    MD |

Appendix D

| Column(s) | Variables and Response Values |
|---|---|
| 44 | Primary occupation 1<br>    0   professional/intellectual<br>    1   not professional/intellectual<br>    9   MD |
| 45 | Primary occupation 2<br>    0   professional revolutionary<br>    1   not professional revolutionary<br>    9   MD |
| 46 | Primary occupation 3<br>    0   government official<br>    1   not government official<br>    9   MD |
| 47 | Primary occupation 4<br>    0   banking/industry<br>    1   not banking/industry<br>    9   MD |
| 48 | Primary occupation 5<br>    0   worker<br>    1   nonworker<br>    9   MD |
| 49 | Primary occupation 6<br>    0   peasant/farmer<br>    1   non-peasant/farmer<br>    9   MD |
| 50 | Primary occupation 7<br>    0   military<br>    1   not military<br>    9   MD |
| 51 | Primary occupation 8<br>    0   landed gentry<br>    1   not landed gentry<br>    9   MD |
| 52 | Father's primary occupation 1<br>    0   professional/intellectual<br>    1   not professional/intellectual<br>    9   MD |
| 53 | Father's primary occupation 2<br>    0   professional revolutionary<br>    1   not professional revolutionary<br>    9   MD |

Appendix D

| Column(s) | Variables and Response Values |
|---|---|
| 54 | Father's primary occupation 3<br>    0   government official<br>    1   not government official<br>    9   MD |
| 55 | Father's primary occupation 4<br>    0   banking/industry<br>    1   not banking/industry<br>    9   MD |
| 56 | Father's primary occupation 5<br>    0   worker<br>    1   nonworker<br>    9   MD |
| 57 | Father's primary occupation 6<br>    0   peasant/farmer<br>    1   non-peasant/farmer<br>    9   MD |
| 58 | Father's primary occupation 7<br>    0   military<br>    1   not military<br>    9   MD |
| 59 | Father's primary occupation 8<br>    0   landed gentry<br>    1   not landed gentry<br>    9   MD |
| 60 | Membership in organizations: extent<br>    0   none<br>    1   few<br>    2   some<br>    3   many<br>    9   MD |
| 61 | Membership in organizations: traditional or legal<br>    0   no<br>    1   yes<br>    9   MD |
| 62 | Membership in organizations: revolutionary or protorevolutionary<br>    0   no<br>    1   yes<br>    9   MD |

| Column(s) | Variables and Response Values |
|---|---|
| 63 | Membership in trade union organization<br>    0    no<br>    1    yes<br>    9    MD |
| 64 | Membership in professional organizations<br>    0    no<br>    1    yes<br>    9    MD |
| 65 | Membership in other organizations<br>    0    no<br>    1    yes<br>    9    MD |
| 66 | Record of arrest: frequency<br>    0    none<br>    1    light<br>    2    moderate<br>    3    extensive<br>    9    MD |
| 67-68 | Record of arrest: total years<br>    Code exact number of years<br>    99    MD |
| 69 | Publications<br>    0    none<br>    1    few<br>    2    some<br>    3    many<br>    9    MD |
| 70 | Type of political ideology to which leader subscribes 1<br>    0    socialist<br>    1    not socialist<br>    9    MD |
| 71 | Political ideology 2<br>    0    communist<br>    1    not communist<br>    9    MD |
| 72 | Political ideology 3<br>    0    nationalist<br>    1    not nationalist<br>    9    MD |

Appendix D

| Column(s) | Variables and Response Values |
|---|---|
| 73 | Political ideology 4<br>   0   communist/nationalist<br>   1   not communist/nationalist<br>   9   MD |
| 74 | Political ideology 5<br>   0   democratic<br>   1   not democratic<br>   9   MD |
| 75 | Origin of political ideology to which leader subscribes<br>   0   primarily indigenous<br>   1   primarily foreign but adapted to indigenous conditions<br>   2   Primarily foreign<br>   9   MD |
| 76 | Personalities the leader admires or identifies with<br>   0   yes: a hero figure exists<br>   1   no: a hero figure does not exist<br>   9   MD |
| 77 | Attitude toward human beings<br>   0   negative<br>   1   fluctuating<br>   3   positive<br>   9   MD |
| 78 | Attitude toward own country<br>   1   negative<br>   2   fluctuating<br>   3   positive<br>   9   MD |
| 79 | Attitude toward international society<br>   0   negative<br>   1   fluctuating<br>   2   positive<br>   4   dualistic<br>   9   MD |

# Bibliography

NOTE: This bibliography is in three parts: theoretical and empirical studies, general data sources, regional and country studies. The third part is by no means exhaustive, incorporating, as it does, two types of sources: those containing data relevant to presentations in Parts II and III of the text, those important for understanding a particular context as that context shapes the outlook of political leaders.

## THEORETICAL AND EMPIRICAL STUDIES

Aberbach, Joel D., Robert D. Putnam, and Bert A. Rockman. *Bureaucrats and Politicians in Western Democracies*. Cambridge: Harvard University Press, 1981.

Adler, Alfred. *Understanding Human Nature*. Garden City: Garden City Publishing Co., 1927.

———. *The Individual Psychology of Alfred Adler*. Edited by H. L. Ansbacher and R. R. Ansbacher. New York: Harper & Row, 1964.

———. "The Psychology of Power" [1928]. *Journal of Individual Psychology* 22 (1966): 166-72.

Ayling, S. E. *Portraits of Power*. 4th ed. London: George G. Harrap, 1967.

Barber, James David. *The Lawmakers: Recruitment and Adaptation to Legislative Life*. New Haven: Yale University Press, 1965.

Bass, Bernard M. *Stogdill's Handbook of Leadership*. Revised and expanded ed. New York: Free Press, 1981.

Beck, Carl et al. *Comparative Communist Political Leadership*. New York: David McKay, 1973.

Bellows, Robert. *Creative Leadership*. Englewood Cliffs: Prentice Hall, 1959.

Berman, Paul. *Revolutionary Organization*. Lexington, Mass.: Lexington Books, 1974.

Blanchard, William H. *Revolutionary Morality: A Psychosexual Analysis of Twelve Revolutionists*. Santa Barbara, CA: ABC-Clio, 1984.

Blondel, Jean. *Government Ministers in the Contemporary World*. Beverly Hills: Sage Publications, 1985.

――――― . *World Leaders: Heads of Government in the Postwar Period*. Beverly Hills: Sage Publications, 1980.

Brinton, Crane. *The Jacobins: An Essay in the New History*. New York: Macmillan, 1930.

Broh, C. Anthony. "Adler on the Influence of Siblings in Political Socialization." *Political Behavior* 1 (1979): 175-200.

――――― . "Siblings and Political Socialization: A Closer Look at the Direct Transmission Thesis." *Political Psychology* 3 (Spring-Summer 1982): 173-83.

Browning, Rufus P., and Herbert Jacob. "Power Motivation and the Political Personality." *Public Opinion Quarterly* 28 (1964): 75-90.

Buck, Phillip W. *Amateurs and Professionals in British Politics 1918-1959*. Chicago: University of Chicago Press, 1963.

Bunce, Valerie. *Do New Leaders Make a Difference?* Princeton: Princeton University Press, 1981.

Burns, James M. *Leadership*. New York: Harper & Row, 1978.

Bychowski, Gustav. *Dictators and Disciples: From Caesar to Stalin*. New York: International Universities Press, 1948.

Camus, Albert. *The Rebel: An Essay on Man in Revolt*. New York: Vintage Books, 1956.

Carlyle, Thomas. *On Heroes, Hero-Worship, and the Heroic in History* [1841]. London: Oxford University Press, 1957.

Cowley, W. H. "Three Distinctions in the Study of Leaders." *Journal of Abnormal and Social Psychology* 23 (March-April 1928): 144-57.

Cox, Catherine M. *The Early Mental Traits of 300 Geniuses*. Stanford: Stanford University Press, 1926.

Crozier, Brian. *The Study of Conflict*. London: Institute for the Study of Conflict, 1970.

Czudnowski, Moshe M., ed. *Does Who Governs Matter?* DeKalb: Northern Illinois University Press, 1982.

――――― . *Political Elites and Social Change*. DeKalb: Northern Illinois University Press, 1983.

Daly, William T. *The Revolutionary: A Review and Synthesis*. Beverly Hills: Sage Publications, 1972.

Davies, James C. *Human Nature in Politics*. New York: John Wiley & Sons, 1963.

Davis, Jerome. "A Study of 163 Outstanding [Russian] Communist Leaders." *American Sociological Review* 24 (1929): 42-55.

Debray, Régis. *Revolution in the Revolution? Armed Struggle and Political Struggle in Latin America*. New York: Grove Press, 1967.

Dogan, Mattei, ed. *The Mandarins of Western Europe: The Political Role of Top Civil Servants*. Beverly Hills: Sage Publications, 1975.

Downton, James V., Jr. *Rebel Leadership: Commitment and Charisma in the Revolutionary Process*. New York: Free Press, 1973.

Easton, David. *The Political System*. New York: Alfred A. Knopf, 1953.

Edinger, Lewis J. "The Comparative Analysis of Political Leadership." *Comparative Politics* 7 (1975): 253-69.

———. "Political Science and Political Biography: Reflections on the Study of Leadership." *Journal of Politics* 26 (May & August 1964): 423-39, 648-76.
Edinger, Lewis J., ed. *Political Leadership in Industrialized Societies.* New York: Wiley, 1967.
Edinger, Lewis J., and Donald D. Searing. "Social Background in Elite Analysis: A Methodological Inquiry." *American Political Science Review* 61 (June 1967): 428-45.
Erikson, Erik H. *Gandhi's Truth: On the Origins of Militant Nonviolence.* New York: W. W. Norton, 1969.
———. *Young Man Luther: A Study in Psychoanalysis and History.* New York: W. W. Norton, 1962.
Fiedler, Fred E. "A Contingency Model of Leadership Effectiveness." In *Advances in Experimental Social Psychology*, Leonard Berkowitz, ed., vol. 1. New York: Academic Press, 1964.
———. *Leadership.* Morristown, NJ: General Learning Press, 1971.
Force, George T., and Jack R. Van Der Slik. *Theory and Research in the Study of Political Leadership.* Revised ed. Carbondale: Southern Illinois University, Public Affairs Research Bureau, 1972.
Forer, Lucille, and Henry Still. *The Birth Order Factor.* New York: David McKay, 1976.
George, Alexander. "Power as a Compensatory Value for Political Leaders." *Journal of Social Issues* 3 (1968): 29-49.
Gibb, Cecil A. "An International View of the Emergence of Leadership." *Australian Journal of Psychology* 10 (1958): 101-10.
———. "Leadership." In *Handbook of Social Psychology*, Gardner Lindzey and Elliot Aronson, eds., vol. 4. Reading, MA: Addison-Wesley, 1969.
———. "Leadership: Psychological Aspects." *International Encyclopedia of the Social Sciences*, vol. 9. New York: Macmillan, 1968.
Gilbert, G. M. *The Psychology of Dictatorship.* New York: Ronald Press, 1970.
Goertzel, Mildred G., Victor Goertzel, and Ted G. Goertzel. *Three Hundred Eminent Personalities.* San Francisco: Jossey-Bass, 1978.
Goertzel, Victor, and Mildred G. Goertzel. *Cradles of Eminence.* Boston: Little, Brown, 1962.
Gouldner, Alvin W., ed. *Studies in Leadership: Leadership and Democratic Action.* New York: Harper & Bros., 1950.
Greenstein, Fred I. *Personality and Politics.* Chicago: Markham, 1969.
Groth, Alexander. *Revolution and Elite Access: Some Hypotheses on Aspects of Political Change.* University of California, Davis: Institute of Governmental Affairs, 1966.
Gurr, Ted Robert. *Why Men Rebel.* Princeton: Princeton University Press, 1970.
Gusfield, Joseph R. "Functional Areas of Leadership." *Sociological Quarterly* 7 (1966): 137-56.
Guttsman, W. L. *The British Political Elite.* New York: Basic Books, 1964.
Harris, John S., and Thomas V. Garcia. "The Permanent Secretaries: Britain's Top Administrators." *Public Administration Review* 26 (1966): 31-44.
Hemphill, John K. *Situational Factors in Leadership.* Ohio State University: Bureau of Educational Research, 1948.

Hermann, Margaret G., ed. *A Psychological Examination of Political Leaders.* New York: Free Press, 1977.

_____ . *Political Psychology.* San Francisco: Jossey-Bass, 1986.

Hersey, Paul. *The Situational Leader.* New York: Warner Books, 1984.

Hollander, Edwin P. *Leadership Dynamics.* New York: Free Press, 1978.

Hollander, Edwin P., and J. W. Julian. "Leadership." In *Handbook of Personality Theory and Research*, Edgar P. Borgatta and W. W. Lambert, eds. Chicago: Rand McNally, 1968.

Hoogenboom, Ari. "Industrialism and Political Leadership: A Case Study of the United States Senate." In *The Age of Industrialism in America*, Frederic C. Jaher, ed. New York: Free Press, 1968.

Hook, Sidney. *The Hero in History.* Boston: Beacon Press, 1955.

Huntington, Samuel P. *Political Order in Changing Societies.* New Haven: Yale University Press, 1968.

Iremonger, Lucille. *The Fiery Chariot: A Study of British Prime Ministers and the Search for Love.* London: Secker & Warburg, 1970.

Janda, Kenneth F. "Toward the Explication of the Concept of Leadership in Terms of the Concept of Power." *Human Relations* 30 (1960): 345-63.

Janowitz, Morris. "The Systematic Analysis of Political Biography." *World Politics* 6 (1954): 405-12.

Johnson, R. W. "The British Political Elite, 1955-1972." *European Journal of Sociology* (Paris) 14 (1973): 35-77.

Katz, Daniel. "Patterns of Leadership." In *Handbook of Political Psychology*, Jeanne N. Knutson, ed. San Francisco: Jossey-Bass, 1973.

Kautsky, John H. "Revolutionary and Managerial Elites in Modernizing Regimes." *Comparative Politics* 1 (July 1969): 441-67.

Kavanaugh, Dennis, "Political Leadership: The Labours of Sisyphus." In *Challenge to Governance: Studies in Overload Politics*, Richard Rose, ed. Beverly Hills: Sage Publications, 1980.

Kellerman, Barbara, ed. *Leadership: Multidisciplinary Perspectives.* Englewood Cliffs: Prentice-Hall, 1984.

_____ . *Political Leadership: A Source Book.* Pittsburgh: University of Pittsburgh Press, 1986.

Klapp, Orrin R. *Symbolic Leaders: Public Drama and Public Men.* Chicago: Aldine Publishing Co., 1964.

Knutson, Jeanne N., ed. *Handbook of Political Psychology.* San Francisco: Jossey-Bass, 1973.

Korten, D. C. "Situational Determinants of Leadership Structure." *Journal of Conflict Resolution* 6 (1962): 222-35.

Lacouture, Jean. *The Demigods: Charismatic Leadership in the Third World.* New York: Alfred A. Knopf, 1970.

Laski, Harold J. "The Personnel of the British Cabinet, 1801-1924." *American Political Science Review* 22 (1928): 12-31.

Lasswell, Harold D. *Power and Personality* [1948]. New York: The Viking Press, 1962.

_____ . *Psychopathology and Politics* [1930]. New York: The Viking Press, 1960.

Lasswell, Harold D., and Daniel Lerner, eds. *World Revolutionary Elites.* Cambridge: M.I.T. Press, 1965.
Lasswell, Harold D., Daniel Lerner, and C. Easton Rothwell. *The Comparative Study of Elites.* Stanford: Stanford University Press, 1952.
Le Bon, Gustave. *The Psychology of Revolution.* New York: G. P. Putnam's Sons, 1913.
Lee, Ming T. "The Founders of the Chinese Communist Party: A Study in Revolutionaries." *Civilisations* 13 (1968): 113-27.
Madsen, Douglas. "A Biochemical Property Relating to Power Seeking in Humans." *American Political Science Review* 79 (June 1985): 448-57.
_____. "Power Seekers are Different: Further Biochemical Evidence." *American Political Science Review* 80 (March 1986): 261-70.
Magnusson, David, ed. *Toward a Psychology of Situations: An Interactional Perspective.* Hillsdale, NJ: Lawrence Erlbaum Associates, 1981.
Magnusson, David, and Norman S. Endler, eds. *Personality at the Crossroads: Current Issues in Interactional Psychology.* Hillsdale, NJ: Lawrence Erlbaum Associates, 1977.
Martin, James Kirby. *Men in Rebellion.* New Brunswick: Rutgers University Press, 1973.
Marvick, Dwaine, ed. *Political Decision-Makers.* Glencoe, IL: Free Press, 1961.
Maslow, Abraham H. *Motivation and Personality.* Revised ed. New York: Harper & Row, 1970.
Matthews, Donald R. *The Social Background of Political Decision-Makers.* New York: Doubleday, 1954.
_____. *U.S. Senators and Their World.* Chapel Hill: University of North Carolina Press, 1960.
Mazlish, Bruce. *The Revolutionary Ascetic.* New York: Basic Books, 1976.
McLelland, David C. *The Achieving Society.* Princeton: Van Nostrand, 1961.
McLelland, David C. et al. *The Achievement Motive.* New York: Appleton-Century-Croft, 1953.
Mellors, Colin. *The British MP: A Socio-Economic Study of the House of Commons.* Westmead, Farnborough, Eng.: Saxon House, 1978.
Moore, Barrington, Jr. *Injustice: The Social Bases of Obedience and Revolt.* White Plains, NY: M. E. Sharpe, 1978.
Mullaney, Marie M. *Revolutionary Women: Gender and the Socialist Revolutionary Role.* New York: Praeger Publishers, 1983.
Paige, Glenn D., ed. *Political Leadership.* New York: Free Press, 1972.
Paige, Glenn D. *The Scientific Study of Political Leadership.* New York: Free Press, 1977.
Payne, James L. et al. *The Motivations of Politicians.* Chicago: Nelson-Hall, 1984.
Pigors, Paul. *Leadership or Domination.* Boston: Houghton Mifflin, 1935.
Post, Ken. "Individuals and the Dialectic: A Marxist View of Political Biographies." In *The Making of Politicians: Studies from Africa and Asia,* W. H. Morris-Jones, ed. University of London: Athlone Press, 1976.
Putnam, Robert D. *Beliefs of Politicians.* New Haven, CT: Yale University Press, 1973.

———. *The Comparative Study of Political Elites*. Englewood Cliffs: Prentice-Hall, 1976.
Quandt, William B. *The Comparative Study of Political Elites*. Beverly Hills: Sage Publications, 1970.
Raser, John R. *Personal Characteristics of Political Decision-Makers*. La Jolla, CA: Western Behavioral Sciences Institute, 1965.
Rejai, M. *The Comparative Study of Revolutionary Strategy*. New York: David McKay, 1977.
———. "Theory and Research in the Study of Revolutionary Personnel." In *Handbook of Political Conflict: Theory and Research*, T. R. Gurr, ed. New York: Free Press, 1980.
Rejai, M., and K. Phillips. *Leaders of Revolution*. Beverly Hills, CA: Sage Publications, 1979.
———. *World Revolutionary Leaders*. New Brunswick: Rutgers University Press, 1983.
Robins, Robert S., ed. *Psychopathology and Political Leadership*. New Orleans: Tulane University Press, 1977.
Rosenbach, William E., and Robert L. Taylor, eds. *Contemporary Issues in Leadership*. Boulder: Westview Press, 1984.
Rustow, Dankwart A. "The Study of Elites: Who's Who, When, and How." *World Politics* 18 (1966): 690-717.
Scalapino, Robert A., ed. *The Communist Revolution in Asia*. 2nd ed. Englewood Cliffs: Prentice-Hall, 1969.
Schlesinger, Joseph A. *Ambition and Politics: Political Careers in the United States*. Chicago: Rand McNally, 1966.
Schweitzer, Arthur. *The Age of Charisma*. Chicago: Nelson-Hall, 1984.
Searing, Donald D. "Models and Images of Man and Society in Leadership Theory." *Journal of Politics* 31 (1969): 3-31.
Seligman, Lester G. "Leadership: Political Aspects." *International Encyclopedia of the Social Sciences*, vol. 9. New York: Macmillan, 1968.
Selznick, Philip. *The Organizational Weapon: A Study of Bolshevik Strategy and Tactics*. New York: McGraw-Hill, 1952.
Simonton, Dean Keith. *Genius, Creativity, and Leadership*. Cambridge, MA: Harvard University Press, 1984.
Stewart, Louis H. "Birth Order and Political Leadership." In *A Psychological Examination of Political Leaders*, Margaret G. Hermann, ed. New York: Free Press, 1977.
Stogdill, Ralph M. *Handbook of Leadership: A Survey of Theory and Research*, New York: Free Press, 1974.
Stone, Lawrence. "Prosopography." *Daedalus* 106 (Winter 1971): 46-79.
Strauss, Harlan J. "Revolutionary Types: Russia in 1905." *Journal of Conflict Resolution* 17 (1973): 297-316.
Strozier, Charles B., and Daniel Offer, eds. *The Leader: Psychobiographical Essays*. New York: Plenum Press, 1985.
Suedfeld, Peter. "Authoritarian Leadership: A Cognitive-Interactionist View." Unpublished ms., University of British Columbia, 1983.
Suedfeld, Peter, and A. Dennis Rank. "Revolutionary Leaders: Long-Term Success as a Function of Changes in Conceptual Complexity." *Journal of Personality and Social Psychology* 34 (1976): 169-78.

Sutton-Smith, Brian, and B. G. Rosenberg. *The Sibling.* New York: Holt, Rinehart & Winston, 1970.
Taintor, Zebulon C. "Assessing the Revolutionary Personality." In *Revolution and Political Change*, Claude E. Welch, Jr., and Mavis Bunker Taintor, eds. North Scituate, MA: Duxbury Press, 1972.
Tannenbaum, Arnold S. "Leadership: Sociological Aspects." *International Encyclopedia of the Social Sciences*, vol. 9. New York: Macmillan, 1968.
Tucker, Robert C. "Personality and Political Leadership." *Political Science Quarterly* 92 (Fall 1977): 383-93.
_____ . *Politics as Leadership.* Columbia: University of Missouri Press, 1981.
Van Thal, Herbert, ed. *The Prime Ministers.* 2 vols. London: Allen & Unwin, 1974, 1975.
Verba, Sidney. *Small Groups and Political Behavior: A Study of Leadership.* Princeton: Princeton University Press, 1961.
Wiatr, Jerzy. "Political Elites and Political Leadership." *Indian Journal of Politics* 17 (1973): 139-48.
Walter, James A. "Studying Political Leaders from a Distance: The Lessons of Biography." *Political Psychology* 2 (1980): 150-67.
Walzer, Michael. *The Revolution of the Saints.* Cambridge: Harvard University Press, 1965.
Welch, William A. *Leaders and Elites.* New York: Holt, Rinehart & Winston, 1979.
_____ . "Toward a Multiple-Strategy Approach to Research on Comparative Communist Political Elites." In *Communist Studies and the Social Sciences*, Frederic J. Fleron, Jr., ed. Chicago: Rand McNally, 1969.
Willner, Ann R. *Charismatic Political Leadership: A Theory.* Princeton: Center of International Studies, 1968.
_____ . *The Spellbinders: Charismatic Political Leadership.* New Haven: Yale University Press, 1984.
Winter, David G. *The Power Motive.* New York: Free Press, 1973.
Wolfenstein, E. Victor. *Revolutionary Personality: Lenin, Trotsky, Gandhi.* Princeton: Princeton University Press, 1967.

## GENERAL DATA SOURCES

Ali, Tariq. *The New Revolutionaries: A Handbook of the International Radical Left.* New York: William Morrow, 1969.
Banks, Arthur S. et al., eds. *Political Handbook of the World 1975-1985.* New York: various publishers, 1975-1985.
Banks, Arthur S., and Robert B. Textor. *A Cross-Polity Survey.* Cambridge: M.I.T. Press, 1963.
Banks, Arthur S. et al. *Cross Polity Time Series Data.* Cambridge: M.I.T. Press, 1971.
Beal, Carleton. *Great Guerrilla Warriors.* Englewood Cliffs: Prentice-Hall, 1970.
Beck, Carl, and J. T. McKechnie. *Political Elites: A Select and Computerized Bibliography.* Cambridge: M.I.T. Press, 1968.
*Biography Index.* 10 vols. New York: H. W. Wilson Co., 1946-1976.
Blackey, Robert. *Modern Revolutions and the Revolutionists: A Bibliography.* Santa Barbara, CA: Clio Press, 1976.
Chaliand, Gérard. *Revolution in the Third World.* New York: Viking Press, 1978.

Clark, Barrett H. *Great Short Biographies of the World.* New York: Robert M. McBride and Co., 1928.
*Conflict Studies.* Nos. 1-103. London: Institute for the Study of Conflict, 1970-1979.
Crozier, Brian. *The Rebels: A Study of Post-War Insurrections.* London: Chatto & Windus, 1960.
*Current Biography.* New York: H. W. Wilson Co., 1940-1977.
*Current Biography Yearbook.* New York: H. W. Wilson Co., 1940-1985.
*Current World Leaders: Almanac.* Pasadena, CA: Almanac of Current World Leaders, 1957-1980.
*Current World Leaders: Biography and News.* Pasadena, CA: Almanac of Current World Leaders, 1957-1980.
*Deadline Data on World Affairs.* New York: McGraw-Hill, 1955-1979.
Dean, Vera M. *Builders of Emerging Nations.* New York: Holt, Rinehart & Winston, 1961.
*Dictionary of International Biography.* London: Rowman, 1963-1977.
Encyclopedia of World Biography. 12 vols. New York: McGraw-Hill, 1973.
*Facts on File.* New York: Facts on File, 1942-1977.
Fairbairn, Geoffrey. *Revolutionary Guerrilla Warfare: The Countryside Version.* Middlesex, Eng.: Penguin Books, 1974.
Fernworth, Lawrence, ed. *Dictators and Democrats.* New York: Robert M. McBride & Co., 1941.
Fishman, W. J. *The Insurrectionists.* London: Methuen, 1970.
Hanna, Willard A. *Eight Nation Makers.* New York: St. Martin's Press, 1964.
Hodges, Donald C., and A. E. Abu Shanab. *National Liberation Fronts, 1960-1970,* New York: William Morrow, 1972.
*International Who's Who, The.* London: Europa Publications and Allen & Unwin, 1935-1985.
*International Yearbook and Statesmen's Who's Who, The.* London: Burke's Peerage, 1953-1980.
Lacouture, Jean. *The Demigods: Charismatic Leadership in the Third World.* New York: Alfred A. Knopf, 1970.
Lartéguy, Jean. *The Guerrillas.* New York: World Publishing Co., 1970.
Malin, Jay, ed. *Terror and Urban Guerrillas.* Coral Gables: University of Miami Press, 1971.
Moss, Robert. *Urban Guerrillas.* London: Temple Smith, 1972.
Palmer, Alan. *Who's Who in Modern History, 1860-1980.* London: Weidenfeld & Nicolson, 1980.
Robinson, Donald. *The 100 Most Important People in the World Today.* New York: G. P. Putnam's Sons, 1970.
Russett, Bruce M. et al., *World Handbook of Political and Social Indicators.* New Haven: Yale University Press, 1964.
Smith, Godfrey, ed. *1000 Makers of the Twentieth Century.* Newton Abbot, Eng.: David & Charles, 1971.
Swearingen, Roger, ed. *Leaders of the Communist World.* New York: Free Press, 1971.

Taylor, Charles L., and Michael C. Hudson. *World Handbook of Political and Social Indicators*. 2nd ed. New Haven: Yale University Press, 1972.
Taylor, Charles L., and David A. Jodice. *World Handbook of Political and Social Indicators*. 3rd ed. New Haven: Yale University Press, 1983.
Thorne, J. O., ed. *Chamber's Biographical Dictionary*. New York: St. Martin's Press, 1962.
United Nations, Department of Economic and Social Affairs. *Growth of the World's Urban and Rural Population, 1920-2000*. New York: United Nations, 1969.
*Webster's Biographical Dictionary*. Springfield, MA: G. & C. Merriam Co., 14 eds., 1943-1980.
*Who's Who in the World*. Chicago: Marquis Who's Who, 1971-1975.
*Who Was Who*. 6 vols. London: A. & C. Black, 1920-1972.
*World Biography*. 5th ed. Bethgage, NY: Institute for Research in Biography, 1954.
*Yearbook on International Communist Affairs*. Stanford: The Hoover Institution, 1966-1978.

## REGIONAL AND COUNTRY STUDIES: AFRICA

Abshire, David M., and Michael A. Samuels. *Portuguese Africa: A Handbook*. New York: Frederick A. Praeger, 1969.
*Africa Encyclopedia*. London: Oxford University Press, 1974.
*Africa Yearbook and Who's Who*. London: Africa Journal, 1976.
Andelman, David A. "Profile: Amilcar Cabral." *Africa Report* 15 (May 1970): 18-19.
Arnold, Millard, ed. *Steve Biko: Black Consciousness in South Africa*. New York: Random House, 1978.
Barber, James. *Rhodesia: The Road to Rebellion*. London: Oxford University Press, 1967.
Barnett, Don, and Roy Harvey. *The Revolution in Angola: MPLA Life Histories and Documents*. Indianapolis: Bobbs-Merrill Co., 1972.
Behr, Edward. *The Algerian Problem*. New York: W. W. Norton, 1962.
Bender, Gerald. *Angola Under the Portuguese*. Berkeley: University of California Press, 1978.
Benson, Mary. *Chief Albert Lutuli [Luthuli] of South Africa*. London: Oxford University Press, 1963.
Blackey, Robert. "Fanon and Cabral: A Contrast in Theories of Revolution for Africa." *Journal of Modern African Studies* 12 (1974): 191-209.
Brace, Richard, and Joan Brace. *Ordeal in Algeria*. Princeton: D. Van Nostrand, 1960.
Bromberger, Serge. *Les Rebelles Algériens*. Paris: Librairie Plon, 1958.
Burchett, Wilfred. *Southern Africa Stands Up: The Revolutions in Angola, Mozambique, Zimbabwe, Namibia, and South Africa*. New York: Urizen Books, 1978.
Cabral, Amilcar. *Guinée "Portugaise": Le Pouvoir des Armes*. Paris: François Maspero, 1970.

_____. *Our People are Our Mountains*. London: Committee for Freedom in Mozambique, Angola and Guinea, n.d. [1971?].
_____. *Return to the Sources: Selected Speeches*. Edited by African Information Service. New York: Monthly Review Press, 1976.
_____. *Revolution in Guinea*. New York: Monthly Review Press, 1969.
Callan, Edward. *Albert John Luthuli and the South African Race Conflict*. Kalamazoo, MI: Western Michigan University Press, 1962.
Chabal, Patrick. *Amilcar Cabral*. Cambridge: Cambridge University Press, 1983.
Chaliand, Gérard. *Armed Struggle in Africa*. New York: Monthly Review Press, 1969.
Chilcote, Ronald H. *Emerging Nationalism in Portuguese Africa: Documents*. Stanford: Hoover Institution Press, 1972.
_____. "The Political Thought of Amilcar Cabral." *Journal of Modern African Studies* 6 (1968): 373-88.
_____. *Portuguese Africa*. Englewood Cliffs, NJ: Prentice-Hall, 1967.
_____. *Protest and Resistance in Angola and Brazil*. Berkeley: University of California Press, 1972.
Clark, Michael K. *Algeria in Turmoil: A History of the Rebellion*. New York: Praeger Publishers, 1959.
Courrière, Yves. *Les Fils de la Toussaint*. Paris: Fayard, 1968.
Davezies, Robert. *La Guerre d'Angola*. Bordeaux: Guy Ducros, 1968.
Davidson, Basil. *Angola*. London: Union of Democratic Control, 1961.
_____. *In the Eye of the Storm: Angola's People*. Middlesex, Eng.: Penguin Books, 1975.
_____. *The Liberation of Guiné: Aspects of an African Revolution*. Baltimore: Penguin Books, 1969.
_____. "The Liberation Struggle in Angola and Portuguese Guinea." *Africa Quarterly* 10 (April-June 1970): 25-31.
Davidson, Basil et al. *Southern Africa*. Bungay, Eng.: The Chaucer Press, 1976.
Dickie, John, and Alan Rake. *Who's Who in Africa*. London: African Buyer and Trader, 1973.
*Dictionary of African Biography*. London: Melrose Press, 1971.
DuBois, Shirley G. *Gamal Abdel Nasser: Son of the Nile*. New York: The Third Press, 1972.
Duffy, James. *Portugal in Africa*. Cambridge: Harvard University Press, 1962.
"Eduardo Chitlangu Chivambu Mondlane, 1920-1969" [obituary]. *Genève Afrique* 8 (1969): 46-49.
Estier, Claude. *Pour l'Algérie*. Paris: François Maspero, 1964.
Evans, L. O. *Emerging African Nations and Their Leaders*. 2 vols. Yonkers, NY: Educational Heritage, 1964.
Fernández-Armesto, Felipe. *Sadat and His Statecraft*. London: The Kensal Press, 1982.
Gibson, Richard. *African Liberation Movements: Contemporary Struggles Against White Minority Rule*. London: Oxford University Press, 1972.
Gillespie, Joan. *Algeria: Rebellion and Revolution*. London: Ernest Benn, 1960.
Gordon, David C. *The Passing of French Algeria*. London: Oxford University Press, 1966.

Green, Reginald H. et al., eds. *Namibia: The Last Colony*. Essex, U.K.: Longman Group, 1981.
Grundy, Kenneth W. *Guerrilla Struggle in Africa*. New York: Grossman Publishers, 1971.
Hall, Richard. *Kaunda: Founder of Zambia*. Lusaka: Longmans of Zambia, 1964.
———. *The High Price of Principles: Kaunda and the White South*. New York: Africana Publishing, 1969.
Harcourt, Melville. *Portraits of Destiny*. New York: Sheed and Ward, 1966.
Hatch, John. *Two African Statesmen: Kaunda of Zambia and Nyerere of Tanzania*. London: Secker and Warburg, 1976.
Heggoy, Alf Andrew. *Insurgency and Counterinsurgency in Algeria*. Bloomington: Indiana University Press, 1972.
Heikal, Mohamed. *Autumn of Fury: The Assassination of Sadat*. New York: Random House, 1983.
Henries, A. Doris Bank. *A Biography of President William V. S. Tubman*. London: Macmillan, 1967.
Henriksen, T. H., "The Revolutionary Thought of Eduardo Mondlane." *Genéve Afrique* 12 (1973): 37-52.
Hirst, David, and Irene Beeson. *Sadat*. London: Faber & Faber, 1981.
Horne, Alistair. *A Savage War of Peace: Algeria 1954-1962*. New York: Viking Press, 1977.
Humbaraci, Arslan. *Algeria: A Revolution That Failed*. New York: Praeger Publishers, 1966.
Hymans, Jacques Louis. *Léopold Sédar Senghor: An Intellectual Biography*. Edinburgh, Eng.: Edinburgh University Press, 1971.
Italiaander, Rolf. *The New Leaders of Africa*. Englewood Cliffs: Prentice-Hall, 1961.
Jackson, Robert H., and Carl G. Rosberg. *Personal Rule in Black Africa: Prince, Autocrat, Prophet, Tyrant*. Berkeley: University of California Press, 1982.
Joesten, Joachim. *The New Algeria*. Chicago: Follett Publishing Co., 1964.
———. *Nasser: The Rise to Power*. London: Odhams Press, 1960.
Junod, Violaire I., and Idrian N. Resnick. *The Handbook of Africa*. New York: New York University Press, 1963.
Kaula, Edna M. *Leaders of the New Africa*. New York: World, 1966.
Kaunda, Kenneth D. *A Humanist in Africa*. London: Longmans, Green, 1966.
———. *Zambia Shall be Free: An Autobiography*. London: Heinemann, 1962.
Kitchen, Helen. "Conversation With Eduardo Mondlane." *Africa Report* 12 (November 1967): 31-32, 49-51.
Kraft, Joseph. *The Struggle for Algeria*. New York: Doubleday & Co., 1961.
Kurtz, Laura S. *Historical Dictionary of Tanzania*. Metuchen, N.J.: Scarecrow Press, 1978.
Lacouture, Jean. *Nasser: A Biography*. New York: Alfred A. Knopf, 1973.
Legum, Colin, ed. *Africa Contemporary Record*. London: various publishers, 1968-1979.
Legum, Colin, and Tony Hodges. *After Angola: The War Over Southern Africa*. New York: Americana Publishing Co., 1976.

Legum, Colin, ed. *Zambia: Independence and Beyond: The Speeches of Kenneth Kaunda.* London: Thomas Nelson & Sons, 1966.
Listowel, Judith. *The Meaning of Tanganyika.* London: House & Maxwell, 1965.
Lowenkopf, Martin. *Politics in Liberia: The Conservative Road to Development.* Stanford: Hoover Institution Press, 1976.
Luthuli, Albert. *Let My People Go.* New York: McGraw-Hill, 1962.
Machel, Samora. *Establishing People's Power to Serve the Masses.* Toronto: Toronto Committee for the Liberation of Southern Africa, 1976.
_____. *Mozambique: Revolution or Reaction.* Richmond, B.C.: Liberation Support Movement Press, 1975.
_____. *Mozambique: Sowing the Seeds of Revolution.* London: Committee for the Liberation of Mozambique, Angola, and Guinea, 1974.
_____. *The Tasks Ahead.* New York: Afro-American Information Service, 1975.
MacPherson, Fergus. *Kenneth Kaunda of Zambia: The Times and the Man.* Lusaka, Zambia: Oxford University Press, 1974.
Magubane, Bernard. "Amilcar Cabral: Evolution of Revolutionary Thought." *UFAHAMU* 2 (Fall 1971): 17-87.
Mansfield, Peter. *Nasser.* London: Methuen Educational, 1969.
Marcum, John. *The Angolan Revolution*, vol 1: *The Anatomy of An Explosion.* Cambridge: M.I.T. Press, 1969.
_____. *The Angolan Revolution*, vol. 2: *Exile Politics and Guerrilla Warfare.* Cambridge: M.I.T. Press, 1978.
Markovitz, Irving L. *Léopold Sédar Senghor and the Politics of Negritude.* New York: Atheneum, 1969.
Matthews, Tanya. *War in Algeria: Background for Crisis.* New York: Fordham University Press, 1961.
McCollester, Charles. "The Political Thought of Amilcar Cabral." *Monthly Review* 24 (March 1973): 10-21.
Melady, Thomas P., ed. *Kenneth Kaunda of Zambia: Selections from His Writings.* New York: Frederick A. Praeger, 1964.
_____. *Profiles of African Leaders.* New York: Macmillan, 1961.
Merle, Robert. *Ahmed Ben Bella.* New York: Walker & Co., 1967.
Mondlane, Eduardo. *The Struggle for Mozambique.* Baltimore: Penguin Books, 1969.
Moore, Clement H. *Tunisia Since Independence.* Berkeley: University of California Press, 1965.
Moser, Pierre A. *La Révolution Angolaise.* Tunis: Société d'Edition et de Presse, 1966.
Nash, Rebecca. "Interview with Dr. Masipula Sithole [brother of Ndabaningi Sithole]." Dayton, Ohio: University of Dayton, African Studies Department, November 4, 1977.
Nasser, Gamal Abdel. *Egypt's Liberation: The Philosophy of Revolution.* Introduction by Dorothy Thompson. Washington: Public Affairs Press, 1955.
_____. *The Philosophy of the Revolution.* Cairo: Dar al-Maaref, n.d.
Nyerere, Julius K. *Freedom and Development.* Dar es Salaam: Oxford University Press, 1973.

———. *Freedom and Socialism*. Dar es Salaam: Oxford University Press, 1968.
———. *Freedom and Unity*. Dar es Salaam: Oxford University Press, 1967.
———. *Ujamaa*: *The Basis of African Socialism*. Dar es Salaam: Oxford University Press, 1962.
O'Ballance, Edgar. *The Algerian Insurrection, 1954-1962*. Hamden, CT: Archon Books, 1967.
Ottaway, David, and Marina. *Algeria*: *The Politics of a Socialist Revolution*. Berkeley: University of California Press, 1970.
"Portrait: Portuguese Guinea Rebel [Amilcar Cabral]." *West Africa* (London), April 18, 1964, p. 427.
Quandt, William B. *Revolution and Political Leadership*: *Algeria, 1954-68*. Cambridge: M.I.T. Press, 1969.
*Revolution in Angola*. London: Merlin Press, 1972.
Roder, Wolf, ed. *Voices of Liberation in Southern Africa*. Waltham, MA: African Studies Association, 1972.
Rosberg, Carl G., and William H. Friedland, eds. *African Socialism*. Stanford: Stanford University Press, 1964.
Rotberg, Robert I. "From Moderate to Militant: The Rise of Joshua Nkomo and Southern Rhodesian Nationalism." *African Report* 7 (March 1962): 3-4, 8, 22.
———. *Rebellion in Black Africa*. London: Oxford University Press, 1971.
Rotberg, Robert I., and Ali A. Mazrui, eds. *Protest and Power in Black Africa*. New York: Oxford University Press, 1970.
Sadat, Anwar el-. *In Search of Identity*: *An Autobiography*. New York: Harper & Row, 1977.
———. *Revolution on the Nile*. London: Allan Wingate, 1957.
Segal, Ronald. *African Profiles*. Baltimore, MD: Penguin Books, 1962.
———. *Political Africa*: *A Who's Who of Personalities and Parties*. London: Steven and Sons, 1961.
Senghor, Léopold Sédar. *On African Socialism*. New York: Frederick A. Praeger, 1964.
Shore, Herb. "Mondlane, Machel and Mozambique: From Rebellion to Revolution." *Africa Today* 24 (Winter 1974): 3-12.
Sithole, Ndabaningi. *African Nationalism*. 2nd ed. New York: Oxford University Press, 1968.
———. *Threshold of Revolution*. London: Oxford University Press, 1977.
Smith, William E. *Nyerere of Tanzania*. London: Victor Gollancz, 1973.
Stephane, Roger. *La Tunisie de Bourguiba*. Paris: Librairie Plon, 1958.
Stephens, Robert. *Nasser*: *A Political Biography*. New York: Simon & Schuster, 1971.
Stubbs, Aelred, ed. *Steve Biko*: *I Write What I Like*. London: Bowerdean Press, 1978.
Taylor, Sidney, ed. *The New Africans*. New York: G. P. Putnam's Sons, 1976.
Townsend, E. Reginald. *The Official Papers of William V. S. Tubman, President of the Republic of Liberia*. London: Longmans, Green, 1968.
Vatikiotis, P. J. *Nasser and His Generation*. London: Croom Helm, 1978.

Venter, Al J. *Black Leaders of Southern Africa*. London: Siesta Publications, 1976.
Wheeler, Douglas L., and René Pélissier. *Angola*. New York: Praeger Publishers, 1971.
Wilkinson, Anthony R. *Insurgency in Rhodesia*. London: International Institute for Strategic Studies, 1973.
Woods, Donald. *Biko*. New York: Paddington Press, 1978.
Wynn, Wilton. *Nasser of Egypt*: *The Search for Dignity*. Cambridge, MA: Arlington Books, 1959.

## REGIONAL AND COUNTRY STUDIES: ASIA AND THE MIDDLE EAST

Abu-Lughod, Ibrahim, ed. *The Transformation of Palestine*. Evanston: Northwestern University Press, 1971.
Alami, Musa al-. "The Lesson of Palestine." *Middle East Journal* 3 (1949): 373-405.
Alencastre, Amilcar. *El Fatah: os Comandos Arabes da Palestine*. Rio de Janeiro: Gráfica e Editora Tacaratu Ltda., 1969.
Armstrong, John P. *Sihanouk Speaks*. New York: Walker, 1964.
Ba Maw. "U Nu Psychoanalyzed." *The Nation* (Rangoon), October 11, 1959, pp. 5, 8.
Berkov, Robert. *Strong Man of China*: *The Story of Chiang Kai-shek*. Boston: Houghton Mifflin, 1938.
*Biographical Service*. No. 1-158. Hong Kong: Union Research Service, 1956-1957.
Boorman, Howard L., ed. *Biographical Dictionary of Republican China*. 4 vols. New York: Columbia University Press, 1967-1971.
_____ . "Mao Tse-tung: The Lacquered Image." *The China Quarterly* 16 (November-December 1963): 1-55.
Bouscaren, Anthony T. *The Last of the Mandarins*: *Diem of Vietnam*. Pittsburgh: Duquesne University Press, 1965.
Burchett, Wilfred G. *Mekong Upstream*. Hanoi: Red River Publishing House, 1957.
Butwell, Richard. *U Nu of Burma*. Stanford: Stanford University Press, 1963.
Chaliand, Gérard. *The Palestinian Resistance*. Baltimore: Penguin Books, 1972.
Champassak, Sisouk Na. *Storm Over Laos*: *A Contemporary History*. New York: Frederick A. Praeger, 1961.
Ch'en, Jerome, ed. *Mao*. Englewood Cliffs: Prentice-Hall, 1969.
Ch'en, Jerome. *Mao and the Chinese Revolution*. New York: Oxford University Press, 1967.
Chiang Kai-shek. *China's Destiny*. New York: Roy, 1947.
*Chinese Communist Who's Who*. 2 vols. Taipei: Institute of International Relations, 1971-1972.
Coaley, John. *Green March—Black September*. London: Cass and Co., 1973.
Crozier, Brian. *The Man Who Lost China*. New York: Charles Scribner's Sons, 1967.
Curtis, Michael et al., eds. *The Palestinians*. New Brunswick: Transaction Books, 1975.
Day, Beth. *The Philippines*: *Shattered Showcase for Democracy in Asia*. New York: M. Evans & Co., 1974.

Denoyan, Gilbert. *El Fath Parle*: *Les Palestiniens Contre Israel*. Paris: Editions Albin Michel, 1970.
Dîem, Ngo Dinh. *Major Policy Speeches*. 2nd ed. Saigon: Presidency of the Republic of Vietnam, Press Office, 1956. (Includes brief biographical sketch.)
Dittmer, Lowell. *Liu Shao-ch'i and the Chinese Cultural Revolution*. Berkeley: University of California Press, 1974.
Dobson, Christopher. *Black September*: *Its Short, Violent History*. New York: Macmillan, 1974.
Dommen, Arthur J. *Conflict in Laos*: *The Politics of Neutralization*. Rev. ed. New York: Praeger Publishers, 1971.
Elegant, Robert S. *China's Red Masters*: *Political Biographies of the Chinese Communist Leaders*. New York: Twayne Publishers, 1951.
Emi Siao. *Mao Tse-tung*: *His Childhood and Youth*. Bombay: People's Publishing House, 1953.
Epp, Frank. *The Palestinians*. Scottdale, PA: Herald Press, 1976.
Fall, Bernard B., ed. *Ho Chi Minh on Revolution*. New York: Frederick A. Praeger, 1967.
_____ . *The Two Vietnams*: *A Political and Military Analysis*. 2nd ed. New York: Frederick A. Praeger, 1967.
_____ . *The Viet-Minh Regime*. New York: Institute of Pacific Relations, 1956.
_____ . "Vo Nguyên Giap—Man and Myth." In Giap, *People's War, People's Army*. New York: Frederick A. Praeger, 1962.
Fenn, Charles. *Ho Chi Minh*: *A Biographical Introduction*. New York: Charles Scribner's Sons, 1973.
Furlong, Geoffrey. *Palestine Is My Country*: *The Story of Musa Alami*. New York: Praeger Publishers, 1969.
Furuya, Feiji. *Chiang Kai-shek*: *His Life and Times*. New York: St. John's University Press, 1981.
Hahn, Emily. *Chiang Kai-shek*: *An Unauthorized Biography*. New York: Doubleday, 1955.
_____ . *The Soong Sisters*. New York: Doubleday, Doran & Co., 1941.
Halberstam, David. *Ho*. New York: Random House, 1971.
Hamid, Rashid. "What is the PLO?" *Journal of Palestine Studies* 4 (Summer 1975): 90-122.
Hammer, Ellen J. *The Struggle for Indochina*. Stanford: Stanford University Press, 1954.
Han Suyin. *The Morning Deluge*: *Mao Tse-tung and the Chinese Revolution. 1893-1954*. Boston: Little, Brown, 1972.
_____ . *Wind in the Tower*: *Mao Tse-tung and the Chinese Revolution, 1949-1975*. Boston: Little, Brown, 1976.
Hartzell, Spense. *Marcos of the Philippines*: *A Biography*. New York: World Publishing, 1969.
Heradstveit, Daniel. "A Profile of the Palestine Guerrillas." *Cooperation and Conflict* 7 (1972): 13-36.
Hinton, Harold C. *Leaders of Communist China*. Santa Monica, CA: The RAND Corporation, RM-1845, 1956.
Ho Chi Minh. *Prison Diary*. Hanoi: Foreign Languages Publishing House, 1972.

Holden, David. "Which Arafat?" *New York Times Magazine*, March 20, 1975, pp. 11+.
Honey, P. J. *Communism in North Vietnam*. Cambridge: M.I.T. Press, 1963.
_____. *North Vietnam Today*. New York: Frederick A. Praeger, 1962.
Hsu, Kai-yu. *Chou En-lai: China's Gray Eminence*. New York: Doubleday Anchor Books, 1969.
Hsüeh, Chün-tu, ed. *Revolutionary Leaders of Modern China*. New York: Oxford University Press, 1971.
Hussain, Mehmood. *The Palestine Liberation Organization*. Delhi, India: University Publishers, 1975.
Huyen, N. Khac. *Vision Accomplished? The Enigma of Ho Chi Minh*. New York: Collier Books, 1971.
Juradini, Paul, and William Hazen. *The Palestinian Movement in Politics*. Lexington, MA: Lexington Books, 1976.
Kadi, Leila S., ed. *Basic Political Documents of the Armed Palestinian Resistance Movement*. Beirut: Palestine Liberation Organization Research Center, 1969.
Kazziha, Walid W. *Revolutionary Transformation in the Arab World: Habash and His Comrades from Nationalism to Marxism*. New York: St. Martin's Press, 1975.
Khadduri, Majid. *Arab Contemporaries*. Baltimore: Johns Hopkins University Press, 1973.
Kiernan, Thomas. *Arafat: The Man and the Myth*. New York: W. W. Norton, 1976.
Klein, Donald W., and Ann B. Clark. *Biographic Dictionary of Chinese Communism, 1921-1965*. 2 vols. Cambridge: Harvard University Press, 1971.
Kuo, Warren et al. *Who's Who in Communist China*. Taiwan: Institute of International Relations, 1968.
Lacouture, Jean. *Ho Chi Minh: A Political Biography*. New York: Random House, 1968.
Laffin, John. *Fedayeen: The Arab-Israeli Dilemma*. London: Cassell & Co., 1973.
Langer, Paul F., and Joseph J. Zasloff. *North Vietnam and the Pathet Lao: Partners in Struggle for Laos*. Cambridge: Harvard University Press, 1970.
*Leaders of Communist China*. Washington: U.S. Department of State, Division of Biographic Information, n.d.
Lee, Ming T. "The Founders of the Chinese Communist Party: A Study in Revolutionaries." *Civilisations* 13 (1968): 113-27.
Lesch, Anne Mosely. *Arab Politics in Palestine 1917-1939*. Ithaca: Cornell University Press, 1979.
Lifton, Robert J. *Revolutionary Immortality: Mao Tse-tung and the Chinese Cultural Revolution*. New York: Random House, 1968.
Loh, Pinchon P. Y. *The Early Chiang Kai-shek: A Study of His Personality and Politics*. New York: Columbia University Press, 1971.
Mao Tse-tung. *Selected Works*. 5 vols. Peking: Foreign Languages Press, 1961-1971.
Marcos, Ferdinand E. *The Democratic Revolution in the Philippines*. Englewood Cliffs: Prentice-Hall International, 1974.
Mertz, Anton. "Why George Habash Turned Marxist." *Mid East: A Middle East-North African Review* 11 (August 1970): 31-37.

*The Middle East and North Africa* [Yearbook]. London: Europa Publications, 1948-1978.

Migdal, Joel S. *Palestinian Society and Politics*. Princeton: Princeton University Press, 1980.

Mishal, Shaul. *West Bank/East Bank*. New Haven: Yale University Press, 1978.

Morwood, William. *Duel for the Middle Kingdom: The Struggle Between Chiang Kai-shek and Mao Tse-tung for Control of China*. New York: Everest Books, 1980.

Neumann-Hoditz, Reinhold. *Portrait of Ho Chi Minh*. Hamburg: Herder and Herder, 1972.

Nu, U. "Man, The Wolf of Man." *The Guardian* (Rangoon) 1 (June-October 1954) and 2 (November 1954-January 1955).

_____ . *The People Win Through*. New York: Taplinger Publishing, 1957. (A play with a biographical introduction by Edward Hunter.)

_____ . *U Nu: Saturday's Son* [An Autobiography]. New Haven: Yale University Press, 1975.

O'Ballance, Edgar. *Arab Guerrilla Power, 1967-1972*. London: Faber & Faber, 1974.

O'Neill, Robert J. *General Giap: Politician and Strategist*. New York: Frederick A. Praeger, 1969.

Payne, Robert. *Chiang Kai-shek*. New York: Weybright & Talley, 1969.

_____ . *Mao Tse-tung*. New York: Weybright & Talley, 1969.

Perleberg, Max. *Who's Who in Modern China*. Hong Kong: Ye Olde Printerie, 1954.

"Profiles [of Vietnamese Leaders]." Portion of a typescript (pp. 25-50) supplied by Vietnam Working Group, U.S. Department of State, Washington, 1973.

Pye, Lucian W. *Mao Tse-tung: The Man in the Leader*. New York: Basic Books, 1976.

Quandt, William B. et al. *The Politics of Palestinian Nationalism*. Berkeley: University of California Press, 1973.

Sainteny, Jean. *Ho Chi Minh and His Vietnam: A Personal Memoir*. Chicago: Cowles Book Co., 1972.

Scalapino, Robert A., ed. *The Communist Revolution in Asia*. 2nd ed. Englewood Cliffs: Prentice Hall, 1969.

Schiff, Zeev, and Raphael Rothstein. *Fedayeen: Guerrillas Against Israel*. New York: David McKay, 1972.

Schram, Stuart. *Mao Tse-tung*. Baltimore: Penguin Books, 1967.

_____ . *The Political Thought of Mao Tse-tung*. Rev. Ed. New York: Frederick A. Praeger, 1969.

Seagrave, Sterling. *The Soong Dynasty*. New York: Harper & Row, 1985.

Sharabi, H. B. *Nationalism and Revolution in the Arab World*. Princeton: D. Van Nostrand, 1966.

Shimoni, Jaacov, and E. Levine. *Political Dictionary of the Middle East in the 20th Century*. New York: Quadrangle Books, 1974.

Silverstein, Joseph. *Burmese Politics: The Dilemma of National Unity*. New Brunswick: Rutgers University Press, 1980.

Smedley, Agnes. *The Great Road: The Life and Times of Chu Teh*. New York: Monthly Review Press, 1956.

Snow, Edgar. *Red Star Over China* [1938]. New York: Grove Press, 1961.
Spencer, Cornelia. *Three Sisters*. New York: John Day, 1939.
Tinker, Hugh. "Nu, The Serene Statesman." *Pacific Affairs* 30 (June 1957): 120-37.
Tong, Hollington K. *Chiang Kai-shek*. Taipei: China Publishing Co., 1953.
Vatikiotis, P. J., ed. *Revolution in the Middle East*. Totowa, NJ: Rowman and Littlefield, 1972.
Vo Nguyên Giap. *Banner of People's War, the Party's Military Line*. New York: Praeger Publishers, 1970.
_____. *Big Victory, Great Task*. New York: Frederick A. Praeger, 1968.
_____. *The Military Art of People's War*. New York: Monthly Review Press, 1970.
_____. *People's War, People's Army*. New York: Frederick A. Praeger, 1962.
Wales, Nym. *Red Dust: Autobiographies of Chinese Communists as Told to Nym Wales*. Stanford: Stanford University Press, 1952.
Walinsky, Louis J. "The Rise and Fall of U Nu." *Pacific Affairs* 38 (1965-1966): 269-81.
Warner, Denis. *The Last Confucian*. New York: Macmillan, 1963.
*Who's Who in Communist China*. Hong Kong: Union Research Institute, 1966.
*Who's Who in Communist China*. 2 vols. Hong Kong: Union Research Institute, 1969-1970.
*Who's Who of the Republic of South Vietnam*. Saigon: Editions Giai Phong, 1969.
Yaari, Ehud. *Strike Terror: The Story of Fatah*. New York: Sabra Books, 1970.
Zasloff, Joseph J. *The Pathet Lao: Leadership and Organization*. Lexington, MA: Lexington Books, 1973.

## REGIONAL AND COUNTRY STUDIES: LATIN AMERICA

Alexander, Robert J. *Bolivia: Past, Present, and Future of its Politics*. New York: Praeger Publishers, 1982.
_____. *The Bolivian National Revolution*. New Brunswick: Rutgers University Press, 1958.
_____. *Prophets of Revolution: Profiles of Latin American Leaders*. New York: Macmillan, 1962.
Alexandre, Marianne, ed. *Viva Che! Contributions in Tribute to Ernesto "Che" Guevara*. New York: E. P. Dutton & Co., 1968.
Alphonse, Max. *Guerrillas in Latin America*. The Hague: International Documentation and Information Center, 1971.
Alvarez Garcia, John, ed. *Camilo Torres: Biographia, Platforma, Mensajes, Medellin*. Bogotá: Ediciones Carpel-Antorcha, n.d. (1966?).
Alvarez Garcia, John, and Christian Restrepo Calle, eds. *Camilo Torres: Priest and Revolutionary*. London: Sheed & Ward, 1968.
Añi Castillo, Gonzalo. *Historia Secreta de las Guerrillas*. Lima: Ediciones "Mas Alla," 1967.
Bambirra, Vanie et al. *Diez Años de Insurrección en América Latina*. Santiago, Chile: Ediciones Prensa Latinoamericana, 1971.
Batista, Fulgencio. *Cuba Betrayed*. New York: Vantage Press, 1962.
_____. *The Growth and Decline of the Cuban Republic*. New York: Devin-Adair, 1964.

Bibliography 169

Beals, Carleton. "Fulgencio Batista." In *Dictators and Democrats*, L. Fernworthy, ed. New York: Robert M. McBride & Co., 1941.
Belaúnde Terry, Fernando. *Peru's Own Conquest*. Lima: American Studies Press, 1965.
Blanco, Hugo. *El Camino de Nuestra Revolución*. Lima: Revolución Peruana, 1964.
_____. *Land or Death: The Peasant Struggle in Peru*. New York: Pathfinder Press, 1972.
_____. *Workers and Peasant to Power!: A Revolutionary Program for Peru*. New York: Pathfinder Press, 1978.
Bonachea, Rolando E., and Nelson Q. Valdés, eds. *Che: The Selected Works of Ernesto Guevara*. Cambridge: M.I.T. Press, 1969.
_____. *Revolutionary Struggle, 1947-1958: The Selected Works of Fidel Castro*, vol. 1. Cambridge: M.I.T. Press, 1972.
Bourne, Richard. *Political Leaders of Latin America*. Baltimore: Penguin Books, 1969.
Bourricaud, François. *Power and Society in Contemporary Peru*. New York: Praeger Publishers, 1970.
Broderick, Walter J. *Camilo Torres: A Biography of the Priest-Guerrillero*. New York: Doubleday & Co., 1975.
*Carlos Marighella* [biography and selected writings]. Havana: Tricontinental, 1970.
Castro, Fidel. *History Will Absolve Me*. New York: Fair Play for Cuba Committee, 1961.
_____. *The Road to Revolution in Latin America*. New York: Pioneer Publishers, 1963.
Casuso, Teresa. *Cuba and Castro*. Trans. from the Spanish by Elmer Grossberg. New York: Random House, 1961.
Chester, Edmund A. *A Sergeant Named Batista*. New York: Henry Holt, 1954.
Costa, Omard. *Los Tupamaros*. México: Ediciones Era, 1971.
Davis, Harold E. *Makers of Democracy in Latin America*. New York: W. H. Wilson Co., 1945.
_____. *Revolutionaries, Traditionalists, and Dictators in Latin America*. New York: Cooper Square Publishers, 1973.
De la Puente Uceda, Luis. "The Peruvian Revolution: Concepts and Perspectives." *Monthly Review* 17 (November 1965): 12-28.
Del Corro, Alejandro, ed. *Camilo Torres: Un Simbolo Controvertido 1962-1967*. Guernavaca: Centro Intercultural de Documentacion, 1967.
Díaz Machiaco, Porfirio. *Historia de Bolivia: Peñaranda, 1940-1943*. La Paz: Editorial JUVENTUD, 1958.
Dix, Robert H. *Colombia: The Political Dimensions of Change*. New Haven: Yale University Press, 1967.
*Dos Rebeldes: Camilo Torres/Carlos Marighella*. Lima: n.p., 1970.
Draper, Theodore. *Castroism: Theory and Practice*. New York: Frederick A. Praeger, 1965.
_____. *Castro's Revolution: Myths and Realities*. New York: Frederick A. Praeger, 1962.
Dubois, Jules. *Fidel Castro: Rebel-Liberator or Dictator?* Indianapolis: Bobbs-Merrill Co., 1959.

Ebon, Martin. *Che: The Making of a Legend*. New York: Universe Books, 1969.
Fellman Velarde, José. *Víctor Paz Estenssoro: El Hombre y la Revolución*. La Paz: Alfonso Tejerina, 1954.
Fiechter, Gewges-André. *Brazil Since 1964: Modernization Under a Military Regime*. London: Macmillan, 1975.
Fluharty, Vernon L. *Dance of the Millions: Military Rule and Social Revolution in Colombia, 1930-1956*. Pittsburgh: University of Pittsburgh Press, 1957.
Frei, Eduardo. *Latin America: The Hopeful Option*. Maryknoll, NY: Orbis Books, 1978.
Gadea Acosta, Ricardo. "Luis de la Puente: To the Measure of Peru." *Tri-Continental* (Havana) 4-5 (1968): 47-55.
Gadea, Hilda. *Ernesto: A Memoir of Che Guevara*. New York: Doubleday & Co., 1972.
Gally, Hector, ed. *Camilo Torres: Con las Armas en la Mano*. Mexico City: Editorial Diógenes, 1971.
Gerassi, John, ed. *Revolutionary Priest: The Complete Writings and Messages of Camilo Torres*. Middlesex, Eng.: Penguin Books, 1973.
───. *Venceremos! The Speeches and Writings of Ernesto Che Guevara*. New York: Macmillan, 1968.
Gil, Federico G. *The Political System of Chile*. Boston: Houghton Mifflin, 1966.
Gilio, Maria, Esther. *The Tupamaro Guerrillas*. New York: Balantine Books, 1973.
Gonzales, Luis J., and Gustavo A. Sanchez Salazar. *The Great Rebel: Che Guevara in Bolivia*. New York: Grove Press, 1969.
Gott, Richard. *Guerrilla Movements in Latin America*. New York: Anchor Press, 1972.
Gross, Leonard. *The Last Best Hope: Eduardo Frei and Chilean Democracy*. New York: Random House, 1967.
Guevara, Ernesto. *Guerrilla Warfare*. New York: Vintage Books, 1961.
───. *Reminiscences of the Cuban Revolutionary War*. New York: Grove Press, 1968.
Guzmán, Germán. *Camilo Torres*. New York: Sheed & Ward, 1969.
Guzmán Campos, Germán. *El Padre Camilo Torres*. Mexico City: Siglo XXI Editores, 1968.
Habegger, Norberto. *Camilo Torres: El Cura Guerrillero*. Buenos Aires: A. Peña Lillo, 1967.
Halperin, Ernst. *Nationalism and Communism in Chile*. Cambridge: M.I.T. Press, 1965.
───. *Terrorism in Latin America*. Beverly Hills: Sage Publications, 1976.
Harris, Richard. *Death of a Revolutionary: Che Guevara's Last Mission*. New York: W. W. Norton & Co., 1970.
Hilton, Ronald. *Who's Who in Latin America, Part III: Columbia, Ecuador, and Venezuela*. Stanford: Stanford University Press, 1951.
───. *Who's Who in Latin America, Part IV: Bolivia, Chile, and Peru*. Stanford: Stanford University Press, 1947.
───. *Who's Who in Latin America, Part VI: Brazil*. Stanford: Stanford University Press, 1948.
*Homenaje a Luis de la Puente*. Habana: Universidad de la Habana, 1966.

Horowitz, Irving Louis et al., eds. *Latin American Radicalism*. New York: Vintage Books, 1969.
Huberman, Leo, and Paul M. Sweezy, eds. *Régis Debray and the Latin American Revolution*. New York: Monthly Review Press, 1968.
"Hugo Blanco: Peru's Most Successful Reformer." *Atlas* 19 (April 1970): 56-57.
James, Daniel, ed. *The Complete Bolivian Diaries of Che Guevara and Other Captured Documents*. New York: Stein & Day, 1968.
Kantor, Harry. *Patterns of Politics and Political Systems in Latin America*. Chicago: Rand McNally, 1969.
Kenner, Martin, and James Petras, ed. *Castro Speaks*. New York: Grove Press, 1969.
Klein, Herbert S. *Bolivia: The Evolution of a Multi-Ethnic Society*. New York: Oxford University Press, 1982.
_____. *Parties and Political Change in Bolivia, 1880-1952*. Cambridge, Eng.: Cambridge University Press, 1969.
Kohl, James, and John Litt. *Urban Guerrilla Warfare in Latin America*. Cambridge: M.I.T. Press, 1974.
Kuczynski, Pedro-Pablo. *Peruvian Democracy Under Economic Stress: An Account of the Belaúnde Administration, 1963-1968*. Princeton: Princeton University Press, 1977.
Labrousse, Alain. *Les Tupamaros: Guérilla Urbaine un Uruguay*. Paris: Editions du Seuil, 1971.
_____. *The Tupamaros: Urban Guerrillas in Uruguay*. Middlesex, Eng.: Penguin Books, 1973.
*Las Guerrillas en el Perú y su Repression*. Lima: Ministerio de Guerra, 1966.
Lecca, Alcantara L. *Diccionario Biográfico de Figuras de Actualidad*. La Paz: Litografias e Imprentas Unidas, 1929.
Lockwood, Lee. *Castro's Cuba, Cuba's Fidel*. New York: Macmillan, 1967.
Lowenthal, Abraham F. *The Peruvian Experiment: Continuity and Change Under Military Rule*. Princeton: Princeton University Press, 1975.
Maldonado, Oscar et al. *Camilo Torres: Christianismo y Revolución*. Mexico City: Ediciones Era, 1970.
Mallin, Jay, ed. *Che Guevara on Revolution*. New York: Dell Publishing Co., 1969.
Malloy, James M. *Bolivia: The Uncompleted Revolution*. Pittsburgh: University of Pittsburgh Press, 1970.
Malpica, Mario Antonio. *Biografia de la Revolución: Historia y Antología del Pensamiento Socialista*. Lima: Ediciones Ensayos Sociales, 1967.
Marighella, Carlos. *Acción Libertadora*. Paris: François Maspero, 1970.
_____. *For the Liberation of Brazil*. Middlesex, Eng.: Penguin Books, 1971.
_____. *La Guerra Revolucionaria*. 2nd ed. Mexico City: Editorial Diógenes, 1971.
Marrett, Robert. *Peru*. New York: Praeger Publishers, 1969.
Martin, Dolores Moyano. "A Memoir of the Young Guevara." *New York Times Magazine*. August 18, 1968, pp. 48 plus.
Martin, Michael R., and Gabriel H. Lovett. *An Encyclopedia of Latin American History*. New York: Abelard-Schuman, 1956.
Martin, Michael R. et al. *Encyclopedia of Latin American History*. Indianapolis: Bobbs-Merrill, 1968.

Martin, Percy A. "The Career of José Batlle y Ordóñez." *Hispanic American Historical Review* 10 (November 1930): 413-28.
Matthews, Herbert L. *Fidel Castro*. New York: Simon & Schuster, 1969.
Maullin, Richard. *Soldiers, Guerrillas, and Politics in Colombia*. Lexington, MA: Lexington Books, 1973.
Max, Alphonse. *Tupamaros: A Pattern of Urban Guerrilla Warfare in Latin America*. The Hague: International Documentation and Information Centre, 1970.
Mercader, Antonio. *Tupamaros: Estrategia y Acción*. Montevideo: Editorial Alfa, 1969.
Mercado, Rogger. *Las Guerrillas del Perú*. Lima: Fondo de Cultura Popular, 1967.
Mercier Vega, Luis. *Guerrillas in Latin America*. New York: Frederick A. Praeger, 1969.
Nuñez, Carlos. *Los Tupamaros: Vanguardia Armada en Uruguay*. Montevideo: Provincias Unidas, 1969.
Ostria Gutiérrez, Alberto. *The Tragedy of Bolivia: A People Crucified*. New York: Devin-Adair, 1958.
Palmer, David S. *Peru: The Authoritarian Tradition*. New York: Praeger Publishers, 1980.
Pareja, Carlos H. *El Padre Camilo: El Cura Guerrillero*. Mexico City: Editorial Nuestra América, 1968.
Patch, Richard W. "The Last of Bolivia's MNR." *AUFS Reports: West Coast South America Series*, vol. 11. New York: American Universities Field Staff, 1964.
———. "Personalities and Politics in Bolivia." *AUFS Reports: West Coast South America Series*, vol. 9. New York: American Universities Field Staff, 1962.
Payne, James L. *Patterns of Conflict in Colombia*. New Haven: Yale University Press, 1968.
Perry y Cía, Oliverio, ed. *Quién es Quién en Colombia*. 2nd ed. Bogotá: n.p., 1948.
Petras, James. *Politics and Social Structure in Latin America*. New York: Monthly Review Press, 1970.
Petras, James, and Maurice Zeitlin, eds. *Latin America: Reform or Revolution?* New York: Fawcett Books, 1968.
Porzecanski, Arturo C. *Uruguay's Tupamaros*. New York: Praeger Publishers, 1973.
Quartim, Jõao. *Dictatorship and Armed Struggle in Brazil*. New York: Monthly Review Press, 1971.
*Quién es Quién en Bolivia*. La Paz: Quién es Quién en Bolivia, 1959.
Rojo, Ricardo. *My Friend Che*. New York: Dial Press, 1968.
Sauvage, Leo. *Che Guevara: The Failure of a Revolutionary*. Englewood Cliffs: Prentice-Hall, 1973.
Scheer, Robert, ed. *The Diary of Che Guevara*. New York: Bantam Books, 1969.
Sinclair, Andrew. *Che Guevara*. New York: Viking Press, 1970.
Stallings, Barbara. *Class Conflict and Economic Development in Chile, 1958-1973*. Stanford: Stanford University Press, 1978.
Stepan, Alfred, ed. *Authoritarian Brazil: Origins, Policies, and Future*. New Haven: Yale University Press, 1973.

Stephens, Richard H. *Wealth and Power in Peru*. Metuchen, NJ: Scarecrow Press, 1971.
Torres, Camilo. *Revolutionary Writings*. London: Herder & Herder, 1969.
Vanger, Milton J. *José Batlle y Ordóñez of Uruguay*: *The Creator of His Time, 1902-1907*. Cambridge, MA: Harvard University Press, 1963.
_____. *The Model Country*: *José Batlle y Ordóñez of Uruguay, 1907-1915*. Hanover, NH: University Press of New England, 1980.
Villanueva, Victor. *Hugo Blanco y la Rebellión Campesina*. Lima: Editorial Juan Meija Baca, 1967.
Watt, Stewart, and Harold F. Peterson. *Builders of Latin America*. New York: Harper & Bros., 1942.
Wilkerson, Loree A. R. *Fidel Castro's Political Programs from Reformism to "Marxism-Leninism."* Gainesville: University of Florida Press, 1965.

## REGIONAL AND COUNTRY STUDIES: EUROPE AND NORTH AMERICA

Abbott, Wilbur C., ed. *Writings and Speeches of Oliver Cromwell*. 3 vols. Cambridge: Harvard University Press, 1937.
Adamson, J. H., and J. F. Folland. *Sir Henry Vane*: *His Life and Times, 1613-1662*. Boston: Bambit, 1973.
Alec-Tweedie, E. *The Maker of Modern Mexico* [Díaz]. New York: John Lane Co., 1906.
Alvarez, Alfredo. *Madero y su obra*. Mexico City: Talleres Graficos de la Nacion, 1935.
*Appleton's Encyclopedia of American Biography*. James G. Wilson, et al. eds. 8 vols. New York: Appleton & Co., 1888-1918.
Ashley, Maurice P. *Cromwell*. Englewood Cliffs: Prentice-Hall, 1969.
_____. *The Greatness of Oliver Cromwell*. London: Hodder & Stoughton, 1957.
_____. *Oliver Cromwell*: *The Conservative Dictator*. London: J. Cape, 1937.
_____. *Rupert of the Rhine*. London: Hart Davis, MacGibbon, 1976.
Aulard, A. *The French Revolution*. 4 vols. New York: Charles Scribner's Sons, 1910.
Bailyn, Bernard. *The Ideological Origins of the American Revolution*. Cambridge: Harvard University Press, 1967.
_____. *The Ordeal of Thomas Hutchinson*. Cambridge: Harvard University Press, 1974.
Balabanoff, Angelica. *Impressions of Lenin*. Ann Arbor: University of Michigan Press, 1964.
Baldwin, Ernest H. "Joseph Galloway: The Loyalist Politician." *Pennsylvania Magazine of History and Biography* 26 (1902): 161-91, 289-321, 417-42.
Barthou, L. *Mirabeau*. London: Heinemann, 1913.
Basily, Nicholas de. *Memoirs*. Stanford: Hoover Institution Press, 1973.
Bax, Ernest B. *Jean Paul Marat*: *The People's Friend*. Boston: Small, 1901.
Beal, John R. *Pearson of Canada*. New York: Duell, Sloan, and Pearce, 1965.
Beals, Carleton. *Porfirio Díaz*: *Dictator of Mexico*. Philadelphia: J. B. Lippincott Co., 1932.

Beeman, Richard R. *Patrick Henry: A Biography*. New York: McGraw-Hill Book Co., 1974.

Beesley, A. H., *The Life of Danton*. London: Longman's, Green & Co., 1899.

Bellamy, Francis R. *The Private Life of George Washington*. New York: Crowell Publishing Co., 1951.

Belloc, Hilaire. *Danton: A Study*. New York: Charles Scribner's Sons, 1899.

Bence-Jones, Mark. *The Cavaliers*. London: Constable & Co., 1976.

Beraud, Henry. *Twelve Portraits of the French Revolution*. Boston: Little, Brown, 1928.

Berkin, Carol. *Jonathan Sewall: Odyssey of an American Loyalist*. New York: Columbia University Press, 1974.

Bingham, Clive. *The Chief Ministers of England, 920-1720*. New York: E. P. Dutton, 1923.

*Biographical Dictionary of American Colonial and Revolutionary Governors, 1607-1789*. Westport, CT: Meckler Books, 1980.

*Biographical Dictionary of World War One*. Edited by Holger H. Hernig and Neil M. Heyman. Westport, CT: Greenwood Press, 1982.

Boorstein, Daniel J. *The Lost World of Thomas Jefferson*. Boston: Beacon Press, 1963.

Borden, Morton. *George Washington*. Englewood Cliffs: Prentice-Hall, 1969.

Bordiaev, Nikolai A. *The Russian Revolution*. Ann Arbor: University of Michigan Press, 1961.

Bourne, Edward C. E. *The Anglicanism of William Laud*. London: Society for Promoting Christian Knowledge, 1947.

Bowen, Catherine D. *John Adams and the American Revolution*. Boston: Little, Brown, 1950.

Braddy, Haldeen. *Cock of the Walk: The Legend of Pancho Villa*. Albuquerque: University of New Mexico Press, 1955.

Brett, Sidney R. *John Pym, 1583-1643: The Statesman of the Puritan Revolution*. London: J. Murray, 1940.

Brodie, Fawn M. *Thomas Jefferson: An Intimate History*. New York: W. W. Norton, 1974.

Brooke, John. *King George III*. London: Constable & Co., 1972.

Brown, Wallace. *The Good Americans: The Loyalists in the American Revolution*. New York: William Morrow & Co., 1969.

Burghclere, Lady Winifred. *Strafford*. 2 vols. London: Macmillan, 1931.

Butterfield, L. H., ed. *Diary and Autobiography of John Adams*. 3 vols. Cambridge: Harvard University Press, 1961.

──────. *The Earliest Diary of John Adams*. Cambridge: Harvard University Press, 1966.

Calhoun, Robert M. *The Loyalists in Revolutionary America 1760-1781*. New York: Harcourt Brace Jovanovich, 1965.

Camp, Roderic A. *Mexican Political Biographies, 1935-1981*. 2nd ed. Tucson: University of Arizona Press, 1982.

Canfield, Cass. *Samuel Adams's Revolution 1765-1776*. New York: Harper & Row, 1976.

Cannon, John. *The Noble Lord in the Blue Ribbon* [Lord North]. London: The Historical Society, 1970.

# Bibliography

———. "Lord North." In *The Prime Ministers*, vol. 1, Herbert Van Thall, ed. London: George Allen & Unwin, 1974.
Carr, Edward Hallett. *The Bolshevik Revolution, 1917-1923*. Vol. 1. New York: Macmillan, 1951.
Chamberlin, William Henry. *The Russian Revolution, 1917-1921*. 2 vols. New York: Macmillan, 1935.
Chinard, Gilbert. *Honest John Adams*. Boston: Little, Brown, 1933.
Christopher, Robert. *Danton: A Biography*. New York: Doubleday & Co., 1967.
Clarendon, Earl of. *Clarendon: Selections from "The History of the Rebellion and Civil Wars" and "The Life by Himself."* London: Oxford University Press, 1955.
Cobban, Alfred. *The Social Interpretation of the French Revolution*. Cambridge: Cambridge University Press, 1965.
Cockcroft, James D. *Intellectual Precursors of the Mexican Revolution 1900-1913*. Austin: University of Texas Press, 1968.
Cocks, H. F. L. *The Religious Life of Oliver Cromwell*. London: The Independent Press, 1960.
Coffin, Robert P. T. *Laud: Storm Center of Stuart England*. New York: Brentano's, 1930.
Collins, William, ed. *Archbishop Laud Commemoration, 1895*. New York: Burt Franklin, 1969.
Coltman, Irene. *Private Men and Public Causes: Philosophy and Politics in the English Civil War*. London: Faber & Faber, 1962.
Conquest, Robert. *V. I. Lenin*. New York: Viking Press, 1972.
Conroy, Mary S. *Peter Arkadievich Stolypin: Practical Politics in Late Tsarist Russia*. Boulder, CO: Westview Press, 1976.
Corbin, John. *The Unknown Washington*. New York: Charles Scribner's Sons, 1930.
Craik, Sir Henry. *The Life of Edward, Earl of Clarendon*. 2 vols. London: Smith, Elder & Co., 1911.
Creelman, James. *Díaz: Master of Mexico*. New York: D. Appleton & Co., 1911.
Cronin, Vincent. *Louis and Antoinette*. London: William Collins & Sons, 1974.
Cumberland, Charles C. *Mexican Revolution: Genesis Under Madero*. Austin: University of Texas Press, 1952.
Dakin, Douglas. *Turgot and the Ancient Régime in France*. London: Methuen & Co., 1939.
De Jouvenel, Henry. *The Stormy Life of Mirabeau*. New York: Book League of America, 1929.
Deutscher, Isaac. *Lenin's Childhood*. London: Oxford University Press, 1970.
———. *The Prophet Armed: Trotsky, 1879-1921*. New York: Oxford University Press, 1954.
———. *Stalin: A Political Biography*. New York: Oxford University Press, 1949.
*Dictionary of American Biography*. Allen Johnson et al., eds. 16 vols. New York: Charles Scribner's Sons, 1927-1981.
*Dictionary of National Biography*. George Smith et al., eds. 22 vols. New York: Oxford University Press, 1917-1965.
Dill, Alonzo T. *Governor Tryon and His Palace*. Chapel Hill: University of North Carolina Press, 1955.

Drinkwater, John. *John Hampden's England*. London: Thorton, Butterworth, 1933.
_____ . *Oliver Cromwell: A Character Study*. New York: Doubleday & Co., Inc., 1927.
Dromundo, Baltasar. *Vida de Emiliano Zapata: Biográfia*. Mexico City, 1934.
Fallows, Samuel. *Sam Adams: A Character Sketch*. New York: Instructor Publishing Co., 1958.
Faÿ, Bernard. *Louis XVI*. Chicago: Henry Regnery Co., 1968.
Ferling, John E. *The Loyalist Mind: Joseph Galloway and the American Revolution*. University Park: Pennsylvania State University Press, 1977.
Firth, Charles H. *Oliver Cromwell and the Rule of the Puritans in England*. New York: G. P. Putnam's Sons, 1900.
Fischer, Louis. *The Life of Lenin*. New York: Harper & Row, 1964.
Flexner, James T. *George Washington*. . . . 4 vols. Boston: Little, Brown, 1965-1972.
Flick, Alexander C. *Loyalism in New York During the American Revolution*. New York: Columbia University Press, 1902.
Fraser, Antonia. *Cromwell: The Lord Protector*. New York: Alfred A. Knopf, 1973.
Gardiner, Samuel R. *Cromwell's Place in History*. London: Longman, Green & Co., 1910.
_____ . *The First Two Stuarts and the Puritan Revolution*. London: Longman, Green & Co., 1888.
_____ . *History of the Great Civil War, 1642-1649*. 4 vols. London: Longman, Green & Co., 1893.
_____ . *Oliver Cromwell*. London: Goupil and Co., 1899.
Gill, Carlos B., ed. *The Age of Porfirio Diaz*. Albuquerque: University of New Mexico Press, 1977.
Gosselin, L. T. *Robespierre's Rise and Fall*. London: Hutchinson & Co., 1927.
Gottschalk, Louis R. *Jean Paul Marat: A Study in Radicalism*. New York: Benjamin Blom, 1966.
Graves, J. T. et al., eds. *Eloquent Sons of the South*, vol. 1. Boston: Chapple Publishing Co., 1909.
Gurko, Vladimir I. *Features and Figures of the Past: Government and Opinion in the Reign of Nicholas II*. Stanford: Stanford University Press, 1939.
Guzmán, Martín Luis. *The Memoirs of Pancho Villa*. Austin: University of Texas Press, 1965.
Haddox, John H. *Vasconcelos of Mexico: Philosopher and Prophet*. Austin: University of Texas Press, 1967.
Hall, E. B. *The Life of Mirabeau*. New York: G. P. Putnam's Sons, 1912.
Hannay, David. *Dîaz*. New York: Henry Holt, 1917.
Haraszti, Zoltan. *John Adams and the Prophets of Progress*. Cambridge: Harvard University Press, 1952.
Harbron, John D. *This Is Trudeau*. Don Mills, Ontario: Longmans Canada, 1968.
Hare, Richard. *Portraits of Russian Personalities Between Reform and Revolution*. London: Oxford University Press, 1959.
Harlow, Ralph V. *Samuel Adams: Promoter of the American Revolution*. New York: Henry Holt & Co., 1923.

D'Haussonville, Vicomte. *The Salon of Madame Necker*. 2 vols. London: Chapman & Hall, 1882.
Hérbert, Jacques, and Pierre Elliott Trudeau. *Two Innocents in Red China*. Toronto: Oxford University Press, 1968.
Hexter, J. H. *The Reign of King Pym*. London: Oxford University Press, 1941.
Hill, Christopher. *God's Englishman: Oliver Cromwell and the English Revolution*. New York: Dial Press, 1970.
──────. *Lenin and the Russian Revolution*. New York: Macmillan, 1950.
──────. *Puritanism and Revolution*. London: Secker and Warburg, 1958.
──────. *The World Turned Upside Down: Radical Ideas During the English Revolution*. New York: Viking Press, 1972.
Hilton, Ronald. *Who's Who in Latin America, Part I: Mexico*. Stanford: Stanford University Press, 1945.
Hingley, Ronald. *Joseph Stalin: Man and Legend*. London: Hutchinson and Co., 1974.
Hodgson, W. B. *Turgot: His Life, Times, and Opinions*. London: Trubner & Co., 1870.
Hosmer, James K. *The Life of Thomas Hutchinson*. Boston: Houghton Mifflin, 1896.
──────. *Samuel Adams*. Baltimore: Johns Hopkins University Press, 1884.
──────. *Young Sir Henry Vane*. Boston: Houghton Mifflin and Co., 1899.
Hutton, William H. *William Laud*. Boston: Houghton Mifflin, 1895.
Iswolsky, Alexander. *Recollections of a Foreign Minister*. New York: Doubleday, Page & Co., 1921.
Jameson, J. Franklin. *The American Revolution Considered as a Social Movement*. Princeton: Princeton University Press, 1967.
Jensen, Merrill. *The Founding of a Nation*. New York: Oxford University Press, 1968.
Jolly, Pierre. *Necker*. Paris: Les Oeuvres Françaises, 1947.
Judson, Margaret A. *The Political Thought of Sir Henry Vane the Younger*. Philadelphia: University of Pennsylvania Press, 1969.
Kalmykow, Andrew D. *Memoirs of a Russian Diplomat: Outposts of the Empire 1893-1917*. New Haven: Yale University Press, 1971.
Keys, Alice M. *Cadwallader Colden: A Representative Eighteenth Century Official*. New York: Columbia University Press, 1906.
Knollenberg, Bernhard. *George Washington: The Virginia Period, 1732-1775*. Durham: Duke University Press, 1964.
──────. *Washington and the Revolution: A Reappraisal*. New York: Macmillan, 1940.
Koch, Adrienne. *The Philosophy of Thomas Jefferson*. Gloucester, MA: Peter Smith Publishers, 1957.
Korngold, Ralph. *Robespierre and the Fourth Estate*. New York: Modern Age Books, 1941.
Krupskaya, N. K. *Reminiscences of Lenin*. New York: International Publishers, 1970.
Kuntzleman, Oliver C. *Joseph Galloway: Loyalist*. Philadelphia: Temple University, 1941.

Lacey, Robert. *Robert, Earl of Essex*. New York: Atheneum Press, 1971.
Lefebvre, Georges. *The Coming of the French Revolution*. Princeton: Princeton University Press, 1947.
_____. *The French Revolution: From Its Origins to 1783*. New York: Columbia University Press, 1962.
Lenin, V. I. *Selected Works*. 12 vols. New York: International Publishers, 1943.
Lewis, George Henry. *The Life of Maximilien Robespierre*. London: Chapman and Hall, 1899.
Lister, Thomas H. *Life and Administration of Edward, First Earl of Clarendon*. 3 vols. London: Longman, Green & Co., 1838.
Lodge, Eleanor C. *Sully, Colbert, and Turgot: A Chapter in French Economic History*. Port Washington, NH: Kennikat Press, 1970.
Lucas, Reginald. *Lord North 1732-1792*. 2 vols. London: Arthur L. Humphreys, 1913.
Luckett, Richard. *The White Generals: An Account of the White Movement and the Russian Civil War*. London: Longman, 1971.
Macdiarmid, John. *Lives of British Statesmen*. London: Longman, Hurst, Reese and Orme, 1807.
Madelin, Louis. *Danton*. New York: Alfred A. Knopf, 1921.
_____. *Figures of the Revolutions*. Freeport, NY: Books for Libraries Press, 1968.
Madero, Francisco I. "Mis Memorias." *Anales del Museo Nacional de Arquelogia Historia y Etnografia*, Mexico City, 1922.
Magaña, Gildardo. *Emiliano Zapata y el Agrarismo en México*. 3 vols. Mexico City, 1938.
Maier, Pauline. *The Old Revolutionaries: Political Lives in the Age of Samuel Adams*. New York: Knopf, 1980.
Malone, Dumas. *Jefferson and His Times*. 6 vols. Boston: Little, Brown, 1952-1981.
Margaret, Duchess of Newcastle. *The Life of William Cavendish, Duke of Newcastle* [1667]. Ed. by C. H. Firth. 2nd ed. London: George Routledge & Sons, n.d. [1906].
Mathiez, Albert. *The French Revolution*. New York: Knopf, 1928.
*McGraw-Hill Encyclopedia of Russia and the Soviet Union*. Edited by Michael T. Florinsky. New York: McGraw-Hill, 1961.
Meade, Robert. *Patrick Henry: Patriot in the Making*. Philadelphia: J. B. Lippincott Co., 1957.
Mehlinger, Howard D., and John M. Thompson. *Count Witte and the Tsarist Government in the 1905 Revolution*. Bloomington: Indiana University Press, 1972.
Mignet, F. A. *History of the French Revolution*. London: George Bell & Sons, 1891.
Miller, George. *Edward Hyde, Earl of Clarendon*. Boston: Twayne Publishers, 1983.
Miller, John C. *Sam Adams: Pioneer in Propaganda*. Stanford: Stanford University Press, 1936.
Millon, Robert P. *Zapata: The Ideology of a Peasant Revolutionary*. New York: International Publishers, 1969.

Morf, Gustave. *Terror in Quebec: Case Studies of the FLQ*. Toronto: Clarke, Irwin & Co., 1970.
Morley, John Viscount. *Biographical Studies*. London: Macmillan, 1923.
Morrah, Patrick. *Prince Rupert of the Rhine*. London: Constable & Co., 1976.
Morris, Richard B. *Seven Who Shaped Our Destiny: The Founding Fathers as Revolutionaries*. New York: Harper & Row, 1973.
Namier, Lewis, and John Brooke. *The House of Commons 1754-1790*. vol. 3. New York: Oxford University Press, 1964.
Nelson, William H. *The American Tory*. Oxford: Oxford University Press, 1961.
Nettles, Curtis P. *George Washington and American Independence*. Boston: Little, Brown, 1951.
Newcomb, Benjamin H. *Franklin and Galloway: A Political Partnership*. New Haven: Yale University Press, 1972.
Palmer, R. R. *The Age of the Democratic Revolutions*. 2 vols. Princeton: Princeton University Press, 1959, 1964.
Pares, Bernard. *The Fall of the Russian Monarchy*. London: Jonathan Cape, 1939.
Payne, Robert. *The Life and Death of Lenin*. New York: Simon and Schuster, 1964.
Peacock, Donald. *Journey to Power: The Story of a Canadian Election*. Toronto: The Ryerson Press, 1968.
Pearson, Lester B. *Mike: The Memoirs of the Right Honorable Lester B. Pearson*. 2 vols. Toronto: University of Toronto Press, 1972, 1973.
Pearson, Raymond. *The Russian Moderates and the Crisis of Tsarism 1914-1917*. London: Macmillan, 1977.
Pelletier, Gérard. *The October Crisis*. Toronto: McClelland & Stewart, 1971.
Pemberton, W. Baring. *Lord North*. London: Longman, Green & Co., 1938.
Pencak, William. *America's Burke: The Mind of Thomas Hutchinson*. Washington: University Press of America, 1982.
Perry, Laurens B. *Juárez and Díaz: Machine Politics in Mexico*. DeKalb: Northern Illinois University Press, 1978.
Peterson, Merril D. *Thomas Jefferson and the New Nation*. New York: Oxford University Press, 1970.
Petrie, Charles, ed. *King Charles, Prince Rupert, and the Civil War: From Original Letters*. London: Routledge & Kegan Paul, 1974.
Pipes, Richard. *Struve: Liberal of the Left 1870-1905*. Cambridge: Harvard University Press, 1970.
_____. *Struve: Liberal of the Right 1905-1944*. Cambridge: Harvard University Press, 1980.
Provencher, Jean. *René Lévesque: Portraits of a Québécois*. n.p.: Gage Publishing, 1975.
Raab, Felix. *The English Face of Machiavelli [Earl of Clarendon]*. London: Routledge & Kegan Paul, 1964.
Regush, Nicholas M. *Pierre Vallières: The Revolutionary Process in Quebec*. New York: Dial Press, 1973.
Reyes, H. Alfonso. *Emiliano Zapata: Su Vida y Su Obra*. Mexico City, 1963.
Rittenhouse, Floyd. "Emiliano Zapata and the Suriano Rebellion." Ph.D. diss.-tion, Ohio State University, 1947.

Romero Flores, Jesus. *Lázaro Cárdenas: Biográfia de un Gran Mexicano*. Mexico City: Costa-Amic, 1971.
Ross, Stanley R. *Francisco I. Madero: Apostle of Mexican Democracy*. New York: Columbia University Press, 1955.
Rowe, Violet A. *Sir Henry Vane the Younger*. London: The Athlone Press, 1970.
Rudé, George, ed. *Robespierre*. Englewood Cliffs: Prentice-Hall, 1967.
Sabine, Lorenzo. *Biographical Sketches of Loyalists of the American Revolution*. 2 vols. Boston: Little, Brown, 1864.
Schachner, Nathan. *Thomas Jefferson: A Biography*. 2 vols. New York: Appleton Century Crofts, 1951.
Schuz, Heinrich et al., eds. *Who Was Who in the U.S.S.R.* Metuchen, NJ: Scarecrow Press, 1972.
Scott, Eva. *Rupert: Prince Palatine*. New York: G. P. Putnam's Sons, 1899.
Shaw, Peter. *The Character of John Adams*. Chapel Hill: University of North Carolina Press, 1975.
Shub, David. *Lenin*. New York: Doubleday & Co., 1948.
Siebert, Wilbur H. *The Loyalists of Pennsylvania*. Columbus: Ohio State University Press, 1920.
Smith, C. Page. *John Adams*. 2 vols. New York: Doubleday & Co., 1962.
Smith, Charles D. *The Early Career of Lord North, the Prime Minister*. Cranbury, NJ: Associated University Presses, 1979.
Smith, Edward E. *The Young Stalin: The Early Years of an Elusive Revolutionary*. New York: Farrar, Strauss and Giroux, 1967.
Smith, Goldwin. *Three English Statesmen*. London: Macmillan, 1868.
Snow, Vernon F. *Essex the Rebel*. Lincoln: University of Nebraska Press, 1970.
Souvarine, Boris. *Stalin: A Critical Survey of Bolshevism*. London: Longman, Green & Co., 1939.
Stark, James H. *The Loyalists of Massachusetts and the Other Side of the American Revolution*. Boston: J. H. Stark, 1910.
Stephens, W. Walker. *The Life and Writings of Turgot*. London: Longman, Green & Co., 1895.
Stephenson, Graham. *Russia From 1812 to 1945: A History*. New York: Praeger Publishers, 1969.
Stewart, Walter. *Trudeau in Power*. New York: Outerbridge and Dienstfreng, 1971.
Stolypin, Arkadii Petrovich. *P. A. Stolypin*. Paris: Imp. Scientifique et Commerciale, 1927.
Stursberg, Peter. *Lester Pearson and the American Dilemma*. Toronto: Doubleday Canada, 1980.
———. *Lester Pearson and the Dream of Unity*. Toronto: Doubleday Canada, 1978.
Suarez Valles, Manuel. *Lázaro Cárdenas*. Mexico City: Cost-Amic, 1971.
Sullivan, Martin. *Mandate '68*. Toronto: Doubleday Canada, 1968.
Sydnor, Charles. *American Revolutionaries in the Making*. New York: Free Press, 1965.
Tannenbaum, Frank. *Mexico: The Struggle for Peace and Bread*. New York: Alfred A. Knopf, 1950.

Theen, Rolf H. W. *Lenin: Genesis and Development of a Revolutionary*. Philadelphia: J. B. Lippincott Co., 1973.
Thodarson, Bruce. *Lester Pearson: Diplomat and Politician*. Toronto: Oxford University Press, 1974.
_____. *Trudeau and Foreign Policy*. Toronto: Oxford University Press, 1972.
Thomas, Peter D. G. *Lord North*. London: Allen Lane, 1976.
Thompson, James M. *The French Revolution*. New York: Oxford University Press, 1945.
_____. *Leaders of the French Revolution*. New York: Harper Colophon Books, 1967.
_____. *Robespierre*. New York: Appleton, 1936.
Thomson, George M. *Warrior Prince: Prince Rupert of the Rhine*. London: Secker & Warburg, 1976.
Timmis, John H., III. *Thine is the Kingdom: The Trial for Treason of Thomas Wentworth, Earl of Strafford, First Minister to King Charles I, and Last Hope of the English Crown*. University, Alabama: University of Alabama Press, 1974.
Townsend, William Cameron. *Lázaro Cárdenas: Mexican Democrat*. Ann Arbor, MI: George Wahr Publishing Co., 1952.
Treadgold, Donald W. *Lenin and His Rivals*. New York: Frederick A. Praeger, 1955.
Trevor-Roper, H. R. *Archbishop Laud, 1573-1645*. 2nd ed. Hamden, CT: Archon Books, 1963.
_____. *Edward Hyde, Earl of Clarendon*. Oxford: Clarendon Press, 1975.
Trotsky, Leon. *Diary in Exile*. Cambridge: Harvard University Press, 1958.
_____. *The History of the Russian Revolution*. New York: Simon & Schuster, 1936.
_____. *Lenin: Notes for a Biographer*. New York: G. P. Putnam's Sons, 1971.
_____. *My Life: An Attempt at an Autobiography*. New York: Charles Scribners's Sons, 1930.
_____. *Stalin: An Appraisal of the Man and His Influence*. New York: Harper & Bros., 1941.
_____. *The Young Lenin*. Tran. Max Eastman; ed. Maurice Friedberg. New York: Doubleday & Co., 1972.
Trudeau, Margaret. *Beyond Reason*. New York: Paddington Press, 1979.
Trudeau, Pierre Elliott. *Approaches to Politics*. Toronto: Oxford University Press, 1970.
_____. *Conversations with Canadians*. Toronto: University of Toronto Press, 1972.
_____. *Federalism and the French Canadians*. New York: St. Martin's Press, 1968.
Trudeau, Pierre Elliott, ed. *The Asbestos Strike*. Toronto: James Lewis and Samuel, 1974.
Tucker, Robert C. *Stalin as Revolutionary, 1879-1929: A Study in History and Personality*. New York: W. W. Norton & Co., 1973.
Tudor, William. *The Life of James Otis of Massachusetts*. Boston: Wells & Lilly, 1823.

Tyler, Moses C. *Patrick Henry*. New York: Fredrick Ungar Publishing Co., 1898.
Ulam, Adam B. *The Bolsheviks: The Intellectual and Political History of the Triumph of Communism in Russia*. New York: Macmillan, 1965.
_____. *Stalin: The Man and His Era*. New York: Viking Press, 1973.
Umbreit, Kenneth. *The Founding Fathers: Men Who Shaped our Tradition*. Port Washington, NY: Kennikat Press, 1941.
Upton, Leslie, F. S., ed. *Revolutionary versus Loyalist: The First American Civil War*. Waltham, MA: Blaisdell Publishing Co., 1968.
Valentine, Alan. *Lord North*. 2 vols. Norman: University of Oklahoma Press, 1967.
Vallentin, Antonia. *Mirabeau*. New York: Viking Press, 1948.
Vallières, Pierre. *White Niggers of America*. New York: Monthly Review Press, 1971.
Van Tyne, Claude H. *The Loyalists in the American Revolution*. New York: Macmillan, 1902.
Vasconcelos, José. *A Mexican Ulysses: An Autobiography*. Bloomington, IN: Indiana University Press, 1963.
Vassili, Count Paul [Princess Catherine Radziwill, pseud.]. *Behind the Veil at the Russian Court*. New York: John Lane, 1914.
Voline, Boris. *12 Militants Russes*. Paris: Librairie de l'Humanité, 1925.
Von Bock, Maria. *Reminiscences of my Father, Peter A. Stolypin*. Metuchen, NJ: Scarecrow Press, 1970.
Von Laude, Theodore H. *Sergei Witte and the Industrialization of Russia*. New York: Columbia University Press, 1963.
_____. *Why Lenin? Why Stalin? A Reappraisal of the Russian Revolution, 1900-1930*. Philadelphia: J. B. Lippincott, 1964.
Walzer, Michael. *The Revolution of the Saints: A Study in the Origin of Radical Politics*. Cambridge: Harvard University Press, 1965.
Warwick, Charles F. *Mirabeau and the French Revolution*. Philadelphia: J. B. Lippincott Co., 1905.
_____. *Danton and the French Revolution*. Philadelphia: George W. Jacobs & Co., 1908.
Wedgwood, Cicely V. *Oliver Cromwell*. New York: Macmillan, 1956.
Wells, William V. *The Life and Public Service of Samuel Adams*. 3 vols. Boston: Little, Brown, 1888.
Wendel, Hermann. *Danton*. New Haven: Yale University Press, 1935.
Weyl, Nathaniel, and Sylvia Weyl. *The Reconquest of Mexico: The Years of Lázaro Cárdenas*. London: Oxford University Press, 1939.
Williamson, Hugh R. *John Hampden*. London: Hodder and Stoughton, 1933.
Wirt, William, ed. *Patrick Henry: Life, Correspondence and Speeches*. 3 vols. New York: Charles Scribner's Sons, 1891.
Wirt, William. *Sketches of the Life and Character of Patrick Henry*. Philadelphia: Thomas, Cowperthwait & Co., 1841.
Witte, Count Sergei. *The Memoirs of Count Witte*. New York: Doubleday, Page & Co., 1921.
Wolfe, Bertram D. *Three Who Made a Revolution*, rev. ed. New York: Dial Press, 1964.

Womack, John. *Zapata and the Mexican Revolution*. New York: Alfred A. Knopf, 1969.
Woodburn, James A., and Thomas Moran. *The Makers of America*. New York: Longmans, Green, & Co., 1922.
Wormald, B. H. G. *Clarendon*: *Politics, History, and Religion 1640-1660*. Cambridge: Cambridge University Press, 1951.

# Index

Abbas, Ferhat, xvi, xviv, 22, 47, 59
Aberbach, Joel D., 14, 115, 118
access, concept of, 9, 19–22, 39–40, 61, 111–12, 118
Adler, Alfred, 5, 71
Adams, John, xvii, xviv, 33, 47, 75, 79, 86
Adams, Samuel, xvii, 47, 81–82
Alami, Musa el-, xvii, 47
Arafat, Yasir, xvii, 33, 66, 78, 80, 88
asceticism, 11, 71, 72, 79–80, 112

Bailyn, Bernard, xv
Batista, Fulgencio, xvii, 19, 40, 41, 64, 80–81
Batlle, José, xvii, xx, 53, 64, 73
Belaúnde, Fernando, xvii, xx, 53
Ben Bella, Ahmed, xvi, xviv, 86, 100
Biko, Stephen, xvi, xx, 41
Blanchard, William H., 6, 71
Blanco, Hugo, xvii, 47
Blondel, Jean, 3, 13, 14
Bourguiba, Habib, xvi, xviv, 22, 58–59, 75, 97–98
Brienne, Etienne Charles de, xv
Breteuil, Louis Charles, xv
Burns, James MacGregor, 4, 13

Cabral, Amilcar, xvi, xx

Calonne, Charles-Alexandre, xv
Cárdenas, José, xviii, xx, 40, 41, 49, 73, 79, 98
Castro, Fidel, xvii, xviv, 47, 67, 80, 87, 100
Cavendish, William, xvii, 46, 53, 61, 98
chance, role of, 10, 57
Chiang Kai-shek, xvi, xviv, 53, 74–75, 84
child development, study of, 48–49
Chou En-lai, xvi, 47
Chu Teh, xvi, 47, 87
Clausewitz, Karl Von, 100
cohort analysis, 110
Colden, Cadwallader, xvii, 47
control group, absence of, xxi, 107
Cromwell, Oliver, xvii, 33, 40, 86, 100

Danton, Georges Jacques, xviii, 47
data: collection of, xiv–xvi; reliability of, xxi–xxii; sources of, xv–xxii; validity of, xxi–xxii
Debray, Régis, 100–101
deLuca, Anthony R., 14
Devereux, Robert, xvii, 47, 100
Díaz, Porfirio, xviii, 60–61, 81, 98
Diêm, Ngô Dinh, xvii, 24, 47, 53, 58
discriminant analysis, 37–42, 109–110

Dogan, Mattei, 3
Dutra, Eurico, xvii, 53

Easton, David, 4
Edinger, Lewis J., 3
egotism, 11, 71, 72, 74-78
Erikson, Erik H., 71
estheticism, 71, 72, 90-91, 113

factor analysis, 31-36
Fiedler, Fred E., 3
foco theory, 100-101
Frei, Eduardo, xvii, xx, 47, 73
Freud, Sigmund, 3, 5, 71

Galloway, Joseph, xvii, 97, 101-102
generational politics, 110
George, Alexander L., 4, 5, 71
Giap, Vo Nguyên, xvii, 47, 67
Gibb, Cecil A., 3
Gomez, Laureano, xvii, 53, 97
Greenstein, Fred I., 4
Groth, Alexander, 118
Guevara, Ernesto, xvii, 47, 88, 91, 100, 101
Gurr, Ted Robert, 4, 71
Guttsman, W.L., 14

Habash, George, xvii, 66
Hampden, John, xvii
Heifetz, Ronald L., 4
Henry, Patrick, xvii, 47
Hermann, Margaret G., 4
Ho Chi Minh, xvii, 67, 86
Hollander, Edwin P., 3
Horney, Karen, 71
Hosmer, James K., xv
Hutchinson, Thomas, xv, xvii, 47, 62-63, 84, 102
Hyde, Edward, xvii, 47, 61

Iremonger, Lucille, 71

Jefferson, Thomas, xvii, 91, 99
Johnson, R.W., 14
justice, sense of, 11, 73

Kaunda, Kenneth, xvi, xviv, 22, 41, 58-59
Klecka, William R., 42
K'ung, H.H., xvi, 53

Laski, Harold J., 14
Lasswell, Harold D., 3, 4, 5, 6, 71, 83, 88
Laud, William, xvii, 33, 64, 74
leader differences, 18-30, 32, 37-42, 45, 57, 71, 97, 107
leader similarities, 17-18, 29, 32-36, 45, 57, 71, 97, 107
leaders, characteristics of, xiii, 5, 7-9, 17-42, 108-109; age, 7, 22-23; attitudes, 9, 18, 28-29; arrest record, 9, 22, 25; birthplace, 8, 17; education, 8, 18; emergence of, 9-12, 71-95, 112-113; ethnicity, 8, 18; family life, 8, 17; foreign travel, 9, 18; ideologies, 9, 18, 27-28; occupations, 8, 18, 20-21; psychological dynamics, 9-12, 71-95, 112-113; religion, 8, 18, 26; socioeconomic status, 8, 18-19
leaders, modal models of, 114-18
leaders, motivations of, xiii, 4-6, 9-12, 71-95, 112-13
leaders, politicization of, 45-56; in family, 45-49; in school, 49-53; in travel, 53-55
leaders, psychologies of, xiii, 4-6, 9-12, 71-95, 112-13
leaders, social background of, xiii, 5, 7-9, 17-42, 108-109
leaders, socialization of. See leaders, politicization of
leaders, type of: career, 31-36, 109; crisis, 31-36, 109; failed, 128-29; successful, 128-29; transactional, 3, 119; transforming, 4, 119
leadership, comparative studies of, 3-4
leadership, conventional wisdom about, ix, 119
leadership, modal models of, 114-18
leadership, theories of, 3-14, 110-18
leadership positions, access to, 9, 19-22, 39-40, 61, 111-12, 118

leadership situations, 4–5, 7, 9–10, 57–70, 110–12
leadership skills, 4–5, 12, 97–104, 113–14
leadership theory, 4–14, 110–18
Lenin, Nikolai, xviii, 47, 78, 80, 88, 91, 99
Lévesque, René, xviii, xx, 25, 47, 53, 59–60, 83
Lin Piao, xvi
Liu Shao-ch'i, xvi
loyalist, defined, xiii
loyalists-turned-revolutionaries, xxiv–xxi, 22, 128
Luthuli, Albert John, xvi, 40, 41, 79

Machel, Samora Moises, xvi
Madero, Francisco, xviii, 88
Madsen, Douglas, 6
Magnusson, David, 14
Mao Tse-tung, xvi, 67, 80, 87, 89–90, 99, 100
Marat, Jean Paul, xviii, 65, 75, 81
Marcos, Ferdinand E., xvii, 22–23, 53, 64
marginality, 11, 71, 72, 83–88, 113, 115
Marighella, Carlos, xvii, xx
Matthews, Donald R., 3, 71, 118
Maurepas, Jean-Frédéric, xv, xviii, 33, 61–62, 102
Mazlish, Bruce, 5–6, 71
McLelland, David C., 5
Mellors, Colin, 14
Mirabeau, Comte de, xviii, 65, 87–88
Mondlane, Eduardo, xvi

Nassar, Gamal Abdel, xvi, xx, 22, 75, 79, 98
nationalism, 11, 73–74
Necker, Jacques, xv, xviii, 33, 49, 74, 84–85
Nikolaevich, Nikolai, xviii, 33, 46–47, 57, 98
Nkomo, Joshua, xvi, xxiv, 68
North, Frederick, xvii, 47, 53, 61, 85, 102
Nyerere, Julius K., xvi, xix, xx, 41, 53, 58–59, 90, 98

Odría, Manuel, xvii, 40, 41
oedipal conflict, 11, 71, 88–90, 113
Otis, James, xvii, 47

Paige, Glenn D., 3, 13
Payne, James L., 4, 6, 71
Paz Estenssoro, Víctor, xvii, xxiv
Pearson, Lester B., xviii, xx, 47, 53, 63
Peñaranda, Enrique, xvii, 47
Phillips, Katie V., 47
psychological dynamics, 9–12, 71–95, 112–13; asceticism, 11, 71, 72, 79–80, 112; egotism, 11, 71, 72, 74–78; estheticism, 71, 72, 90–91, 113; marginality, 11, 71, 72, 83–88, 113, 115; nationalism, 11, 73–74; oedipal conflict, 11, 71, 88–90, 113; relative deprivation, 11, 71, 72, 80–83, 112; sense of justice, 11, 73; status inconsistency, 11, 71, 72, 80–83, 112; vanity, 11, 71, 72, 74–78
de la Puente, Luis, xvii, xx
Putnam, Robert D., 3, 115, 118
Pym, John, xvii, 33, 40

Quandt, William B., 3

radicalization, patterns of. *See* leaders, politicization of
relative deprivation, 11, 71, 72, 80–83, 112
revolutionaries-turned-loyalists, xxiv, xxi, 22, 127
revolutionary, defined, xiii
Roberto, Holden, xvi
Robespierre, Maximilien, xviii, 47, 79
Rockman, Bert A., 4, 115, 118
Rupert, Prince, xviii, 46, 49, 61, 74, 81, 85, 98

Sabine, Lorenzo, xv, xxiii
Sadat, Anwar el-, xvi, 59, 75
Schrim, François, xviii, xx
Schoeters, Georges, xviii, xx, 67–68, 74
Searing, Donald D., 4
Sendic, Raúl, xvii, xx

Senghor, Léopold Sédar, xvi, xix, 40, 41, 53
Sewall, Jonathan, xvii, 47, 81
siblings, 47–49
Sihanouk, Norodom, xvii, 46, 53, 57–58, 78
Simonton, Dean Keith, 7
Sithole, Ndabaningi, xvi, xix, 65–66, 78
socialization. *See* leaders, politicization of
Soong, T.V., xvi, 47, 53
Souphanouvong, xvii, xix, 47, 87
Stalin, Joseph, xviii, xx
status inconsistency, 11, 71, 72, 80–83, 112
Stogdill, Ralph M., 3
Stolypin, Peter, xviii, 47, 53, 62, 74, 97
Struve, Peter, xviii, 25, 85

Thieu, Nguyên Van, xvii, 47
Torres, Camilo, xvii, xx, 80, 91
Trotsky, Leon, xviii, 47, 75, 86–87
Trudeau, Pierre, xviii, xx, 47, 53, 63
Tryon, William, xv
Tubman, William V.S., xvi, xx, 40, 41, 47

Tuchman, Barbara, 6
Tucker, Robert C., 4
Turgot, Anne-Robert-Jacques, xv, xviii, 61–62, 90, 97

U Nu, xvi, xx, 47, 58, 78

Vallières, Pierre, xviii, xx, 67, 75–76, 82–83, 87
Van Thal, Herbert, 14
Vane, Henry (Harry), xviii, 47
vanity, 11, 71, 72, 74–78
Vasconcelos, José, xviii, 53, 83
Villa, Pancho, xviii

Walzer, Michael, 64, 71
Wang Ching-wei, xvi, xix, 22, 53, 79
Washington, George, xvii, xix, xx, 82
Wentworth, Thomas, xviii, 33, 47, 53, 61
Winter, David G., 5
Witte, Serge, xviii, 47, 53, 62, 81
Wolfenstein, E. Victor, 4, 5, 71, 88, 89
women leaders, 17

Zapata, Emiliano, xviii

# About the Authors

MOSTAFA REJAI received his Ph.D. from UCLA. He is distinguished professor in the department of political science, Miami University, Oxford, Ohio. His publications include *Comparative Political Ideologies* (1984), *The Comparative Study of Revolutionary Strategy* (1977), and *Decline of Ideology* (1971). His articles have appeared in social sciences and humanities journals in the United States and Europe.

KAY PHILLIPS received her Ph.D. from the University of Cincinnati. She is professor of sociology and anthropology and associate provost at Miami University. She is the coauthor with Dr. Rejai of *World Revolutionary Leaders* (1983) and *Leaders of Revolution* (1979). She is currently at work on a project titled "Demographic Change and the Rise of Capitalism."